FUGITIVE TEXTS

FUGITIVE TEXTS

Slave Narratives in Antebellum Print Culture

Michaël Roy

Translated by Susan Pickford

THE UNIVERSITY OF WISCONSIN PRESS

This work received the French Voices Award for excellence in publication and translation. French Voices is a program created and funded by the French Embassy in the United States and FACE Foundation.

The University of Wisconsin Press
728 State Street, Suite 443
Madison, Wisconsin 53706
uwpress.wisc.edu

Gray's Inn House, 127 Clerkenwell Road
London EC1R 5DB, United Kingdom
eurospanbookstore.com

Printed in the United States of America
This book may be available in a digital edition.

Library of Congress Cataloging-in-Publication Data

Names: Roy, Michaël, author. | Pickford, Susan, translator.
Title: Fugitive texts : slave narratives in antebellum print culture /
Michaël Roy ; translated by Susan Pickford.
Other titles: Textes fugitifs. English
Description: Madison, Wisconsin : The University of Wisconsin Press, [2022] |
Originally published in French as Textes fugitifs: le récit d'esclave
au prisme de l'histoire du livre, copyright ©2017 by ENS Éditions. |
Includes bibliographical references and index.
Identifiers: LCCN 2021053056 | ISBN 9780299338404 (hardcover)
Subjects: LCSH: Slave narratives—United States—History and criticism. |
Slaves' writings, American—History and criticism. | Slaves—United
States—Biography. | American literature—African American
authors—History and criticism. | Autobiography—African American
authors—History—19th century. | Autobiography—African American
authors—History and criticism. | Publishers and publishing—United
States—History—19th century.
Classification: LCC PS366.A35 R6913 2022 |
DDC 810.9/206250973—dc23/eng/20220124
LC record available at https://lccn.loc.gov/2021053056

French Voices Logo designed by Serge Bloch

ISBN 9780299338442 (paperback)

For Claire Parfait and Michael Winship

The question then occurred to me, Could I not, by *making a book*, do something to relieve myself and my children. . . . This idea struck me with so much force, that I have yielded to it—that is, to write a short Narrative of my own life, setting forth the trials and difficulties the Lord has brought me through to this day, and offer it for sale to my friends generally, as well as to the public at large.

—NOAH DAVIS, 1859

The fact that Negroes are turning Book makers may possibly serve to remove the popular impression that they are fit only for Bootblacking, and although they may not *shine* in the former profession as they have long done in the latter, I am not without hope that they will do themselves good by making the effort.

—FREDERICK DOUGLASS, 1851

Contents

Contents

Illustrations

Abbreviations

AASS	American Anti-Slavery Society
ACS	American Colonization Society
AFASS	American and Foreign Anti-Slavery Society
AMA	American Missionary Association
CASS	Connecticut Anti-Slavery Society
MASS	Massachusetts Anti-Slavery Society
NYSASS	New York State Anti-Slavery Society
OASS	Ohio Anti-Slavery Society
PASS	Pennsylvania Anti-Slavery Society

FUGITIVE TEXTS

Introduction

Runaway Best Sellers?

A FTER A CENTURY OF "CULTURAL REPRESSION," antebellum slave narratives have taken pride of place in the American literary canon.[1] Once ignored, disparaged, or simply forgotten, these accounts of life in bondage and freedom are now widely read, studied, and anthologized—to the extent that the slave narrative often stands, in surveys of American literature, for the whole of antebellum African American writing. As early as 1995, Carla L. Peterson warned against "privileg[ing] the slave narrative as *the* African-American literary form of the antebellum period" and making it "the metonym for nineteenth-century African-American literary production."[2] There have been numerous calls since then for extending the canon of early Black literature "beyond [Frederick] Douglass," "beyond Douglass and [Harriet] Jacobs," or "beyond the slave narrative."[3] The recent explosion of scholarship on early African American print culture has helped illuminate the host of Black writings that coexisted with or predated the antebellum slave narrative but have been obscured by it.[4] In *Forgotten Readers: Recovering the Lost History of African American Literary Societies* (2002), Elizabeth McHenry has explored the world of literary societies organized by free Black women and men in the urban North and the varied print culture that emerged from them. Eric Gardner has engaged us to look toward "unexpected places"—geographic (Missouri, Indiana, California) as well as generic (newspaper columns, letters to editors, essays)—to widen our understanding of early African American letters and political thought. Contributors to Lara Langer Cohen and Jordan Alexander Stein's *Early African American Print Culture* (2012), George Hutchinson and John K. Young's *Publishing Blackness: Textual Constructions of Race since 1850* (2013), and Brigitte Fielder and Jonathan Senchyne's *Against a Sharp White Background: Infrastructures of African American Print* (2019) have foregrounded a vast and fascinating array of Black-authored print materials,

3

including periodicals, poetry chapbooks, printed orations, and organizational proceedings.[5] As Derrick R. Spires makes clear, these projects "are not just about the recovery of texts or troubling the canon, nor do they seek to diminish the importance of the slave narrative or experiences of enslavement; rather, they are invested in creating a deeper understanding of the expressive print cultures black communities created out of these experiences."[6]

Given this context, a book solely devoted to the antebellum slave narrative might seem like a historiographical anachronism. Most foundational studies of the genre—Frances Smith Foster's *Witnessing Slavery: The Development of Ante-bellum Slave Narratives* (1979), Marion Wilson Starling's *The Slave Narrative: Its Place in American History* (1981), Charles T. Davis and Henry Louis Gates Jr.'s *The Slave's Narrative* (1985), William L. Andrews's *To Tell a Free Story: The First Century of Afro-American Autobiography, 1760–1865* (1986)—were published thirty to forty years ago.[7] Recent scholarship on the slave narrative primarily consists of student-oriented volumes such as Audrey Fisch's *Cambridge Companion to the African American Slave Narrative* (2007) and John Ernest's *Oxford Handbook of the African American Slave Narrative* (2014), confirming, in Fisch's words, that "the African American slave narrative is now recognized as a major genre, firmly established in the academic canon of what should be read and studied."[8] Yet this rich and multifaceted body of work has left unexamined one key aspect of the antebellum slave narrative: its materiality. Nor have African American print culture scholars looked into a genre whose prominence they questioned in the first place. The slave narrative, it seems, went missing in the turn "from black lit to black print."[9] A handful of essays have argued for studying the slave narrative as material text. Laurence Cossu-Beaumont and Claire Parfait note that "the study of slave narratives . . . may benefit from a book history approach," taking as an example the narrative of William Wells Brown. "Despite highly sophisticated readings of the slave narrative as a discursive text and a greatly expanded canon," Teresa A. Goddu adds, "still little is known about the slave narrative as a material artifact—who published the slave narrative, what its original editions looked like, how much it cost, how it was distributed, who read it, and so on." Gardner concurs: "We . . . lack full publication histories for many narratives—senses of the size and character of print runs, publishers' backgrounds and practices, patterns of publisher-author interactions, publishers' catalogs, etc."[10] *Fugitive Texts* is the first book to address these issues.

The only slave narrative that has been thoroughly studied from a book-historical perspective—*The Interesting Narrative of the Life of Olaudah Equiano, or Gustavus Vassa, the African* (1789)—was first published not in the United States but in London. James Green has pieced together its publication history; Vincent Carretta has pointed to Equiano's profits from sales of his book; John Bugg has explored how the narrative was distributed during Equiano's tour of the British Isles; Akiyo Ito has looked at the readership for the narrative's first American edition, finding it consisted largely of New York artisans unconnected to the abolition movement.[11] These scholars have focused on Equiano's personal investment in publishing and distributing his narrative, seeing him as a master of self-promotion with shrewd business acumen. No such comparable analysis has been made of a writer like Douglass, though he, too, expended considerable energy distributing copies of *Narrative of the Life of Frederick Douglass, an American Slave* (1845). Scholarship has tended to downplay Douglass's agency, foregrounding attempts by white abolitionists to control his narrative. This focus on the "white envelope" around the "black message" and on the role of white abolitionists in the publishing process has sidelined the very real contribution most antebellum African American authors— formerly enslaved or not—made to the production and distribution of their writings.[12]

There are undeniably difficulties in approaching African American slave narratives as material objects, due not only to the fact that "scholars of slave culture and print culture have [until recently] rarely shared agendas" but also to the way the narratives were made available in modern editions from the 1960s onward.[13] The publishers who took on this task—Arno Press (with the backing of the *New York Times*), Negro Universities Press, Mnemosyne, Rhistoric Publications, and others—generally reprinted the narratives as facsimiles, with little textual editing. Making slave narratives widely available seemed a more urgent (and, for some, more profitable) project than producing scholarly editions reflecting the various stages the text went through or the author's intentions. The narratives by Douglass, Brown, and Jacobs were to be interpreted first and foremost as literary works and mined as source material for the history of slavery.[14] Today, the online database *Documenting the American South* is the principal point of access to slave narratives for many researchers and students. While it does include dozens of narratives, some of which would otherwise be hard to find, the database offers a single format for texts that are very different in form and in nature. For the antebellum period, for instance, the "Narrative of James Curry, a Fugitive Slave," transcribed by white abolitionist Elizabeth Buffum Chace and published on the front page of William Lloyd Garrison's *Liberator* on 10 January 1840, is given the same presentation as *My Bondage and My Freedom* (1855), the second of Douglass's three autobiographies—a compendious 464-page volume that is closer to memoir than testimony. The materiality of slave narratives is hard to grasp on screen, as are the social worlds in which they were produced, distributed, and consumed. The same issues come to the fore in slave narrative anthologies. Such anthologies were crucial in recovering slave narratives: works such as Gilbert Osofsky's *Puttin' on Ole Massa*, Arna Bontemps's *Great Slave Narratives*, and Robin W. Winks's *Four Fugitive Slave Narratives*, all published in 1969, helped identify the slave narrative as a distinct literary object and contributed to its canonization.[15] The Library of America anthology edited by Gates and Andrews remains a precious classroom resource.[16] Yet the process of gathering slave narratives in anthologies inevitably "erase[s] their diverse material histories."[17] Erasing their individual material histories, in turn, corroborates the idea put forward by James Olney nearly forty years ago of an "overwhelming *sameness*" in slave narratives.[18] While some motifs do recur across narratives, and while approaching slave narratives as a genre makes sense in terms of literary criticism, book history seeks to *undo* the genre of the slave narrative, often seen as monolithic, and approach each narrative as an individual entity in its own right.

Approaching slave narratives with the tools of book history also turns a spotlight on the bibliographical confusion that presides over most discussions of slave narratives—less in specialist research than in overviews of American literature and histories of antebellum America. Mistakes are easy to make given the complexity of some of these narratives' publishing histories. Erroneous titles and dates of publication and mixing up several editions of a single narrative are commonplace. One critic dates the publication of Douglass's first narrative to 1844 instead of 1845 and gives two incorrect titles for Josiah Henson's second narrative (*Truth Stranger and Stronger than Fiction* and *Truth Stronger than Fiction* instead of *Truth Stranger than Fiction*); another records that Lunsford Lane's narrative was printed by "abolitionist J. G. Torrey," confusing the Boston printer Joseph G. Torrey and the antislavery activist Charles T. Torrey, and states that Henry Watson's 1848 narrative was published by Henry Holt, who founded his company after the Civil War. A third writes that the Boston firm Thayer and Eldridge published *Incidents in the Life of a Slave Girl* (1861), which Jacobs in fact self-published.[19] "Most African American authors," Meredith L. McGill writes, "still [await] thorough and exacting bibliographical study."[20] This is especially true of the authors of slave narratives, whose works are no less deserving of bibliographical accuracy than those of Nathaniel Hawthorne, Henry David Thoreau, and Herman Melville. Hawthorne never wrote *The House of the Eight Gables*; neither did Douglass write his *Autobiography*, as one historian claims.[21] *Fugitive Texts* draws less on the Anglo-American bibliographical tradition than on French book history, but it aims to contribute to projects with a more overtly bibliographical slant such as the Black Bibliography Project, under the directorship of McGill and Jacqueline

Goldsby at Rutgers and Yale University.[22] It also responds to Amy E. Earhart's call for an "editorial renaissance" of Black-authored literary texts—one that "recognizes the systemic issues that have affected the production of Black texts."[23]

Some might claim that erroneous publication dates and titles are of minor significance and that the materiality of slave narratives is of secondary importance to their content. Is it not faintly inappropriate to focus on the format and binding of texts recounting the lives of men and women who were prey to exploitation and violence? One reviewer of Henry Bibb's narrative suggested as much: "This is a volume of 204 pages, handsomely printed on good paper, and well bound. But it is not in the execution that the interest lies; it is in the thrilling incidents so well told."[24] Yet one of this book's central tenets is that book history improves our understanding of the status and place of slave narratives in antebellum America. As deeply political literary objects, slave narratives cannot be dissociated from the historical context that produced them and more specifically from their circumstances of publication, circulation, and reception. A lack of appropriate tools means that these circumstances remain little known and are often handled somewhat superficially.

Slave narratives are generally read solely against the backdrop of the abolition movement. Clearly, the sharp rise in slave narratives in the antebellum period was part of the growth of antislavery sentiment, now described by historians of abolition as a second wave in a *longue durée* process that dated back at least as far as the American Revolution.[25] One notable form taken by second-wave abolitionism was a network of interracial (albeit white-led) societies that established an institutional framework for the movement. The American Anti-Slavery Society (AASS), founded in New York in 1833, was its nerve center in the 1830s. The AASS was the crucible for the slave narrative in its modern form, as I show in chapter 1. Yet this by no means suggests that all slave narratives were produced within this institutional setting, or that white abolitionists at the head of such societies made slave narratives a central pillar of their argument. Many narratives were self-published, sometimes with the more or less helpful support of an antislavery society, sometimes wholly independently, on the fringes of the movement; others were printed by mainstream trade publishers and sold commercially. Antislavery circles were unequally receptive to such narratives: some, published and distributed on a small local scale, were never promoted in the antislavery press, while others, published commercially, were read by a wide section of American society. The oft-repeated claim that slave narratives were published "under the auspices of antislavery societies" does not reflect the various dynamics governing their production, dissemination, and reception.[26]

Scholarship has also emphasized the popularity and marketability of slave narratives. Gates describes them as "extraordinarily popular texts"; James Brewer Stewart mentions their "tremendous readership"; Andrews states that "a significant number of antebellum slave narratives went through multiple editions, were translated into several European languages, and sold in the tens of thousands."[27] They point to the print runs of *Narrative of the Life of Frederick Douglass* and Solomon Northup's *Twelve Years a Slave* (1853), estimated at thirty thousand and twenty-seven thousand copies, respectively.[28] This is nothing new: sources at the time equally discussed the popularity of slave narratives, including an article by Ephraim Peabody in the *Christian Examiner* in 1849, regularly quoted in twentieth-century overviews of the slave narrative. Peabody, a Boston-based Unitarian clergyman, was an admirer of slave narratives, counting them among "the most remarkable productions of the age." "The extent of the influence such lives must exert," he went on, "may be judged of, when we learn the immense circulation which has been secured for them. Of Brown's Narrative, first published in 1847, not less than eight thousand copies have been already sold. Douglass's Life, first published in 1845, has in this country alone passed through seven editions, and is, we are told, now out of print. They are scattered over the whole of the North."[29] Peabody's discourse is problematic insofar as it fails to take account of the obstacles to publication encountered by some authors, how hard many authors had to work to put their books in readers' hands, and the low print runs of some narratives intended for small-scale distribution at a local level. Jacobs, whose path to publication for *Incidents in the Life of a Slave Girl* was long and complicated, would have disagreed with the claim that "slave narratives were so popular that almost any victim of slavery could get published." Likewise, Sojourner Truth's narrative, which she largely distributed herself, never "flooded the bookstores."[30]

It has also been claimed that slave narratives were "largely directed toward a northern white audience."[31] White middle-class readers, scholars contend, were at the same time horrified by the brutality of slavery and titillated by the sensationalist content of some narratives. Those converted to the antislavery cause consumed slave narratives serially, purchasing and reading them one after the other.[32] In this sense, slave narratives foreshadow later genres such as westerns and crime novels; they formed a genre in their own right, enjoyed by a wide, though mostly white, readership.[33] Such claims, as Gardner notes, "lack verification, nuance, and context."[34] Since the work of Benjamin Quarles, historians of abolition have focused increasingly on the role of Black activists in the movement.[35] The best known, including Douglass and Brown, wrote their own narratives. African American activists were often marginalized within institutional antislavery yet made vital contributions to the abolitionist cause: they attended antislavery meetings, held Colored Conventions, set up vigilance committees to assist fugitive slaves, founded their own press organs—and read slave narratives. Slave narratives have a Black reception history that deserves more attention. The 1845 copy of *Narrative of the Life of Frederick Douglass* held at the American Antiquarian Society was owned by Henry O. Remington, a leading Black figure in New Bedford, Massachusetts; in the late 1850s and early 1860s, Thomas Hamilton's *Weekly Anglo-African*, the preeminent paper of the northern Black community, carried advertisements for and reviews of *Twelve Years a Slave, My Bondage and My Freedom*, and *Incidents in the Life of a Slave Girl.*[36] Free Black readers invested these texts with specific meanings, as Erica L. Ball has explored.[37] Slave narratives also have a southern history, as the cases of Douglass, Bibb, and James Williams will show, as well as a (more familiar) transatlantic history.

Above all, it is open to question whether slave narratives ever formed as homogeneous and easily identifiable a genre as has been claimed. The slave narrative as we think of it today is essentially a modern construct; the phrase "slave narrative" itself had little currency in antebellum America.[38] Different narratives took different paths, meeting only occasionally on the shelves of an antislavery book depository or in the review section of a Black-owned periodical. A book history approach to the antebellum slave narrative, I argue, illuminates the heterogeneous nature of what is often perceived as a homogeneous whole and ultimately paves the way for a redefinition of the literary form we have come to recognize as "the slave narrative." My aim is not to deny that slave narratives share common features but to take them out of what is sometimes a rather restrictive genre categorization to understand the conditions surrounding the birth of each individual text. This approach allows me to foreground the contingent nature of the processes of writing, publication, and, later, canonization that were in no way ineluctable. It also sheds light on the underexplored issue of African Americans' relationship with print artifacts in the nineteenth century.

Fugitive Texts reconstructs the publication histories of a number of famous and lesser-known narratives published in book form, placing them against the changing backdrop of antebellum print culture. It does so over the course of three chapters organized in roughly chronological fashion. The narratives in chapter 1 were all published and/or disseminated, for at least one point in their publication history, by an antislavery society for purposes that were essentially ideological in nature. These narratives were wholly part of the print network of institutional abolitionism and were seen first and foremost as weapons in the antislavery struggle. The *Narrative of James Williams* (1838), prompted, produced, and distributed by the AASS, is the archetypal example in this category. Most narratives discussed in chapter 2 were self-published. They were

more personal literary-political projects, produced on a smaller, less professional scale. Their publication and distribution depended in large part on the
author's own efforts to find funding, oversee the logistics of printing and distributing the book, and promote it in person at antislavery events. Their publication history is therefore less closely bound up with institutional abolitionism, though the links are never completely severed. These narratives were not
intended solely as denunciations of slavery: they could be a way of protecting
a damaged reputation or generating income for authors in a precarious financial
position. *Narrative of the Life of Frederick Douglass* is one such example. Chapter 3 studies narratives that were brought out by mainstream trade publishers
and distributed via traditional publishing circuits, building on the success of
Harriet Beecher Stowe's 1852 *Uncle Tom's Cabin*. Publishers active in this arena
tended to act less on the basis of political belief than on the hope of profits, as
their publishing tactics demonstrate. Such "commercial" narratives, particularly Northup's *Twelve Years a Slave*, rapidly won a broad, diverse readership.
The chapter closes with the publishing history of Jacobs's narrative, whose journey to commercial publication ended in failure: the narrative was eventually
self-published, demonstrating the longevity of the nonprofessional publishing
model on the eve of the Civil War. The conclusion then shows how a focus on
the materiality of book-length slave narratives leads us to look beyond the book
as the key to understanding the genre. I make the case for reading slave narratives as "fugitive texts" apt to be embodied in various written, oral, and visual
forms. Slave narratives, I argue, owed their popularity in antebellum America
above all to their capacity to shift between formats and media.

   I will conclude this introduction with a few words on the publishing history of *Fugitive Texts*. The book began life in 2012–15 as a doctoral dissertation,
which gave rise to a French publication in 2017. *Textes fugitifs*, as it was originally known, was written for a French readership unfamiliar with African
American slave narratives. This meant a degree of rewriting prior to translation. The French version contained a lengthy opening chapter on the historiography of the slave narrative, outlining its fall from sight and gradual reemergence in the twentieth century as it was rediscovered by literary critics and
historians. The opening chapter has been removed and some aspects reworked
into the introduction and subsequent chapters. I have also incorporated insights
from books and articles published since 2017. African American print culture
studies are a vibrant field, and much recent work has transformed the way I
thought about some aspects of the question. *Fugitive Texts* remains faithful to
the spirit of the French book it arose from. This English-language version
would not exist without Jonathan Senchyne, who encouraged me to work on
it, and Susan Pickford, who translated it. I thank them both.

CHAPTER ONE

"The General Diffusion of Abolition Light"

The Institutional Origins of the Antebellum Slave Narrative

As historian Manisha Sinha reminds us, "People of African descent wrote autobiographies from the early days of racial slavery."[1] Book-length slave narratives were not an entirely new literary form in the early 1830s, when the United States witnessed the emergence of a mass social movement in favor of the immediate abolition of slavery. Formerly enslaved men and women had begun writing (or dictating) narratives in Britain and North America in the latter half of the eighteenth century, with titles including *A Narrative of the Uncommon Sufferings, and Surprizing Deliverance of Briton Hammon, a Negro Man* (1760), *A Narrative of the Most Remarkable Particulars in the Life of James Albert Ukawsaw Gronniosaw, an African Prince* (1770), and *The Interesting Narrative of the Life of Olaudah Equiano, or Gustavus Vassa, the African* (1789). Two narratives by formerly enslaved African American men were published in the 1820s, in New York and London, respectively, as *Life of William Grimes, the Runaway Slave* (1825) and *A Narrative of Some Remarkable Incidents, in the Life of Solomon Bayley, Formerly a Slave, in the State of Delaware, North America* (1825).

Only in the 1830s, however, did the number of such narratives rise significantly and did they achieve a higher profile in the United States. The increasing prominence of slave narratives in the literary and political landscape of antebellum America was due first and foremost to the formerly enslaved men and women who told and retold their own stories. But it was also a consequence of the involvement of the American Anti-Slavery Society (AASS) in publishing and disseminating their accounts. As Trish Loughran and Teresa A. Goddu have shown, in just a few years, the AASS became a powerful organization with an army of salaried speakers and a network of auxiliary societies dispersed across the North. Headquartered in New York City, the society set out to bring the antislavery message "into every nook of the extended republic," including the South, thanks to a sophisticated infrastructure facilitating the distribution of abolitionist literature on a grand scale. AASS-sponsored print culture was rich and diverse. It consisted of newspapers, pamphlets, compendia, prints, almanacs, and slave narratives, which benefited from the sheer impact of what Goddu has termed "institutional antislavery."[2] Slave narratives are most commonly read against this institutional backdrop.

Yet it should immediately be made clear that the AASS only brought out a single slave narrative under its name, the 1838 *Narrative of James Williams, an American Slave*. The unique publication history of this narrative, wholly produced and distributed by the AASS, is worthy of a detailed case study. The other narratives explored in this chapter were all published outside the AASS and were incorporated into institutional antislavery's print culture subsequently. Not all were promoted with the same vigor. Only Charles Ball's *Slavery in the United States*, originally published in 1836, was actively pushed by AASS abolitionists later on. Accordingly, I will explore this case in some detail before turning more briefly to the 1837 *Life of Olaudah Equiano*, the 1832 *Memoir of Mrs. Chloe Spear*, and a handful of other narratives published in the same decade by formerly enslaved individuals. The abolition movement underwent significant structural changes in 1840, following a schism within the ranks of the AASS. The society lost some of its financial resources as a result, impacting the publication and distribution of slave narratives. The 1830s, when the AASS was "at the height of its organizational powers," were therefore a distinct moment in the history of the antebellum slave narrative.[3]

Raindrops, Snowflakes, and Autumn Leaves: Publishing and Circulating Antislavery Literature in the 1830s

AASS publishing practices drew heavily on the religious organizations that were its forerunners. Historians such as David Paul Nord and Candy Gunther Brown have studied the pioneering role of evangelical voluntary associations in using print technology and, more broadly, in developing methods of mass communication even before the rise of commercial publishers in the first half of the nineteenth century.[4]

Typical of these associations was the Society for Propagating the Gospel among the Indians and Others in North America, founded in Massachusetts in 1787 to convert to Christianity the Native Americans and poor white folk living in remote corners of New England. The society saw print as the primary source of religious instruction and launched a major program to distribute reading material including Bibles, New Testaments, devotional books, spelling books, and primers. The use of print by religious organizations, however, only became systematic in the early nineteenth century. For the minister and man of letters Jedidiah Morse, who founded the Massachusetts Society for Promoting Christian Knowledge in 1803, print alone could save lost souls. Yet men and women deprived of religious learning "cannot read without books; and a great proportion of them will never have books, unless they are furnished by the hand of charity."[5] Hoping to put as many (free) Bibles into as many hands as possible, the Philadelphia Bible Society, founded in 1808, decided to start producing its own books rather than purchase them for distribution. The society used a newly developed technique—stereotyping—involving casting solid printing plates from movable type.[6] While producing stereotype plates was an expensive process, it was a long-term investment that meant Bibles could be printed in large quantities at regular intervals.[7] Other innovations in print technology such as steam-powered presses and papermaking machines allowed later evangelical associations—the American Bible Society (founded in 1816), American Sunday School Union (1824), and American Tract Society (1825)— to reach an ever-larger readership. The path to a more intense production process was not always smooth, but such associations indubitably helped pave the way for the era of the "industrial book."[8] They also adopted an innovative two-level structure, with a parent society managing the centralized production of print artifacts that were then distributed by a network of local auxiliaries. There was virtually nobody on U.S. soil that the evangelicals could not reach through print. The AASS took up these innovations in the 1830s.

Alongside this evangelical print practice, the AASS inherited a long-standing tradition of print use by North American and British antislavery campaigners. From the mid-eighteenth century, Quaker abolitionists Anthony Benezet and John Woolman devoted considerable energies to disseminating their own writings to a "broader reading public that [they] hoped to convert to the incipient cause of antislavery." Later, "first movement abolitionists," as Paul J. Polgar calls them, also "turned to the world of print," as illustrated by the numerous volumes of minutes printed by the American Convention of Abolition Societies from 1794 on.[9] In the 1820s, Elihu Embree and Benjamin Lundy founded the first newspapers entirely devoted to the antislavery cause, the *Emancipator* and the *Genius of Universal Emancipation*. Even before antislavery thought coalesced into a mass movement and gradualism yielded to immediatism, print was already seen as a means of persuading Americans of the evils of slavery. The immediatist William Lloyd Garrison learned the ropes of printing and journalism working for the gradualist Lundy.[10] Across the Atlantic, the British abolition movement had long led mass publishing campaigns against slavery and the slave trade, taking advantage of the country's high literacy rate and abundant appetite for reading matter. British abolitionists aimed to flood friends and foes alike with print in the form of tracts, periodicals, pamphlets, and books. "Large-scale deployment of the printed word," David Turley writes, was "a powerful feature of the culture of [English] antislavery."[11] Once slavery was abolished in the British colonies in the 1830s, British activists continued to use print to further the cause in America. The AASS therefore drew on strategies developed by its predecessors in the United States and Britain.

The AASS use of print should also be read in the context of Black literary activism. Second-wave antislavery print tactics, Richard S. Newman argues, "flowed first from black abolitionism."[12] As early as the 1790s, free African Americans such as Richard Allen and Absalom Jones articulated their demands for abolition and racial justice in the form of pamphlets, overseeing their production and distribution. Many of these pamphlets started as oral performances delivered at the new independent Black churches, mutual aid groups, and benevolent societies created in the wake of northern emancipation.[13] Committing a speech or sermon to print served various purposes. First, it extended the audience of the original performance, carrying Black voices to physically distant readers. As Dorothy Porter notes, pamphlets "cost little and . . . were easy to distribute or to carry about."[14] Second, pamphlets disproved claims of Black inferiority by displaying their authors' oratorical skills to a broad readership. Giving an address to the New York African Society for Mutual Relief in 1809, William Hamilton brandished a copy of Peter Williams's 1808 *Oration on the Abolition of the Slave Trade*, saying: "I hold in my hand a specimen of African genius. . . . If we continue to produce specimens like these, we shall soon put our enemies to the blush."[15] Hamilton produced the pamphlet as material evidence of the intellectual capabilities of African Americans. Flimsy though it was, he described it as a "book," a term that downplayed its topicality and emphasized its literariness.[16] Hamilton's "striking moment of self-reflexivity" also suggested that "his own oration and future orations would . . . be printed for distribution."[17] Indeed, Black-authored orations on the abolition of the slave trade were published almost annually between 1808 and 1823. Later in the 1820s, David Walker famously managed to circulate his 1829 *Appeal to the Colored Citizens of the World* in the South. With the help of Black and white sailors, copies were smuggled into the ports of Virginia, North Carolina, Georgia, and Louisiana, causing these states and others to criminalize the circulation of "incendiary" literature.[18]

Thus the AASS used organizational methods and strategies for disseminating print developed by the evangelicals, Anglo-American abolitionists of the first wave, and early Black activists. Reading about antislavery ideas, second-wave abolitionists reasoned, would necessarily persuade people of their truth: as one of them put it in 1838, "Those who can be induced to *read*, will most

assuredly be converted, and *thoroughly* converted."[19] "The creation of a reading public," Robert Fanuzzi rightly notes, became "the principal goal of anti-
slavery agitation, the practical equivalent of abolition itself."[20] Even the mass
mailing of tracts and pamphlets to the South was less an act of provocation
than the result of a genuine (some would say misguided) hope of converting
white southerners to the cause. The urge to see antislavery print reach to the
farthest corner of the United States was expressed through a range of meteorological metaphors. For instance, in an early issue of the *Liberator*, Garrison
called for a nationwide antislavery society "to scatter tracts, like rain-drops,
over the land."[21] In the *North Star*, Frederick Douglass discussed an antislavery
pamphlet "which the friends of God and Truth should aid in scattering like
snow-flakes through the vale," while Angelina Grimké "most heartily desire[d]
to see [abolitionist literature] scattered over our land as abundantly as the
leaves of Autumn."[22] The same language cropped up in slave narratives such as
The Rev. J. W. Loguen, as a Slave and as a Freeman (1859). In the 1830s, Loguen
writes, the New York State Anti-Slavery Society (NYSASS) was busy "scattering their tracts, papers and books, like the leaves of autumn over the State, at
an immense expenditure of money, industry and learning."[23]

Pamphlets, books, and periodicals were the main weapons in the antislavery
arsenal, as stipulated in the Declaration of Sentiments of the AASS, written by
Garrison at its founding convention in 1833.[24] From its numerous newspapers—
the *Emancipator, Human Rights*, the *Anti-Slavery Record*, and the *Slave's
Friend*—to the compendium *American Slavery as It Is: Testimony of a Thousand
Witnesses* (1839) and the Great Postal Campaign of 1835, when sacks of antislavery publications were sent to white southerners, the AASS used a broad range
of print forms in the 1830s, distributing its output every way it could to as
wide an audience as possible: northerners and southerners, whites and free
African Americans, men and women, adults and children.[25] The South soon
retaliated. Censorship laws were strengthened and huge rallies organized to
burn antislavery publications, as was the case in Charleston on 29 July 1835.[26]
This does not mean that print was the sole conduit for the immediatist doctrine. The dissemination of print could only prove effective in combination
with the efforts of agents who traveled round the towns and villages of the
North and a dense network of antislavery societies, as again indicated in the
Declaration of Sentiments.[27] Print nonetheless enjoyed significant status for
abolitionists, compared to the more unpredictable impact of speeches. The
Friend of Man, the NYSASS's official organ, quoted the example of "a Patri-
arch in years, of more than 'three score and ten,' who has long resisted the living
arguments as they fell from the lips of the anti-slavery lecturer or preacher, [but]
has at length . . . '*read* himself out an abolitionist.'"[28]

Establishing a distribution system based on those developed by evangelical associations was an early AASS priority. The society oversaw the publication of books and pamphlets, which were then stocked and sold at book depositories run by auxiliaries at the state, county, or town level. The Connecticut Anti-Slavery Society (CASS) founded its own in 1838, where "all the publications of the American Anti-Slavery Society [could] be obtained at the same prices as at New York"; the Pennsylvania Anti-Slavery Society (PASS) opened its depository a month later.[29] The AASS likewise encouraged the creation of antislavery libraries to connect with those who could not or would not buy their publications. It developed a complex system based on sets of bound volumes and pamphlets at various price points that could be combined to build a complete antislavery collection.[30] Even the local library in Nantucket, Massachusetts, provided "as extensive a collection of the standard Anti-slavery productions of British and American authors, as can be found in any Anti-Slavery depository in the country." The "leading A.S. periodicals" could also be consulted, all for free.[31]

The abolition movement was not alone in placing print front and center of its activities. Most reform organizations that arose at the same time, campaigning for causes such as prison and asylum reform, women's rights, and temperance, made use of similar methods, arguing that information would lead to reform.[32] As Goddu argues, "Reform movements drove the rise of popular print in the antebellum period and . . . print culture in turn facilitated the spread of reform."[33] The philosophy behind such reform efforts can be summed up by a motto often found on their publication mastheads: "READ AND CIRCULATE." "This good old motto has nearly gone out of use with us anti-slavery folks," one abolitionist commented.[34] To meet its goal, reform literature had to circulate constantly, passing from reader to reader. Though print diffusion was supervised by the AASS and its auxiliaries, members were also seen as individually responsible for distributing antislavery publications within their own circles. The AASS's official mouthpiece, the *Emancipator*, made this very clear: "Every abolitionist . . . who comes from a distance to the city [of New York], should make it a matter of conscience to lay in a stock of books and pamphlets for circulation among his neighbors." It then concluded, "Never was there so great a necessity for the general diffusion of abolition light."[35] The joint actions of the AASS, its auxiliaries, and their tens of thousands of members ensured that no one on U.S. soil could escape the powerful rays of "abolition light."

The *Narrative of James Williams* as Antislavery Propaganda

The *Narrative of James Williams* was the only slave narrative controlled at every step of the process, from planning to publication and distribution, by an anti-slavery society—the AASS. The later narratives by Douglass and William

Wells Brown are generally included in the same category, though they were in fact written, published, and disseminated in very different ways from Williams's account. The *Narrative of James Williams* was designed as a propaganda tool from the outset. The text circulated within the AASS's print network until its authenticity was called into question by white southerners who lived in the region where Williams claimed to have been enslaved. The publishing history of the *Narrative of James Williams* was brief, beginning and ending in 1838, but nonetheless highly eventful.[36]

The earliest known reference to Williams's narrative is in the AASS executive committee minutes for 4 January 1838, when the committee resolved that the poet and abolitionist John Greenleaf Whittier should "be employed to write a narrative of the life & escape of a fugitive slave now in this neighborhood, & that the same be published under direction of the Publishing Committee, with a portrait & other embellishments."[37] The fugitive slave was James Williams—or at least that was the name he gave abolitionists when he made it north.[38] His birth name was Shadrach Wilkins. Wilkins was initially enslaved by Joseph and Adelaide Janey in Virginia, then sold in 1834 to the Alabama planter Caleb Tate. Wilkins fled Alabama in 1835, helped by a white man who passed himself off as his master. Their journey came to an unexpected end in Baltimore, when Wilkins—by now calling himself James Williams—was imprisoned, then bought by a slave trader who packed him off to New Orleans. Wilkins fled once again aboard a steamer heading up the Mississippi and Ohio Rivers. He passed himself off as a crew member by the name of Jim Thornton. Eventually reaching the free states, he spent some time in Cincinnati before setting out for New York late in 1837. He traveled across Pennsylvania, helped by the abolitionist Emmor Kimber, and—by now calling himself James Williams again—arrived in New York City on 1 January 1838.

Williams told the broad outline of his story to abolitionists in Pennsylvania and New York but changed a number of details, such as the real names of his various enslavers. He also claimed to have come straight from Alabama. He was probably anxious not to let himself be found. It seems he agreed to share his (somewhat modified) story with white abolitionists so that they would help him leave the United States as soon as possible. Williams set sail for Liverpool in late January 1838, before his narrative was even printed, with a letter of recommendation from Lewis Tappan. Other than one brief mention in a letter from a British abolitionist sent to Tappan shortly after, he was never heard of again. The publication of his narrative, on the other hand, brought his name to public prominence.

Williams did not decide himself to write—or even dictate—his narrative. The driving force behind publication was an AASS abolitionist, most likely

Tappan, who devoted considerable energies to promoting and defending the *Narrative of James Williams*.[39] Tappan may have been inspired by earlier works: he had certainly read Charles Ball's *Slavery in the United States*, reprinted in New York in 1837, and Richard Hildreth's 1836 *The Slave*, the fictional autobiography of an enslaved man by the name of Archy Moore. The AASS was in fact on the verge of suspending sales of the novel from its offices on the grounds that fiction had no place among its publications.[40] It is hardly surprising that at the same time as it was expunging a fictional slave narrative from its catalog, the AASS sought to include a (supposedly) authentic slave narrative, and it is clear why one of its readers saw Williams as "the real Archy Moore."[41] Whittier must have struck the executive committee as one of the best possible choices to shape the book the way they wanted and raise its profile. The editor of the influential *New England Weekly Review* and a founding member of the AASS, Whittier had already published several antislavery works, including *Justice and Expediency, or, Slavery Considered with a View to Its Rightful and Effectual Remedy, Abolition* (1833) and *Poems Written during the Progress of the Abolition Question in the United States* (1837).[42]

A first-person account of slavery transcribed by a renowned literary and intellectual figure and published in a standalone volume was sure to find a readership. A few years previously, the American Tract Society had noted the superiority of narrative form over rhetorical arguments when it came to evangelizing and moralizing: "Tracts are needed in *the most simple style*, and especially *narratives* calculated to engage and fasten the attention."[43] The Williams narrative indeed set out to make its mark on the reader with a plain, genuine account of a man risking his life to flee slavery; at 517 pages, *Slavery in the United States* was overly long, while *The Slave* was a work of fiction. Tappan and James G. Birney later explained that Williams's narrative chimed with audiences "not so much because it revealed atrocities unparalleled by others which were already known of the system of slavery, but because it brought many such together, and connected them in the form of *a regular narrative*, in which the narrator himself was the principal actor, and to most of the particulars of which he could himself testify."[44] Even before the *Narrative of James Williams* was available, Tappan claimed it would be a "thrilling" read—an adjective found in most reviews of slave narratives.[45]

Barely three days after Williams arrived in New York on New Year's Day, the decision was taken to publish his account. On 12 January, Theodore D. Weld told Birney that "J. G. W.'s book," as he tellingly called it, would be "out this week."[46] Whittier in fact needed slightly more time to put the finishing touches on the manuscript, as the date in the preface of 24 January makes clear. The following day, the *Emancipator* announced that "an authentic narrative of

this slave—now a FREEMAN—self-emancipated" would be "speedily published."[47] "Whittier's book," as Weld persistently referred to it, was sent to the
printer's in early February and published later that month as the *Narrative of
James Williams, an American Slave; Who Was for Several Years a Driver on a Cotton Plantation in Alabama.*[48] The title page bore the words "Published by the
American Anti-Slavery Society," which would never feature again on another
slave narrative. The frontispiece was adorned with a portrait by Patrick H. Reason, an African American printmaker active between circa 1835 and 1850 in
New York who carried out numerous portrait commissions for Black and white
abolitionists.[49] Thus the *Narrative of James Williams* was as much the product
of the AASS and its partners as it was of Williams.

The paratext of the first edition was entirely focused on guaranteeing the
truth of the narrative. The portrait depicted the formerly enslaved man as a
recognizable figure, proving his existence, as the aforementioned reader noted:
"James Williams is a reality. That fine portrait . . . is the picture of a *real
MAN.*"[50] Using the technique of pointillism, Aston Gonzalez remarks, the
engraver had produced "a highly detailed representation of Williams's clothing
and face" and thus enhanced his individuality.[51] Whittier's preface presented
the narrative as "the simple and unvarnished story of an AMERICAN SLAVE."
Whittier affirmed that he had been at pains to copy down Williams's words as
accurately as possible, "carefully abstain[ing] from comments of his own"; he
corroborated the horrors in Williams's account by including advertisements
for runaway slaves taken from southern newspapers and invited readers to
check the facts by writing to the abolitionists who had assisted Williams in his
escape—Kimber, Tappan, Birney, and others.[52] He further added an appendix
containing accounts by white southerners of the barbaric practices of Virginia
and Alabama planters. As if that were not enough, a later edition bore the
(inaccurate) title *Authentic Narrative of James Williams, an American Slave* on
its cover, followed by the names of abolitionists who could swear to its truth
(fig. 1). The *Narrative of James Williams* provides an extreme example of what
Robert Stepto's taxonomy of slave narratives categorizes as the "eclectic
narrative"—a polyphonic narrative in which (white) voices surround the text
in abundance to lend credence to the word of the (Black) slave. "The publisher or editor, far more than the former slave," Stepto explains, "assembles
and manipulates the authenticating machinery, and seems to act on the prem-
ise that there is a direct correlation between the quantity of documents or texts
assembled and the readership's acceptance of the narrative as a whole."[53] Yet
unlike other eclectic narratives, very little in the paratext to the *Narrative of
James Williams* proved that the specifics of Williams's account were true: at
most, it could be claimed to be *credible.* By harping on its authenticity, AASS

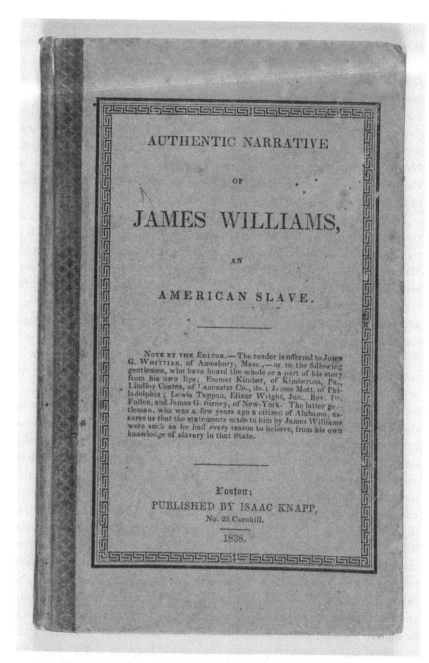

Figure 1. Front cover of *Narrative of James Williams, an American Slave* with inaccurate title (Courtesy of American Antiquarian Society)

abolitionists tried to assert performatively something that they could not demonstrate objectively.

Since Williams had left the United States, it was up to the AASS to promote and distribute the book. The society threw all its resources into the *Narrative of James Williams*. The details of the print runs, recorded in the executive committee minutes, are impressive: five thousand copies printed in February, ten thousand in April, twenty thousand in June and again in September, when the controversy surrounding the title was at its height.[54] The AASS regularly printed pamphlets and books in the tens of thousands, but this was the first time a slave narrative was given such treatment. The society had good grounds for feeling encouraged. In the weeks immediately after publication, many readers wrote to the antislavery press to praise the account. Memento "hope[d] that it [would] be universally read"; A. D. Sargeant, a Methodist preacher, recommended the narrative "to every person who has any desire to know the present condition of slaves on the plantations of the South."[55]

Riding high on the wave of favorable reactions, the AASS decided in April to reprint in a new format. First published in book form at between 18¾ and 25 cents a copy (or between fourteen and seventeen dollars per hundred copies), the *Narrative of James Williams* was reissued in sheets as number 6 of the "Anti-Slavery Examiner." The "cheap" edition, as it was known, sold for one dollar per hundred copies.[56] The temperance advocate Edward C. Delavan was the first to suggest this format: "James Williams should be published on a sheet and sold by the thousand—by the tens of thousands, by the hundreds of thousands."[57] The AASS executive committee took up the idea, resolving that "the 'Narrative of James Williams' be stereotyped, in quarto form, & minion-brevier type, & 10,000 copies printed, on paper like the Advocate of Moral Reform, and sold at $10 per thousand."[58] In a form resembling a newspaper, the new edition of the Williams narrative was cheaper to produce, easier to circulate, and less likely to be excluded from the mail by postal officers who "retained wide discretion over the transmission of tracts, pamphlets, and . . . magazines" but "were required to transmit without discrimination *every* newspaper that had been issued in the proper format," as Richard R. John notes.[59] It could therefore be more readily posted to the South. On 20 October 1838, police in Richmond, Virginia, burned copies of the *Narrative of James Williams* and other publications sent by the AASS.[60] Yet some copies did slip through the censor's net and reached their target. The *Advocate of Freedom* recorded that one Alabama planter was "delighted" with the narrative and "did not hesitate to bear unequivocal testimony to [its] verisimilitude."[61] Birney himself pointed to the society's hard work getting copies of the *Narrative* below the Mason-Dixon line: "Copies were sent to all our exchange papers—to the postmasters, and to multitudes of others persons in that section of the country."[62] The narrative drew the ire of white southerners precisely *because* it was in circulation in the South.

The material changes to the *Narrative of James Williams* did not stop there. The two editions were reprinted in Boston, the first published by Garrison's associate Isaac Knapp, the second reprinted as number three of the Massachusetts Anti-Slavery Society's (MASS's) "Abolitionist's Library." On 8 September 1838, Williams's narrative was also printed in full in *Zion's Watchman*. Editor La Roy Sunderland had altered the layout to fit the eight pages of the cheap edition on two pages of the *Watchman* (fig. 2): "We give this narrative from stereotype plates, which do not exactly tally with the usual form of our paper, but a little attention will show how the columns are to be read. . . . To one and all we say, read it, every word of it."[63] More typically, extracts were featured in major antislavery papers such as the *Liberator* and local press titles like the *Hampshire Gazette*.[64] The narrative was also serialized in the Dover, New Hampshire, *Morning Star* between 18 July and 22 August 1838.

Physically reduced to smaller and smaller spaces—a bound book, sheets, newspaper—and published by a powerful organization, the *Narrative of James Williams* could circulate in many places at the same time. While "4,000 copies of James Williams' Narrative, designed to supply every family in the country," were being disseminated in Litchfield County, Connecticut, the antislavery society of Utica, New York, was circulating it "throughout the city—a copy left with every family, and in every store and office, and two or three copies in boarding houses. It took 1,357 copies; cost, $13.57, and the services of a boy a little over two days."[65] All good antislavery libraries had to have Williams's narrative, which could also be acquired from book depositories in New York, Boston, Hartford, Providence, Philadelphia, Utica, Cincinnati, and Pittsburgh.[66] The agent of the Ohio Anti-Slavery Society (OASS) depository claimed in May that "several hundred copies of 'James Williams' had been called for within a week or two."[67] Rather than waiting for a delivery from New York, the OASS printed six thousand copies at its own cost to be given to delegates at a forthcoming local political convention.[68] Orders poured in from far and wide: 10,000 copies for the Albany Young Men's Anti-Slavery Society, 2,500 for the Wayne County Anti-Slavery Society, and 5,000 for the Onondaga County Anti-Slavery Society from April to July.[69] With the help of its auxiliaries, the AASS supplied the *Narrative of James Williams* through as many venues as possible, and hoped that demand would follow; in many cases, it did not even wait for demand, providing the narrative free of charge. The AASS thus operated in much the same way as other early nineteenth-century religious publishing organizations whose practice was characterized not by

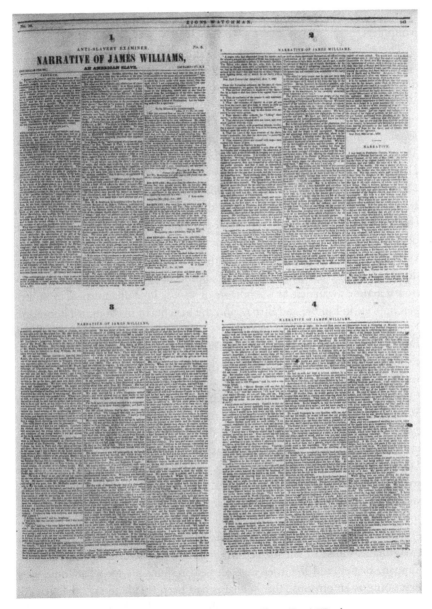

Figure 2. *Narrative of James Williams, an American Slave*, *Zion's Watchman*, 8 September 1838 (Courtesy of Library of Congress, Prints and Photographs Division, sn94096017)

"pure giving or pure selling" but "the mixture of giving and selling" books and pamphlets.[70]

The *Narrative of James Williams* should not be read as separate from other AASS publications. The account was given a higher than usual profile, but its distribution was closely bound up with other categories of antislavery print. Williams's narrative often featured in antislavery newspapers alongside two other titles published the same year, *Emancipation in the West Indies: A Six Months' Tour in Antigua, Barbadoes, and Jamaica, in the Year 1837* by James A. Thome and J. Horace Kimball and *Correspondence, between the Hon. F. H. Elmore, One of the South Carolina Delegation in Congress, and James G. Birney, One of the Secretaries of the American Anti-Slavery Society*. The former demonstrated that the abolition of slavery in the British West Indies had not led to chaos, as predicted by proslavery apologists, but rather had brought positive benefits to the newly emancipated population. The latter was a detailed overview of abolitionist principles, methods, and objectives. Together, the three documents represented three types of approach to the three stages of abolitionist action: awareness of the horrors of slavery in Williams, putting strategies in place in Elmore and Birney, and the benefits of freedom in Thome and Kimball. The three types of texts were most effective when read in combination. The *Emancipator* suggested distributing them together: a community of 1,500 souls could absorb 300 copies of the *Narrative of James Williams*, 25 copies of *Emancipation in the West Indies*, and 124 copies of the *Correspondence*.[71] Other abolitionists saw Thome and Kimball's *Tour* as more significant than Williams.[72] Whatever the order of priority given to the works, the *Narrative of James Williams* should be understood not only in terms of its specificity as an eyewitness account of slavery but also as part of the wider AASS print output. Unlike other slave narratives, Williams's narrative was fully integrated into the society's print culture and distributional system. That was its strength and its weakness. Proslavery southerners saw the narrative as all the more dangerous for being officially sponsored and widely distributed by the AASS.

The earliest criticisms of the *Narrative of James Williams* were addressed less to Williams himself than to the AASS abolitionists who helped publish it. Tappan, Birney, and Whittier were all held responsible for what some were describing as an obvious fake. Williams had been "made to say" the series of lies that composed this "atrocious publication of the abolitionists," and the narrative was regarded as another example of "the multiple artifices by which the American Anti-Slavery Society is perpetually gulling the public."[73] The defamation campaign began just a few weeks after publication. It was orchestrated by John B. Rittenhouse of Greene County, Alabama, where Williams had set the second part of his narrative; Williams had in fact been in Dallas

County. Rittenhouse edited the Greensborough *Alabama Beacon*, which launched the controversy. Aside from a few comments by an anonymous author in the *New York Commercial Advertiser*, the hostilities were mainly confined to the *Emancipator* and the *Beacon* between March and October 1838. The swift communication between the two papers, and therefore the controversy itself, was enabled by the cooperative exchange of newspapers between editors. Any editor was entitled to send copies of their paper to a fellow editor without paying postage. Such exchanges were usually two-way. Political opponents regularly exchanged publications to learn about each other's stances.[74] Rittenhouse had agreed to exchange with the *Emancipator*, acknowledging the reach of the AASS and the need to study its message and strategies.[75] In turn, the AASS was keen to distribute the narrative in the South and readily sent Rittenhouse a copy with the paper.[76]

The *Beacon* soon made its hostility to the narrative clear, firing its opening salvo on 29 March: "We have been politely favored by our correspondent with the lying Abolition pamphlet entitled the 'Narrative of James Williams,' copious extracts from which we find in the paper of that sect. We have not had leisure to give it that perusal which we design doing, but are assured by some of the oldest residents of this county that it is a foul fester of falsehood, a miserably 'weak invention of the enemy.'"[77] Rittenhouse dismissed the narrative in the strongest possible terms. The Larrimore family, Williams's supposed enslavers, simply did not exist, he wrote. None of the most eminent residents of Virginia or Alabama questioned by Rittenhouse had ever heard of them; the Greene County tax records did not list a George Larrimore or any of the neighbors mentioned by Williams. Research by Hank Trent has since demonstrated that George Larimer (a variant spelling) was the son-in-law of Adelaide Janey, Williams's actual enslaver, in Virginia; she lived in Essex County, not Powhatan County as claimed in the narrative. In Alabama, Williams had no further links with the Larimer family. These inaccuracies were awkward for the abolitionists who had to account for them. The AASS carried out a detailed investigation but did not achieve any conclusive results. Williams's departure made the situation even more complicated, as Lydia Maria Child suggested in a letter to Angelina Grimké: "Where *is* James Williams? Can he not be found and cross examined?"[78]

While gathering information on Williams, the AASS abolitionists came to realize his narrative was not entirely rooted in fact. "To you and I, who look on the foundations upon which slavery rests," Child wrote to Weld a few days later, "it is not of the slightest consequence whether James Williams told the truth or not; yet the doubt thrown on his narrative is doing incalculable mischief."[79] Many others were of the same mind. Though some episodes of

Williams's account may not have happened exactly as he claimed, no one could deny the reality of the cruel practices described in the *Narrative of James Williams*. However, Rittenhouse strategically refused to debate this point, restricting the argument to the exact authenticity of the narrative. Since Williams's account was not scrupulously accurate in every detail, the AASS had no business distributing it. In early August, the society decided to halt sales on a temporary basis, though its auxiliaries probably kept disseminating the work.[80] On 16 August, it was agreed that Birney and Tappan would compile a report looking at evidence from both sides of the argument.[81] The report was printed in the *Emancipator* on 30 August with the title "Alabama Beacon versus James Williams." Despite devoting nearly half of the issue to the *Narrative of James Williams*, Birney and Tappan were unable to reach a firm conclusion. Tappan did, however, continue to express his full trust in Williams in his private diary: "I have no doubt whatever of its authenticity. No one who conversed with him at the length I did could question it."[82] It may have been at Tappan's urging that the executive committee decided to print fresh copies of the cheap edition, while Tappan, Birney, and Sunderland spent considerable sums of money on an obstinate quest to pin down the truth about Williams.[83] The verdict came a month later:

> The Special Committee on the Narrative of James Williams reported that the evidence obtained by them from various sources satisfied them that many of the statements made in the said Narrative were false.
>
> Whereupon—Resolved—That the said Special Committee prepare, as soon as may be, a statement in relation to said Narrative, to be inserted in the Emancipator; & that the Publishing Agent be directed to discontinue the sale of the work.[84]

After vindicating the narrative for several months, the AASS admitted defeat. A second report ran in the *Emancipator* on 25 October with the title "'Narrative of James Williams.'" The inclusion of inverted commas eloquently indicated the AASS's wish to distance itself from the text and Williams himself, now "struck off the docket."[85]

Williams's narrative was pulled from distribution nine months after it was published. While other AASS publications were still disseminated by the society as well as other antislavery groups, Williams's narrative gradually fell out of circulation.[86] It still made a few appearances in the OASS book depository catalog for 1839 and the MASS catalog in 1841; abolitionists doubtless did not want to lose money on copies already printed.[87] Even this discreet presence riled the American Colonization Society (ACS), which for two decades had been campaigning for the removal of free African Americans from U.S. soil: "It was with utter amazement that we observed, the other day, in the 'Philanthropist,' the leading Abolition newspaper in the West, published at Cincinnati, *by the Executive Committee of the Ohio Anti-Slavery Society*, advertisements . . . of the renowned narrative for sale."[88] The *Philanthropist* included no further references to the *Narrative of James Williams*. Williams's very name was censored by other authors of slave narratives. Moses Roper's introduction to the third edition of *A Narrative of the Adventures and Escape of Moses Roper, from American Slavery* (1837) features a review of his work from the *Liberator* published just before the Williams controversy broke. "For, be it remembered," the review read originally, "a narrative like that of Charles Ball, or James Williams, or Moses Roper, is not given to the world as an extreme case of suffering, but as the ordinary usage experienced by southern slaves."[89] In the introduction to the new edition, dated June 1839, the quotation was subtly changed: "For, be it remembered, a narrative like that of Charles Ball or Moses Roper, is not given to the world as an extreme case of suffering, but as the ordinary usage experienced by southern slaves."[90] The controversy had clearly reached Roper, then in Britain: he deliberately removed Williams's name to avoid his own narrative being similarly discredited. Leafing through antislavery newspapers, antislavery society reports, and abolitionist correspondence of the 1840s and 1850s, Williams's absence is striking. Other narratives published in the late 1830s, such as Roper's, were regularly referred to.[91] But the *Narrative of James Williams* was taboo.

Following Williams's polemical narrative, no further publishing ventures were attempted on a similar scale. No antislavery society poured so much energy into publishing a slave narrative, though the abolition movement as a whole still encouraged the distribution of a number of such accounts. This was partly due to structural developments across the movement, as I explain in the next chapter. But it must also be attributed in part to the Williams affair: from the point of view of the AASS, the word of a formerly enslaved man was too fragile, too readily undermined, to stand at the heart of abolitionist print culture. This was reflected in the publication of *American Slavery as It Is* a few months later. The "thousand witnesses" heralded in the volume's subtitle did not include a single enslaved person. *American Slavery as It Is* was a compilation of press cuttings from southern newspapers and eyewitness accounts by white individuals, including enslavers, who had lived in the South.[92] Weld's opening note called on "all who have had personal knowledge of the condition of slaves in any of the states of this Union, to forward their testimony with their names and residences," insisting on the vital importance of gathering testimonies that could not be challenged.[93] Weld's publication,

Goddu argues, was meant to draw a veil over Williams's narrative and "reestablish the veracity of the antislavery argument."[94] The Williams affair did not herald the end of the circulation of slave narratives within and beyond the abolition movement, but it did undermine the AASS's credibility and have a lasting impact on the way the society handled later testimonies.

Faithful Portrait, Lawful Weapon:
Charles Ball's *Slavery in the United States*

On 5 January 1838, Weld wrote to Sarah and Angelina Grimké: "We have half a dozen fugitives from southern slavery now in the city—just arrived here all together. Two of them are exceedingly interesting cases. One a man of thirty whose history is as rife with the highest interest as Charles Ball."[95] Weld took Ball as a point of comparison for a fugitive freshly arrived in New York— James Williams. The parallel between Williams and Ball reveals that the two formerly enslaved men's narratives were sharing the same circuits at one point in their publishing history. Yet the history of *Slavery in the United States* proved more complex than that of the *Narrative of James Williams*. It unfolded in three stages. Ball's narrative, initially published in 1836 in Pennsylvania with little fanfare, came to the attention of the AASS and was republished in New York the following year. The narrative later reached the wider commercial market, as I show in chapter 3. This case study of the publication and dissemination of Ball's narrative in the late 1830s draws on newly discovered documents, most notably letters that shed light on the part played by Ball's amanuensis and by the white abolitionists who brought his account into institutional antislavery's print culture.[96]

Slavery in the United States: A Narrative of the Life and Adventures of Charles Ball, a Black Man was originally printed in Lewistown, Pennsylvania, in 1836 (fig. 3). Ball had spent years leading a rootless existence as an enslaved man and later a fugitive, before eventually settling in the state, "fifty miles from Philadelphia," as he explains at the end of his narrative.[97] The work was "printed and published" by John W. Shugert, the editor of the *Lewistown Republican and Working Men's Advocate*.[98] The preface was penned by someone referring to himself as "the writer" or "the compiler."[99] His name—Isaac Fisher—only appeared in the New York edition.

None of the three men involved in writing and publishing *Slavery in the United States* had close links with abolitionist circles. A lawyer and amateur geologist, Fisher had traveled through the southern states, "where he became thoroughly disgusted with the arrogance and self-importance of the slaveholders as a class, and with the iniquities of the institution of slavery."[100] In 1838, he contributed financially to the *Quarterly Anti-Slavery Magazine* and

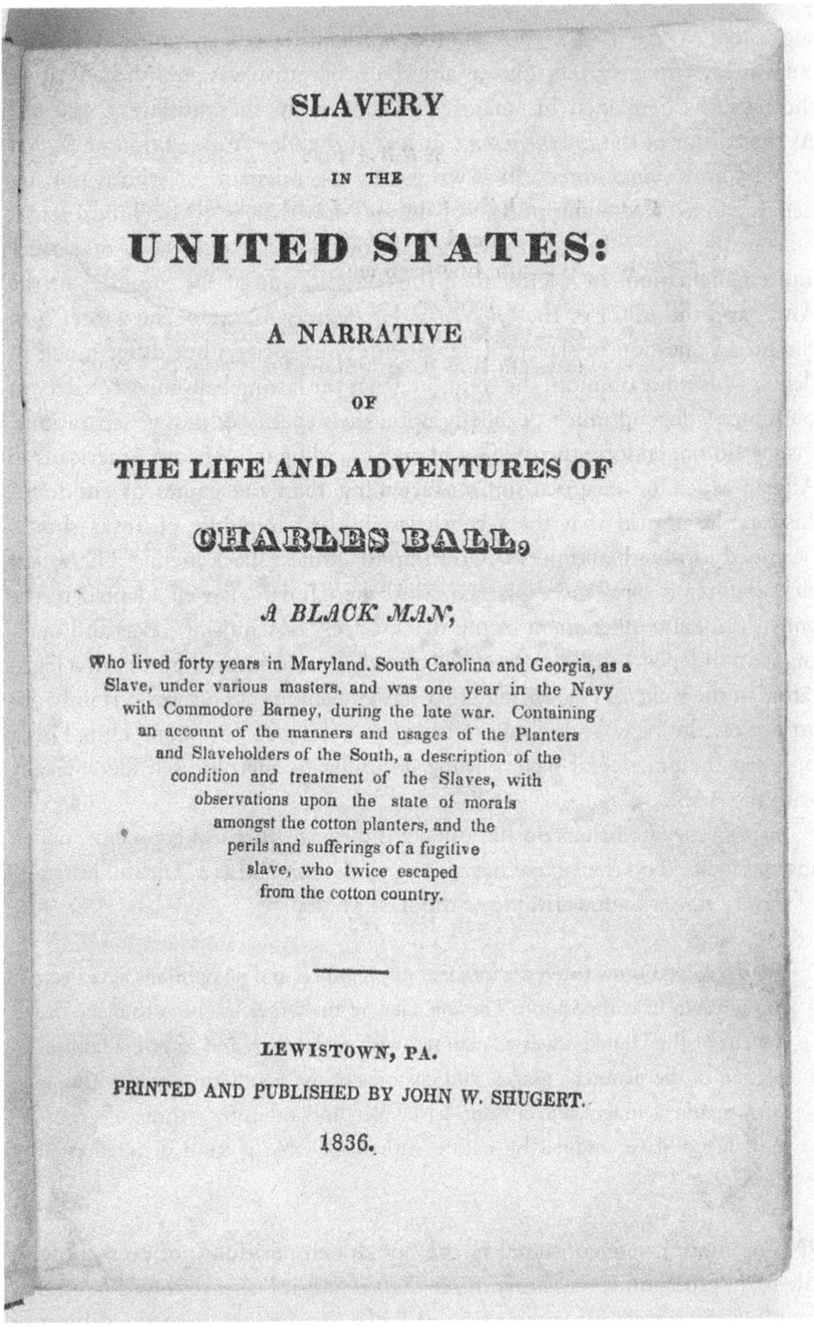

SLAVERY

IN THE

UNITED STATES:

A NARRATIVE

OF

THE LIFE AND ADVENTURES OF

CHARLES BALL,

A BLACK MAN,

Who lived forty years in Maryland. South Carolina and Georgia, as a
Slave, under various masters, and was one year in the Navy
with Commodore Barney, during the late war. Containing
an account of the manners and usages of the Planters
and Slaveholders of the South, a description of the
condition and treatment of the Slaves, with
observations upon the state of morals
amongst the cotton planters, and the
perils and sufferings of a fugitive
slave, who twice escaped
from the cotton country.

———

LEWISTOWN, PA.

PRINTED AND PUBLISHED BY JOHN W. SHUGERT.

1836.

Figure 3. Title page of the 1836 edition of *Slavery in the United States*
(Courtesy of American Antiquarian Society)

suggested to the AASS they should work with Pennsylvania's German-language newspapers, but this was after Ball's narrative was published. Writing the narrative remained his major contribution to the antislavery cause.[101] As the author of the *Emancipator's* review of the New York edition of *Slavery in the United States* noted, "It is written by a gentleman ... who is not, we believe, an avowed abolitionist, nor do we know that, in the technical sense, he is really one."[102] In fact, Fisher had his own idiosyncratic views on slavery and emancipation. In a letter to Elizur Wright, one of the founders of the AASS and the editor of the *Quarterly Anti-Slavery Magazine*, he wrote: "On the broad question of slavery, I agree with your society; but differ much in details." "It is my opinion," he went on, "that the lasting happiness & safety of both races, depend much & chiefly upon their speedy & lasting separation." Fisher did not endorse the ACS's scheme of sending free African Americans to Africa, which he regarded as "more trifling than the games of children." Instead, he argued that the recently established Republic of Texas should be ended forthwith and the soil given up to "honest Black men." "The soil of that country is *good*," he explained, "and the Climate, is well adapted to the constitutional temperament of the Black Race."[103] Acquiring Texas and making it an independent Black state had already been discussed by Virginia legislators in the wake of Nat Turner's 1831 slave rebellion.[104] This was certainly not an option the New York abolitionists were willing to entertain. Thus Fisher opposed the practice of slavery while declining to align himself ideologically with the AASS.

Fisher's specific beliefs on the subject did not feature in his preface, which instead focused on the factual nature of a work designed as a "faithful portrait" of slavery rather than a critique of the slave system:

> The book has been written without fear or prejudice, and no opinions have been consulted in its composition. The sole view of the writer has been to make the citizens of the United States acquainted with each other, and to give a faithful portrait of the manners, usages, and customs of the Southern people, so far as those manners, usages, and customs have fallen under the observations of a common negro slave, endued by nature with a tolerable portion of intellectual capacity.

"No opinions" were consulted in the book's composition, not even those of the main protagonist of *Slavery in the United States*. Fisher's avowed neutrality required the systematic suppression of Ball's "sentiments upon the subject of slavery." Fisher openly presented his case for suppressing the formerly enslaved man's own words:

It might naturally be expected that a man who had passed through so many scenes of adversity, and had suffered so many wrongs at the hands of his fellow man, would feel much of the bitterness of heart that is engendered by a remembrance of unatoned injuries; but every sentiment of this kind has been carefully excluded from the following pages, in which the reader will find nothing but an unadorned detail of acts, and the impressions those acts produced on the mind of him upon whom they operated.[105]

In the words of the *Emancipator*'s reviewer, "the author . . . writes as the historian, and not as the partisan."[106] Ball's narrative is indeed striking for its relatively dispassionate tone—what J. Gerald Kennedy terms its "narrative restraint."[107] Even the most dreadful scenes of torture, of which there are plenty, maintain something of a line between clinical description and critical commentary. In Kennedy's terms, "Fisher mostly foregoes explicit indictment of slavery, allowing the facts to speak for themselves."[108] After a lengthy description of "cathauling," or pulling a cat along a slave's back by its tail so it digs its claws in, Ball/Fisher (exactly who speaks is impossible to determine here) concludes that the punishment is not only "excruciating" but also "dangerous," as "the claws of the cat are poisonous, and wounds made by them are very subject to inflammation." A similar scene in the *Narrative of James Williams* has Williams/Whittier describing "enraged animals" tearing the slave's back "deeply and cruelly."[109] Ball's narrative is devoid of the rhetoric commonly found in narratives emanating from closer to the abolition movement. The most obvious instance is the title, which marginalizes Ball's own role, limiting him to the subtitle; it downplays the autobiographical aspect and therefore the narrative's value as the embodied testimony of a former victim of slavery, focusing rather on its documentary worth.

Fisher seems to have been motivated less by the need to convince his readers of the evils of slavery than by the urge to compile a compendium of knowledge on "slavery in the United States." He saw his task as providing an encyclopedic description of the slave system, including the domestic slave trade, cotton and tobacco farming and the fauna and flora of the Deep South, how the enslaved were clothed and fed, transported and tortured, how they kept themselves entertained, and so on.[110] Ball's personal history was the leitmotif—or, more critically, pretext—for an overview of slavery that was essentially informative in intent. Fisher openly included "incidents" and digressions gleaned from other sources: "There are several . . . incidents, thrown into the Book, not *personal* to Charles, of which he had no knowledge; but all of which have happened . . . as related."[111] At several points, Fisher seemed to quail at the vastness of his undertaking: "It is altogether impossible, to make a person, residing in any of the middle or northern states of the Union, and who has never been in the South, thoroughly acquainted with all the minute particulars of the life of a slave on a cotton plantation." A little later, he went on: "After all that I have written, and all that I shall write, in this book, the reader who has never resided south of the Potomack, will never be able to perceive things, precisely as they present themselves to my vision."[112] It can be argued that the voice here is Ball expressing the impossibility of transmitting the lived experience of slavery, but it seems likely that the first-person narrative voice is also Fisher's, sharing his own difficulty in capturing every detail of the portrait he set out to paint. The reference to the act of writing and the book itself materializes the amanuensis's presence.

This concern for exhaustiveness and objectivity was part of the work's political agenda, which cannot be wholly overlooked. *Slavery in the United States* may not initially have been conceived as abolitionist propaganda, but it did paint a stark picture of the horrors of slavery. The work's opening paragraphs point unambiguously to its ideological roots. Some sentences would be equally at home in the *Liberator* or the *Emancipator*—for instance, when it is claimed that "the entire white population [of the Deep South] is leagued together by a common bond of the most sordid interest, in the torture and oppression of the poor descendants of Africa."[113] One (abolitionist) reviewer summed up the work's stance as follows: "Though it comments with just severity upon some of the atrocities of slavery, it broaches no theory in regard to it, nor proposes any mode or time of emancipation."[114] Fisher may not have wished to make Ball's narrative overtly polemical, but his printer and editor, Shugert, took the opposite tack in promoting it in the press. The reader, Shugert claimed, "will here see portrayed in the language of truth, by an eye witness and a slave, the sufferings, the hardships, and the evils which are inflicted upon the millions of human beings, in the name of the *law of the land* and of the constitution of the United States."[115] Shugert went so far as to claim that *Slavery in the United States* offered "a faithful view of the opinions and feelings of the colored population," though Fisher admitted in the preface to having "cautiously omitted" many of Ball's "opinions."[116] Shugert gave a political spin to the work that was then taken up by many abolitionists.

The same advertisement gave rise to a second horizon of expectation, framing the work as a tale of adventure: "To those who take delight in lonely and desperate undertakings, pursued with patient and unflinching courage, we recommend the flight and journey from Georgia to Maryland, which exhibits the curious spectacle of a man wandering six months in the United States without speaking to a human creature."[117] The figure of Robinson Crusoe, often brought up in reviews of slave narratives, is an implicit presence here, hinting at the extraordinary nature of Ball's adventures. The subtitle of *Slavery in the United States—A Narrative of the Life and Adventures of Charles Ball, a Black Man*—points the same way in including the term "adventures." Ball's narrative features alligators, panthers, and even a lion, as well as kidnapped slaves and British sailors during the War of 1812. The work's underlying structure, based on numerous embedded narratives, echoes picaresque novels such as Tobias Smollett's *The Adventures of Roderick Random* (1748). The digressions include the story of Lydia, a young girl forcibly separated from her beloved mistress and sold to a Deep South slaver; the story of the fugitive slave Paul, whose life ends in suicide; and the tale of two enslaved lovers, Frank and Lucy, who turn to crime.[118] Whether or not Fisher was aware of this literary heritage, it was certainly a useful selling point for Shugert.

The advertisement written by Shugert for the *Liberator* ("Prospectus of a New Work, Entitled Slavery in the United States") is one of the main sources of information for how Ball's narrative came into being. It not only gave notice of publication but called for subscribers. The practice of publishing by subscription, which arose in seventeenth-century England and was later imported to colonial America, allowed a publisher—or printer or author—to have a clear idea up front of how many books they would sell, thereby minimizing the financial risk of publication. The publisher would run a call for subscribers in the press ahead of printing, detailing the type and content of the book, number of pages, price, and so on. They would also distribute the call as a prospectus where anyone interested in purchasing a copy would sign up. Upon reaching a certain number of signatures, the publisher would be confident of not losing money on the publication. The copies would be printed and sent to subscribers, who would then pay up either the whole sum or the balance. The list of subscribers, particularly those with a public profile, sometimes appeared at the end of the volume.[119] The practice fell out of favor with the growth of large commercial publishers in the early nineteenth century—or rather the nature of subscription publishing changed, drawing on an army of agents who traveled across large geographic areas to find buyers for the books on their list. This more modern form of subscription publishing, however, only truly developed after the Civil War; the publication of Ball's narrative was based on the earlier model.[120]

The call for subscribers in the *Liberator* might have been expected to draw the attention of abolitionist readers to Ball's work in large numbers, but this was not the case. Whereas such calls were commonly printed in the same newspaper for months at a time, the prospectus dated 29 August 1835 was never reprinted in the *Liberator* or any other antislavery publication. It is likely that some *Liberator* readers did show an interest in the book as a result of the prospectus, but there cannot have been many of them. No further trace of the call is found until it reappeared in Shugert's own paper, the *Lewistown Republican and Working Men's Advocate*, in late 1835 and early 1836.[121] *Slavery in the United States*, then, was more actively promoted in the *Republican* than it was in the *Liberator*.

This background sheds light on the nature of the first edition of *Slavery in the United States*. It has all the characteristics of a work with a small print run intended for a readership local to Ball. Subscription publication meant printing to meet demand—"No more copies of the work will be printed than shall be subscribed for"—and demand could only arise where the work was promoted.[122] Fisher's correspondence tells us that three thousand copies were printed and sold by a single agent in Lewistown and three counties in Ohio, doubtless the ones adjoining Pennsylvania.[123] A review of the 1837 edition pointed out that the 1836 edition was only distributed locally: "It has as yet had only a limited circulation, the first edition having been small."[124] One historian also noted in 1883, "Only a small edition was printed, and it is difficult to obtain a copy of it now."[125] Today, far more copies of the New York edition of 1837 survive in U.S. libraries than of the 1836 edition, to the point that it is frequently claimed that *Slavery in the United States* was first published in 1837. Ball's case demonstrates why it is problematic to talk of the undeniable success of slave narratives across the board: claims that the first edition of Ball's narrative "met with immediate success" and that "the 1836 edition had sold out before the end of the year" (as if it were a best seller sold out in a few weeks due to insatiable customer demand) tend to overlook the particular circumstances of its publication.[126]

In fact, Ball's account received little attention from the press, including antislavery titles. The sole original review appeared in the *Quarterly Anti-Slavery Magazine* in July 1836, probably the work of its editor, Elizur Wright. As was common practice, Wright copied out entire passages of *Slavery in the United States* word for word—almost twenty pages in total—and paraphrased the rest of the narrative.[127] This was the best way to contribute to raising awareness of a narrative that would otherwise have immediately been forgotten. At a time when books were still financially a stretch for many Americans, reviews of this sort could substitute for the work itself.[128] In this instance, abolitionists learned about Ball's narrative not so much via the circulation of the book itself as via lengthy extracts printed in the *Quarterly Anti-Slavery Magazine*, which were then taken up in other antislavery papers such as the *Philanthropist* and *Zion's Watchman*, by virtue of the antebellum "culture of reprinting."[129] The article headings clearly indicate that the two papers were reprinting the extracts at second hand; neither office had seen a copy of the book itself. The same was true of the *Anti-Slavery Record* of December 1836: "'A narrative of the life and adventures of Charles Ball,' formerly a slave in Georgia, is about to be published at Lewistown, Pa. . . . From a portion of it, published in the Lewistown Republican, we take the following paragraphs."[130] Not only did the *Anti-Slavery Record* reproduce the extracts from the *Republican*, but the editor was unaware that the book was already out. Its publication seems to have only been announced in the *Republican*, which back in April had made it known that *Slavery in the United States* was "just printed" and "ready for delivery."[131] The print run of three thousand copies may have been higher than the number of subscribers: Shugert invited readers to place orders for a dollar, the same price as in the call for subscriptions. This made the book relatively costly, at a day's wages for a skilled white male worker.[132] Given the length of the work and the care taken in producing it—the volume was "handsomely printed on good paper"—it could scarcely have been priced any cheaper.[133] The price did, however, limit its purchase to the middle classes in Lewistown and the surrounding area rather than the "working man" to whose interests the *Republican* was primarily devoted.

While it is possible to outline how the first edition of Ball's narrative came to be published and distributed, it is hard to pin down exactly how the idea for the work came into being. Nothing is known of how Ball, Fisher, and Shugert met, nor which of the three was the driving force behind the project. What is certain is that the publication of *Slavery in the United States* was the result of a private agreement, outside the established circuits of institutional antislavery and commercial publishing. One possible scenario is that Fisher or Shugert came up with the idea for the book to help Ball, by then an old man, with the profits from its sales. *Slavery in the United States* is likely to have been targeted first and foremost at the Lewistown community, where Ball was known and liked and his word trusted—"his account of himself, is universally believed here," Fisher commented in a letter—and where his precarious financial circumstances were common knowledge.[134] Two years previously, when his enslaver turned up in Lewistown to claim Ball as his property, the population apparently raised $250 to purchase his freedom.[135] This can only be a hypothesis, as nothing in Fisher's correspondence or Shugert's call for subscribers explicitly points to a charitable purpose for the book. Whatever the arrangement, *Slavery in the United States* was not initially "a noted anti-slavery book" intended for abolitionists but rather a blend of documentary record and entertainment, published by and for the Lewistown community on a relatively small scale.[136]

Yet Ball's narrative eventually came to the attention of abolitionists by means of extracts reproduced in newspapers. *Slavery in the United States* may not have been an overt critique of slavery, but it did hold up a "mirror . . . of the very best plate glass" to the institution, opening a "window" onto life on southern plantations at a time when it was little known to those living in the North.[137] This made it a useful tool for abolitionists, who incorporated it into institutional antislavery's print culture even before the publication of Williams's account.

Unlike the *Narrative of James Williams*, the 1837 edition of *Slavery in the United States* did not appear under the AASS imprint but with the New York publisher John S. Taylor, who specialized in works on religion and for young readers (fig. 4). Taylor's catalog also reflects a particular interest in the issue of slavery. It includes, for instance, *A View of the American Slavery Question* (1836) by Elijah Porter Barrows and a biography of Elijah P. Lovejoy, who died in 1837 defending the building where he printed his antislavery newspaper in Alton, Illinois. The best known of Taylor's publications was an 1836 reprint of Lydia Maria Child's *Appeal in Favor of that Class of Americans Called Africans* (1833), financed by the AASS, though Taylor kept his own name on the title page.[138] This was a fine example of commission publishing, where Taylor "served as production agent with responsibility for overseeing the manufacture of [the] work." Taylor acted on behalf of "an institution outside the book trade"—the AASS—"who paid all the costs of production plus a fee or commission to the firm for its services and who distributed the resulting publication" through its own infrastructure.[139] The AASS, it should be noted, had no press of its own.[140] In 1838, the society ordered a thousand copies of William Jay's 1835 *Inquiry into the Character and Tendency of the American Colonization, and American Anti-Slavery Societies*, again under Taylor's name.[141] Similarly, the AASS may have (partially) financed the new edition of *Slavery in the United States*, entrusting Taylor with the production of the weighty volume, which called for some technical expertise.

The paratext to the Taylor edition of *Slavery in the United States* bears multiple traces of AASS intervention. The edition was planned as the third volume of the "Cabinet of Freedom" series, established by Lewis Tappan—later to help publish Williams's account—and led by three antislavery activists, William Jay, Gerrit Smith, and George Bush.[142] Jay, an eminent jurist and the son of Founding Father John Jay, suggested Ball's narrative should be part of the series.[143] In September 1836, he wrote enthusiastically to Smith, "Have you read 'A narrative of the life & adventures of Charles Ball, a black man.' If not, I beseech you to procure it. Its interest is that of a first rate romance. It is admirably written, & makes you almost as familiar with Southern Slaves & plantations, as if you were an overseer. . . . I want you to consider the propriety of republishing the book in the 'Cabinet.'"[144] The first title in the series was an

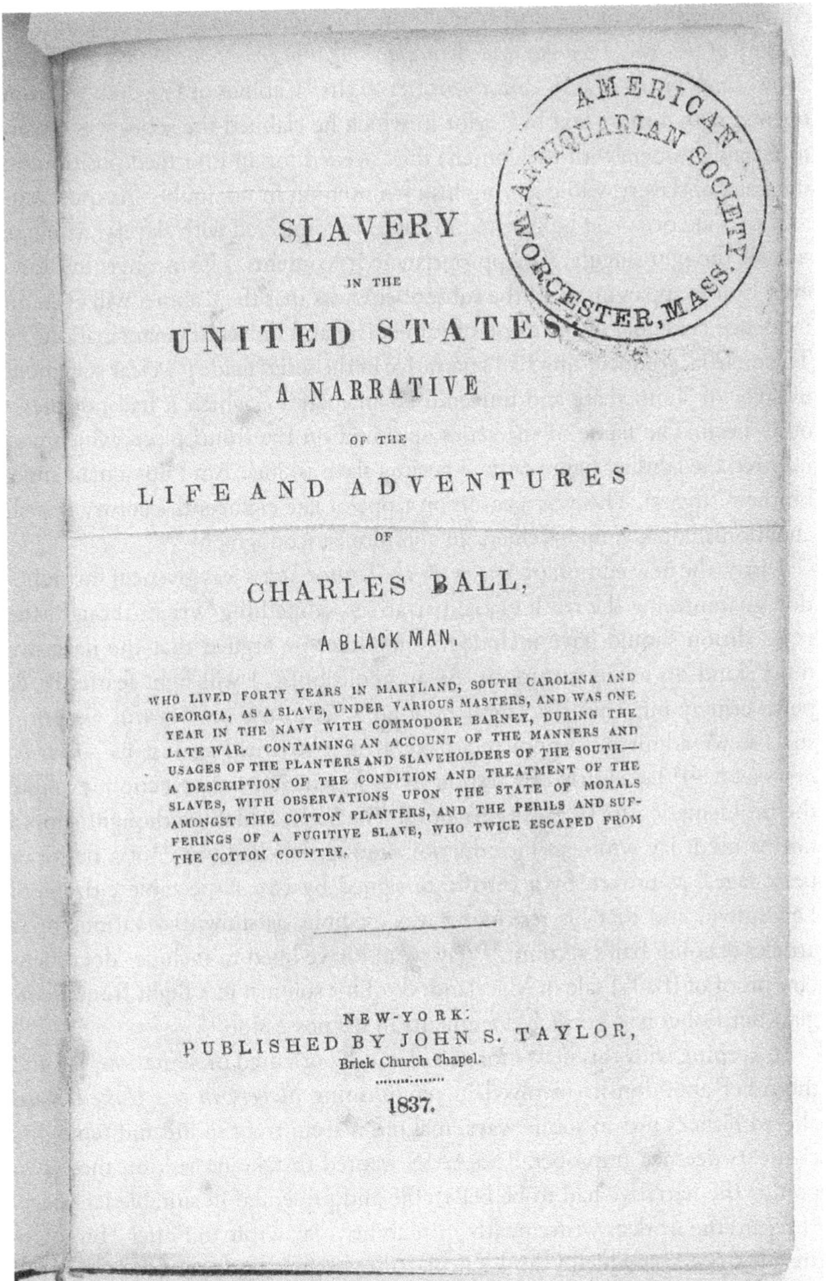

SLAVERY

IN THE

UNITED STATES:

A NARRATIVE

OF THE

LIFE AND ADVENTURES

OF

CHARLES BALL,

A BLACK MAN,

WHO LIVED FORTY YEARS IN MARYLAND, SOUTH CAROLINA AND
GEORGIA, AS A SLAVE, UNDER VARIOUS MASTERS, AND WAS ONE
YEAR IN THE NAVY WITH COMMODORE BARNEY, DURING THE
LATE WAR. CONTAINING AN ACCOUNT OF THE MANNERS AND
USAGES OF THE PLANTERS AND SLAVEHOLDERS OF THE SOUTH—
A DESCRIPTION OF THE CONDITION AND TREATMENT OF THE
SLAVES, WITH OBSERVATIONS UPON THE STATE OF MORALS
AMONGST THE COTTON PLANTERS, AND THE PERILS AND SUF-
FERINGS OF A FUGITIVE SLAVE, WHO TWICE ESCAPED FROM
THE COTTON COUNTRY.

NEW-YORK:
PUBLISHED BY JOHN S. TAYLOR,
Brick Church Chapel.

1837.

Figure 4. Title page of the 1837 edition of *Slavery in the United States*
(Courtesy of American Antiquarian Society)

American edition of the British abolitionist Thomas Clarkson's compendious *History of the Rise, Progress, and Accomplishment of the Abolition of the African Slave-Trade by the British Parliament* (1808). Its "Cabinet of Freedom" edition opened with a short text by Taylor in which he claimed the series was meant to provide readers with the content they needed for an informed position on the issue of slavery, while leaving his own opinion in no doubt: "As the CABI-NET OF FREEDOM will be devoted to subjects connected with slavery, its name may be thought singularly inappropriate to its contents. The incongruity, how-ever, is only apparent, since the subscriber trusts that the Cabinet will exert an influence favorable to the cause of immediate and universal emancipation."[145] The mere fact of including Ball's narrative in the series made it a clear statement in favor of "immediate and universal emancipation," which it had not previ-ously been. The name of the series appeared on the frontispiece, which also featured the familiar figure of the kneeling slave asking, "Am I not a man and a brother?" (fig. 5). This was a common trope of late eighteenth-century British abolitionism, taken up in American abolitionist iconography.[146]

Lastly, the new edition of *Slavery in the United States* was given an introduc-tion guaranteeing the truth of the narrative—something Wright thought the 1836 edition should have included.[147] Jay likewise argued that the narrative must stand up to investigation: "As an abolitionist, I will fight fearlessly, & perseveringly but I want to fight honorably & to use only lawful weapons, such as we admit our opponents have a right to wield against us—*facts & arguments*."[148] Jay clearly saw testimony as legitimate, unlike fiction, evoking the problematic case of Hildreth's novel *The Slave*, which he thought should not be used. Jay wrote an introduction stating that Ball was "not a fictitious personage," as proven by a certificate signed by two respectable citizens of Lewistown, and that his testimony was credible, as shown by various press articles echoing Ball's account.[149] Jay would have liked to include "documen-tary proof of [Ball's] sale in Maryland; & of his sojourn in a flight from Geor-gia," but Fisher had no such documents in his possession.[150]

In keeping with this new, more ideologically oriented presentation, Jay and the other abolitionists involved in republishing *Slavery in the United States* altered Fisher's text in subtle ways, making it seem truer to life and removing elements deemed improper. The AASS wanted to take no risk on these two points: the narrative had to be believable and presented in suitable language. "I regard the work as written with great ability," Jay wrote to Fisher, "but there are a few passages which I think calculated to excite scepticism & which it will therefore be expedient to omit." The material removed by Jay included entire paragraphs of direct speech in chapter 8 and a tirade by Ball's enslaver on the U.S. Constitution that Ball could not have remembered word for word—and

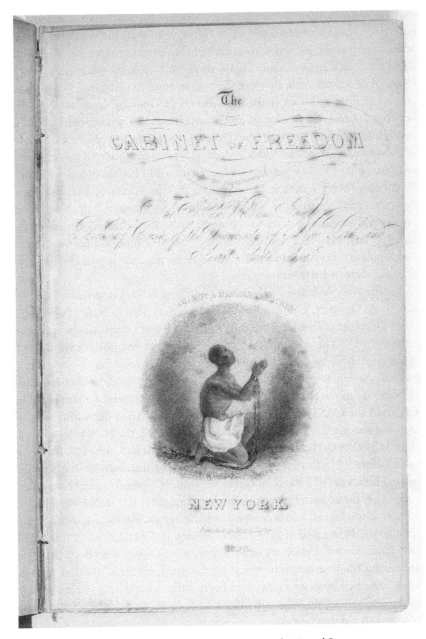

Figure 5. Frontispiece to the 1837 edition of *Slavery in the United States*
(Courtesy of American Antiquarian Society)

that he did not have the intellectual capacities to understand, added Jay, betraying a degree of racial prejudice common to even the most committed white abolitionists. Jay was also concerned that elements of the narrative were liable to shock female readers: "Again there are here & there sentences which it would be scarcely delicate to read aloud in a mixed company."[151] One passage in chapter 13 in which Ball alluded to the impassable physical barrier between the enslaved Black man and his white mistress was removed from the new edition. Fisher's text was edited to meet the moral and racial expectations of the white, middle-class AASS leadership. This amounted to a twofold form of censorship of Ball's voice: having been stripped of his "opinions" by Fisher, Ball then saw his narrative altered to fit Jay's principles of likelihood and decency. From the paratext, which established an image of Ball as a generic, impersonal supplicant slave, to the text itself, which silenced aspects of the narrative deemed unrealistic or disturbing, the New York abolitionists framed and regulated the work to meet their own propaganda needs, thereby suppressing some of Ball's individuality.

Yet the AASS's "reframing" of Ball's narrative helped improve its circulation.[152] As David N. Gellman has noted, including *Slavery in the United States* in the "Cabinet of Freedom" not only legitimized Ball's story but also extended its audience.[153] The abolitionist espousal of the work was not just symbolic: it made it possible to distribute the book far more widely via the AASS and auxiliary society networks. Ball's narrative was, for instance, included in lists of books on sale at antislavery offices and book depositories. Copies could be had from the OASS depository in Cincinnati, the MASS depository in Boston, and the AASS office in New York; as late as 1846, the book was on sale at the PASS office in Philadelphia, not far from where it had come into being ten years before.[154] Indicating the change of scale of distribution, the societies offered bulk sales of a hundred copies for $100, compared to $1.25 for a single copy. The Taylor edition was pricier than Shugert's. But unlike the Shugert edition, it was loaned free of charge by antislavery societies which set up libraries, like the New London Anti-Slavery Society in Connecticut.[155] "We think that CIRCULATING LIBRARIES of abolition books—loaned without charge— are among the best means of spreading the good doctrine," the *Emancipator* read. "The best book we know of, to begin with, is the deeply interesting narrative of Charles Ball. Who will follow the fashion, for it is already started, of buying half a dozen or a dozen copies to lend?"[156]

Ball's account was now available for purchase or loan in all major urban centers across the North. Being available did not mean, however, it was pushed with as much energy and efficiency as Williams's work. *Slavery in the United States* did not bear the AASS stamp after all; nor was it written by an abolitionist. The society was keen to see it available but did not pour as much effort into distributing it as they later did for Williams. It would have been a challenge for them to do so anyway: there were obvious financial and practical barriers to providing free copies of a book over five hundred pages long to the entire population of a town, as they did with the "cheap" edition of the *Narrative of James Williams* in Utica. The sheer length of Ball's narrative was a hindrance to its distribution—something the AASS leadership was well aware of. They considered printing an abridged version at one point: "*Resolved . . .* to inquire & report on the purchase of the copy right of Charles Ball, & the expediency of abridging it for general circulation."[157] The project never came to fruition, possibly because Fisher refused. He had already proved protective of his rights when negotiating the "Cabinet of Freedom" edition: "I have no objection to the reprint of C. Ball in the 'Cabinet of Freedom' provided nothing is done to injure or endanger my Copy Right, which has been secured according to act of Congress."[158]

The lack of an abridged version of *Slavery in the United States* suitable for widespread distribution did not stop Ball's narrative from moving between media within antislavery print culture. From April to July 1838, the *Advocate of Freedom* printed lengthy extracts and invited readers to acquire "the work itself."[159] Other extracts appeared in the *Liberator*, *Zion's Watchman*, and *Zion's Herald* and were sometimes picked up in publications less closely associated with the antislavery cause.[160] The *Salem Gazette* ran extracts from the New York *Plaindealer*, which had taken them from the Taylor edition.[161] Goddu rightly notes that as Ball's narrative moved from one periodical to another, it acquired a more diverse readership. Passages selected for the AASS-sponsored *Slave's Friend* were meant to be read by children; those in *Slavery in America* were intended for a British audience.[162] Nor was its circulation restricted to periodicals, as extracts were also included in La Roy Sunderland's *Anti-Slavery Manual* (1837), from where they were taken up a decade later in a volume printed in London by the British abolitionist Joseph Barker, *Interesting Memoirs and Documents Relating to American Slavery* (1846).[163] An abolitionist flicking through his antislavery almanac in April 1838 would have seen an engraving of an enslaved man hanging from a tree: the caption told readers this was Paul, the fugitive in chapter 15 of Ball's narrative who committed suicide.[164] The distribution of physical copies of *Slavery in the United States* took place in parallel with a more diffuse, looser kind of circulation in the form of press extracts and other ephemera. Many readers of antislavery newspapers, books, and almanacs only knew Ball's account through such indirect sources.

This seems to have brought Ball's narrative a degree of success. The finest illustration is found in another slave narrative, *Chains and Freedom: or, The*

Life and Adventures of Peter Wheeler, published in 1839. When his amanuensis/ interviewer Charles Edward Lester tells Peter Wheeler he will be writing down his narrative, Wheeler chuckles, "I s'pose then you've got an idee of makin' out some sich a book as Charles Ball, and that has done a sight of good. But it seems to me I've suffered as much as Charles Ball, and I've sartinly travelled ten times as fur as he ever did. But I should look funny enough in print, shouldn't I? The Life and Adventers of Peter Wheeler—!! ha! ha!! ha!!!"[165] That Wheeler should mention *Slavery in the United States* indicates that Ball's narrative eventually achieved some visibility and recognition, at least in the abolitionist sphere, which comprised the main audience for the 1837 edition.

Paradoxical Presences:
The Narratives of Olaudah Equiano and Chloe Spear

The *Narrative of James Williams* and the second edition of *Slavery in the United States* are both examples of slave narratives that were wholly integrated into the AASS print network. Both accounts were actively promoted and distributed by the society, leaving an abundance of archival material recording their respective editorial trajectories. Other slave narratives that were circulating at the same time met with less enthusiasm from the AASS and its networks of readers. I will focus briefly on two of these: the narratives of Olaudah Equiano (1837) and Chloe Spear (1832). Though regularly featured in lists of publications sold by antislavery societies, both narratives—and others, including Wheeler's—spilled much less ink than those by Williams and Ball. Their relative neglect by the AASS sheds light on the type of testimony the society chose to foreground in the 1830s.

It might seem surprising to find Equiano discussed alongside Williams and Douglass in a book on antebellum slave narratives. *The Interesting Narrative of the Life of Olaudah Equiano, or Gustavus Vassa, the African* was published in London in 1789, just as the British Parliament was beginning to debate abolishing the slave trade. There were several successive editions in Britain, thanks to Equiano's efforts to publish and disseminate the work, but it only had one American edition at that time, printed in 1791.[166] The book soon dropped out of sight in the United States, only resurfacing occasionally and indirectly: some ten or so pages on Equiano were included in David Baillie Warden's 1810 translation of Henri Grégoire's *De la littérature des nègres* (1808), which Lydia Maria Child drew on in *An Appeal in Favor of That Class of Americans Called Africans*, acknowledging that she had not been able to access a full copy of the work. The Quaker abolitionist Abigail Mott's *Biographical Sketches and Interesting Anecdotes of Persons of Colour* (1826) similarly paraphrased Equiano's narrative, for young readers in this instance. Mott later abridged it in the pamphlet *The Life and Adventures of Olaudah Equiano* (1829).[167] Equiano's original narrative remained out of print, but his name was familiar from such transatlantic circulations between Britain, France, and the United States. This sense of knowing Equiano's narrative through the writings of white activists is doubtless what prompted the author of an article in the *Anti-Slavery Record* to claim erroneously that it had been "repeatedly republished in America."[168]

The Interesting Narrative of the Life of Olaudah Equiano was only reprinted in the United States in 1837. After being repeatedly paraphrased and abridged in the early decades of the nineteenth century, Equiano's text finally reappeared in the author's own words. Only the title changed slightly, to *The Life of Olaudah Equiano, or Gustavus Vassa, the African*. The abolitionist Charles C. Burleigh's announcement of the new edition confirmed that American readers only knew the narrative at second hand, if at all: "The readers of Mrs. Child's Appeal are probably familiar with the name of Gustavus, as he is favorably noticed in that work; but to others it will not be amiss to say, that this simple narrative of a native African . . . will be found to contain much entertaining matter, and much that is instructive."[169] The two volumes of the original edition were brought into one single volume of three hundred pages of closely packed text. The new format certainly proved useful in distributing the whole narrative as a single textual unit.

The new edition was driven by the Boston branch of the abolition movement, represented by William Lloyd Garrison and the *Liberator* printer Isaac Knapp. This was not the first time that the two saw the work of a Black author into print. The African American activist Maria W. Stewart had her early pamphlets printed by Garrison and Knapp, including the 1831 *Religion and the Pure Principles of Morality* and the 1832 *Meditations from the Pen of Mrs. Maria W. Stewart*, as Garrison recalled:

> Soon after I started the publication of *The Liberator* you made yourself known to me by coming into my office and putting into my hands, for criticism and friendly advice, a manuscript embodying your devotional thoughts and aspirations, and also various essays pertaining to the condition of that class with which you were complexionally identified. . . . I not only gave you words of encouragement, but in my printing office put your manuscript into type, an edition of which was struck off, in tract form, subject to your order.[170]

A few years later, Garrison and Knapp brought out Hosea Easton's *A Treatise on the Intellectual Character, and Civil and Political Condition of the Colored People of the U. States* (1837). At the same time, they reprinted the works of two late eighteenth-century Black authors, Phillis Wheatley and Equiano. In 1838,

Knapp republished Wheatley's *Poems on Various Subjects, Religious and Moral*, printed in London in 1773, as *Memoir and Poems of Phillis Wheatley, a Native African and a Slave*, allowing her poetry, as Max Cavitch writes, "to enter . . . the imagination—and publishing marketplace—of the new abolitionism."[171] The same was true of Equiano's narrative. Reprinted under Knapp's imprint, *The Life of Olaudah Equiano* was conscripted into the American anti-slavery struggle, though the plantations of the U.S. South featured marginally in the narrative. Equiano spent most of his years of slavery at sea, on slave ships and British navy vessels, in England and the West Indies. The narrative did provide a striking description of the Middle Passage and revealed the violence of slavery. Its very existence was also a counterargument to racist discourse on Black intellectual inferiority. The sheer bulk of the new edition—Mott's abridgment of the *Interesting Narrative* had been published as a slender pamphlet—was significant. As Joseph Rezek has demonstrated, Wheatley's poems "were not used as evidence in serious arguments for or against the enslavement of Africans" before they appeared in book form. "Format," Rezek argues, "was an important factor in shaping readers' aesthetic [and political] judgments."[172] The book format likewise lent Equiano's narrative cultural authority.

Yet *The Life of Olaudah Equiano* seems not to have left a lasting impression on antebellum Americans' hearts and minds. The book was available in antislavery book depositories and was read by some abolitionists, Black and white—William Wells Brown likely had it in mind when he penned his travelogue *Three Years in Europe* (1852)—but references to Equiano's narrative in antislavery print culture are few and far between.[173] Equiano's necessarily anachronistic narrative was no match in popularity for the more recent accounts by Ball and, later, Williams, which focused on the experience of the enslaved in the United States. Even so, the brief revival of Equiano's narrative ensured it a foothold in American literary memory.

AASS print culture of the 1830s included a single female slave narrative. The *Memoir of Mrs. Chloe Spear, a Native of Africa, Who Was Enslaved in Childhood, and Died in Boston, January 3, 1815. . . . Aged 65 Years*, came out in 1832, seventeen years after Spear's death. The work recounted her kidnap as a child in Africa, her arrival in Philadelphia in the late 1770s, her life in Massachusetts as an enslaved servant, then as a free woman once slavery was abolished in the state. The author remained anonymous, described only as "A Lady of Boston" on the title page and "A Member of the Second Baptist Church in Boston" in the preface. Scholars have established that she was either Mary Webb, a white Bostonian involved in various benevolent societies, or Rebecca Warren Brown, a prolific author of children's books.[174]

Marion Wilson Starling makes the *Memoir of Mrs. Chloe Spear* "one of the first ventures of the Boston branch of the American Anti-Slavery Society."[175] While the AASS did not yet exist in 1832, the claim does usefully locate Spear's narrative in proximity to the institutional sphere it was brought into some years later. The *Memoir of Mrs. Chloe Spear* was published by James Loring, a Boston-based printer and bookseller specializing in religious works for young readers. Loring's other publications included another work now better known than Spear's narrative, the *Memoir of James Jackson* (1835), the biography of a "little colored boy" who died at the age of six, written by his Black school-teacher Susan Paul to "[break] down that unholy prejudice which exists against color."[176] The *Memoir of Mrs. Chloe Spear* was similarly aimed at a young readership and had powerful religious overtones, focusing first and foremost on Spear's spiritual development while also reflecting on the evils of slavery—a topic that "affords a melancholy evidence of the wickedness of man."[177] Loring only published a handful of antislavery works, but he was certainly close to the MASS abolitionists. His bookstore served as an antislavery book depository before specific depositories were established by the antislavery societies.[178]

Given the lack of infrastructure for distributing antislavery literature on a large scale in 1832, the *Memoir of Mrs. Chloe Spear* could only circulate within a restricted sphere. It was mentioned in the *Liberator*, which printed several extracts and the frontispiece, while the *American Baptist Magazine* also featured a few lines on the narrative, whose author and protagonist both belonged to Boston's Second Baptist Church.[179] Once past the first stage of its publishing history, however, it sank from sight until 1837, when the AASS was in the process of implementing a major new strategy to put books in the hands of readers, including children.[180] By adding the *Memoir of Mrs. Chloe Spear* to its catalog and guaranteeing its availability, the society gave it greater prominence than before, as it was then doing for Ball's account. This trajectory was more obvious in Spear's case, her narrative having been published in Boston; Loring's was close to the MASS both ideologically and geographically. Like Ball's narrative, once Spear's work was co-opted by institutional antislavery, it moved into a new "economy," in the sense of Leon Jackson's multiple "authorial economies" governing the circulation of texts in antebellum America.[181] The *Memoir of Mrs. Chloe Spear* was initially published in 1832 as part of a charitable economy— the preface states that "the avails of the copy-right will be devoted to the *benefit of Schools in Africa*"—but in the late 1830s shifted to a less embodied institutional economy.[182] The text itself did not change, but the object did. On the shelves of an antislavery book depository in Philadelphia, in Knapp's office in Boston, or in the antislavery library of New London, Connecticut, Spear's spiritual narrative turned into an antislavery polemic buttressing the ideology of the

AASS.[183] How successful it was remains unclear. As in Equiano's case, there is little evidence of the book's circulation.

The preceding pages have built up a list of slave narratives that shared the same print cultural space—that of the AASS before it splintered in 1840, when it still had the wherewithal to finance major print and distribution campaigns. Alongside the narratives of Williams, Ball, Equiano, and Spear were accounts by Wheeler, Thomas Cooper (*Narrative of the Life of Thomas Cooper*, 1832), and Moses Roper (*A Narrative of the Adventures and Escape of Moses Roper, from American Slavery*, 1837). The latter circulated mainly in Britain, following a dynamic that foreshadowed the journeys of Douglass and Brown in the next chapter. Williams, Ball, Equiano, Spear, Cooper, Wheeler, and Roper are the names found in the catalogs of publications on the last page of the *Liberator* and the paper wrappers of antislavery almanacs. Their publishing fortunes were very different. Williams's narrative was an AASS project from start to finish; the accounts by Ball, Equiano, and Spear were drawn into institutional antislavery as a second step—fifty years after the original publication in Equiano's case, just one year in Ball's. What these narratives have in common is that they were all distributed using AASS infrastructure in the latter half of the 1830s. It seems to have been relatively easy for anyone living in a large northern urban center to get hold of Spear's and Wheeler's narratives: they simply had to find the nearest antislavery book depository, which would sell copies singly, by the dozen, or even by the hundred. Copies could also be borrowed from antislavery libraries. Other narratives that might have benefited from the same system, notably those published in 1825 by William Grimes and Solomon Bayley, slipped through the AASS net and were forgotten until the late twentieth century.[184]

The mere fact that a book was available does not mean that it was purchased. These narratives shared the same milieu but were received differently. Williams's narrative was promoted and distributed on an unprecedented scale: rather than waiting for readers to discover it, the AASS actively brought it to their attention, handing out tens of thousands of copies of the cheap edition across the North and South. Ball's narrative was also given significant support, though to a lesser extent. The accounts by Equiano, Spear, and Wheeler, published independently of the AASS, were distributed, but not actively promoted by the society. They were useful insofar as they represented the point of view of enslaved individuals on slavery but only partially met the AASS's needs in terms of content and style. Neither *The Life of Olaudah Equiano* nor the *Memoirs of Mrs. Chloe Spear* gave detailed descriptions of life on the southern plantations. Nor did *Chains and Freedom*, the first two-thirds of which recounted Wheeler's life as a slave in the states of New York and New Jersey at the onset of gradual emancipation. The last third gave an account of his adventures at sea and his religious conversion. "Though antislavery in tone and commentary," Graham Russell Gao Hodges writes, Wheeler's autobiography "recalls more the eighteenth-century tradition of salvation narratives than the politicized antislavery memoirs of the antebellum decades."[185] *Chains and Freedom* also takes the unusual form of an interview between Wheeler and the man who describes himself on several occasions as the "author" of the book, the historian and Presbyterian preacher Charles Edward Lester. Lester takes over the book's liminal spaces and margins—the preface, footnotes, and chapter endings—to the point that his presence is strikingly intrusive.[186] A hybrid text that came out a few months after the Williams affair, Wheeler's narrative likely left the AASS leadership hesitant. The *Narrative of James Williams* and *Slavery in the United States*, on the other hand, focused on southern slavery and were more traditional in narrative form. This made them useful tools for the ideological struggle led by the AASS. The *Narrative of James Williams* is the only example of a narrative shaped by the society itself to meet its needs.

It is challenging to evaluate the extent to which these narratives made an impact. Williams's work was distributed across much of the United States, but does that mean it was read? As John Nerone points out, "A million copies [of an antislavery pamphlet] would have reached nowhere near a million readers."[187] What did the inhabitants of Utica think on being given pamphlets they never asked for, containing extraordinary tales of angry cats dragging their claws down the backs of slaves? Many copies of the cheap edition of the *Narrative of James Williams* may simply have been thrown away, recycled, or destroyed, in North and South alike. It may not be too much of a stretch to see this edition of Williams's narrative as an antebellum equivalent of spam emails, junked unread.[188] The "rejection history" of the *Narrative of James Williams*, to borrow from Leah Price, is probably as interesting as its "reception history."[189] Likewise, there is no way of knowing whether Spear's and Wheeler's narratives on sale in antislavery book depositories and elsewhere were actually purchased, read, or lent out. Hodges notes that Wheeler's narrative quickly fell into disuse.[190] No reviews are known to exist; the title crops up relatively frequently in antislavery newspapers, but only as passing mentions in lists of publications on sale at the PASS, CASS, or MASS depositories.[191] The presence of these narratives is paradoxical: there is a discrepancy between their apparent availability and the fact that they seem to have been more or less unacknowledged and unread.

One reason for this is the physical absence of the formerly enslaved men and women in question. As the following chapter shows, Douglass, Brown, and Sojourner Truth played an important role in the distribution of their own narratives in the United States and Britain. In most cases, the protagonists of the 1830s narratives were not behind the publication of their own narrative and played no part in its distribution. Equiano and Spear were long dead when *The Life of Olaudah Equiano* and the *Memoirs of Mrs. Chloe Spear* came out; Williams left the United States prior to the publication of his narrative; Ball stated clearly at the end of *Slavery in the United States* that he had no intention of becoming a public figure. Roper's narrative circulated more widely in Britain, where he lived and held meetings, than in the United States, even though his account was on sale in antislavery book depositories across the North.[192] In the absence of the author or protagonist of the story and without substantial support from the AASS, slave narratives had every chance of going unnoticed.

Despite these limitations, the AASS did raise the profile of slave narratives as a genre, enabling them to be identified as a literary form in their own right and become more popular. The AASS did not undertake any further publishing projects along the lines of the *Narrative of James Williams*. But the formerly enslaved Black activists who became central to the abolition movement published their own narratives and distributed copies as widely as possible, with the support of the antislavery community as a whole. The next chapter explores their experiences.

CHAPTER TWO

"My Narrative Is Just Published"

Agency, Itinerancy, and the Slave Narrative

I N A REVIEW OF EZRA Greenspan's 2014 biography of William Wells Brown, *William Wells Brown: An African American Life*, Nell Irvin Painter points out that scholars of African American literature and culture have shown increasing interest in Brown, who long stood in Frederick Douglass's shadow. Painter attributes the trend to "the flowering of two other fields crucial to a full appreciation of Brown's public life—the history of the book and performance art."[1] The link between Brown's own life and book history, a field in which Greenspan is a leading figure, is of particular interest for this chapter. Many nineteenth-century Black authors had their own unique approach to what they sometimes called "book making." Far from being simply the end product of their intellectual or creative labor, books were fundamental expressions of their political views and self-identity as well as a source of income. The process of producing a book was often bound up with the author's affect, as demonstrated by the following exchange between the African American travel writer Nancy Prince, author of *A Narrative of the Life and Travels, of Mrs. Nancy Prince* (1850), and George B. Ide, a white Baptist minister of Springfield, Massachusetts:

> *Mrs. Prince*—I called to see if you would buy my book (hands him the book, together with certain papers certifying to her good character, &c.)
> *Dr. Ide* (turning over the book and papers spitefully)—What could *you* make a book of?
> *Mrs. Prince*—I do not carry the papers so much to help me sell my book as to protect me from insult, as we coloured people are liable to be insulted.
> *Dr. Ide*—*You* insulted! *You* are constantly insulting *us*; how you carried on down there in Philadelphia—making such a fuss about your rights. I don't want your book. I'll give you some change.

> *Mrs. Prince*—I would like to have you take the book for your Sabbath School
> library.
> *Dr. Ide*—I don't want your book; it's nothing but a humbug.
> *Mrs. Prince* (rising and indignantly catching her book and papers)—Don't you
> say that my book is a humbug, you villain! I'll expose you wherever I go; I'll
> expose you in the public prints for insulting me. *Exit.*[2]

The scene reveals how the selling of her book was much more than a mere economic transaction for Prince. It was intensely personal, not only because the narrative was about herself and her past experiences but also because she had put considerable effort into producing the book—writing, publishing, and distributing it. Prince had crafted this object with care, which made Ide's rebuke all the more intolerable. Books were central to Prince's life and those of other antebellum Black authors. For this reason, they now open a window into the experiences of individuals who were marginalized at the time.

This holds particularly true of the formerly enslaved men and women who published their autobiographical narratives in the 1840s. While James Williams and Charles Ball were only tangentially involved in publishing and distributing their respective narratives, Douglass, Brown, and others were the driving forces behind the production and dissemination of their works in the United States as well in Britain. In a tense institutional context where rival organizations now argued over the best methods to combat slavery, many of these authors turned to an artisanal model of publication that placed financial and physical demands on them. Of course, they were helped by antislavery societies and individual abolitionists, both white and Black, but the days of major print propaganda campaigns were over and slave narrative authors had to rely on their own resources and sense of entrepreneurship. Their access to antislavery distribution networks was unequal and several narratives by authors with few connections in abolitionist circles failed to reach a wider audience beyond their home region. This chapter pieces together the publishing history of well-known narratives by Douglass, Brown, Henry Bibb, and Sojourner Truth, as well as the less widely known narrative of Leonard Black, with a view to defining the characteristics of what I term "itinerant" narratives.

Marginality, Itinerancy, and Reform in Antebellum America

The abolition movement underwent significant structural transformations after 1840, which reshaped the strategies of institutional antislavery and in particular its relationship with print culture. The systematic use of print as a weapon in the fight against slavery was largely driven by the American Anti-Slavery Society (AASS) in the 1830s. Abolitionists still distributed pamphlets, books, and newspapers in the following decades, but by then it was just one of a number of strategies used to campaign for abolition.

The late 1830s were a period of increasing strain within the abolition movement, leading to what historians generally refer to as the AASS schism.[3] Abolitionists were divided on religion, politics, and the place of women in antislavery societies. Whereas the followers of William Lloyd Garrison in Boston began to take a harder line against northern churches, accused of being the chief bulwarks of slavery, the New York faction led by Lewis Tappan and the executive committee of the AASS insisted that religious institutions had to undergo necessary reform. Similarly, Garrisonians refused to take part in political activities when the opposing camp set out to defend the antislavery cause electorally. The Boston group also argued that women should play an active role in the movement, including in leadership positions at the AASS—a point of view rejected by Tappan, James G. Birney, and other male representatives. This dispute proved the final straw. When young Abby Kelley was elected to the business committee at the annual convention of the AASS in May 1840, Tappan and his followers seceded and founded the American and Foreign Anti-Slavery Society (AFASS). Garrison took control of the AASS, shifting the center of gravity toward New England, while the AFASS set up its headquarters in New York. The schism fundamentally reshaped American abolitionism. Once a united movement led by a single national organization, abolitionism fragmented into a decentralized jigsaw in which various forms of opposition to slavery coexisted. The schism, Teresa A. Goddu writes, led to "the dissolution of the AASS's centralized institutional structure." Both the AFASS and the Garrison-controlled AASS "were nearly powerless," Merton L. Dillon adds. They continued their activities, "though on a diminished scale."[4] The Panic of 1837 also took its toll on the movement. The wealthy philanthropists Arthur and Lewis Tappan were no longer in a position to bankroll vast operations such as the Great Postal Campaign of 1835. In these circumstances, print was bound to be less central to the antislavery struggle in the 1840s than it had been a decade before.

Abolitionists never stopped using print to inform, unite, and rally their readers. New antislavery newspapers launched in the 1840s included Douglass's *North Star* in Rochester, New York, and the *Anti-Slavery Bugle* in Ohio. There, Kelley and Jane Elizabeth Hitchcock sold "the best AASS tracts" alongside other publications.[5] The two faithful Garrisonian abolitionists devoted considerable energy to distributing antislavery print material.[6] Antislavery societies in New York, Boston, and Philadelphia still stocked publications for sale on their premises. Nor was the South forgotten. Established by the AFASS in 1846, the American Missionary Association (AMA) hoped to attain the abolition of slavery through the peaceful means of establishing antislavery churches in the South and distributing Bibles and antislavery literature, including among the enslaved. "The concept of preaching a whole gospel in the South," Stanley Harrold notes, "was a . . . departure from the postal campaign of 1835, when northern abolitionists scrupulously aimed their propaganda exclusively at slaveholders."[7] Enslaved men and women should be informed of their political rights through the written word.

Despite the best efforts of the various groups that now composed institutional antislavery, print output seems to have tailed off and reached a smaller audience over the years—a trend pointed out by contemporary commentators. "We need more Anti-Slavery tracts in this country," wrote the *National Anti-Slavery Standard* when Wilson Armistead's *Five Hundred Thousand Strokes for Freedom* was published in London in 1853.[8] Likewise, the British abolitionist and printer Joseph Barker declared in the early 1850s that "the circulation of tracts and books on [the subject of slavery] has been too much neglected" in the United States. "In my travels up and down this country," he went on, "I have seen but comparatively few anti-slavery books, except in the houses of avowed and well-known anti-slavery characters."[9] A few years earlier, Barker had established his own series of works of history, science, poetry, and biography. The first volume of the Barker Library, *Interesting Memoirs and Documents Relating to American Slavery, and the Glorious Struggle Now Making for Complete Emancipation* (1846), included Lewis and Milton Clarke's slave narratives and extracts from Ball's account.[10]

Barker's appeal was heard. In the fall of 1854, the AASS established the Tract Fund, planned along the lines of the major projects of the 1830s. The Tract Fund published twenty pamphlets of varying lengths, some by leading white abolitionist writers such as Harriet Beecher Stowe (*The Two Altars; or, Two Pictures in One*), Thomas Wentworth Higginson (*Does Slavery Christianize the Negro?*), and Richard Hildreth (*The "Ruin" of Jamaica*). More than three hundred thousand copies were printed in five years.[11] Yet there was no question of "scattering" the entire country with pamphlets "like rain-drops" (to return to the meteorological metaphor seen in chapter 1), as had been the case twenty years previously. The AASS could barely afford the costs of publication, so it was important that copies ended up in the hands of people who might actually be won over—as opposed to white southerners who would burn them. The society set up a distribution system that relied on individual members, who were expected to obtain and distribute copies around them: "We would again say to all friends in New England who desire tracts for gratuitous distribution, that the least expensive way of procuring them is to call at our office in person, or to request friends coming from their respective towns to do so."[12] The

AASS prioritized "gratuitous distribution" to reach a broad readership. But this came at a cost, and the society was forced to appeal for donations in the antislavery press to keep the Tract Fund afloat. "The cost of stereotyping a tract of eight pages, and publishing *five thousand copies* of it, is about Fifty Dollars," the AASS informed its members. "The cost of *stereotyping* is not far from one dollar and fifty cents per page."[13]

The finances of the AASS improved slightly in the late 1850s thanks to an unexpected bequest from the Boston businessman Charles F. Hovey, who supported various movements for social reform. On his death in 1859, Hovey left $50,000 to fund the fight against slavery, and once that was achieved, other causes such as women's rights and temperance. A committee was established to allocate the money, led by Wendell Phillips, with members including Garrison, Kelley, and Kelley's husband, Stephen S. Foster.[14] Alongside other projects, the committee ring-fenced some of the Hovey Fund for antislavery publications. Harriet Jacobs's *Incidents in the Life of a Slave Girl* (1861) was one of the works to benefit from the scheme, as the next chapter will show. Yet despite Hovey's cash injection, neither the AASS not the AFASS were in a position to finance anything like the major propaganda campaigns of the 1830s.

Furthermore, as the example of the Tract Fund reveals, antislavery societies now tended to focus their print strategies on ephemera such as newspapers and pamphlets, which were cheaper to produce and distribute. Book production was not discouraged per se. But a noticeable proportion of antislavery books dating from the 1840s and 1850s were self-published—financed by the author rather than by an antislavery society acting as publisher. In the *Liberator*, William Goodell confided that he had published his six-hundred-page *Slavery and Anti-Slavery* (1852) "with my own funds, on my own account."[15] Phillips also published his 1847 *Review of Lysander Spooner's Essay on the Unconstitutionality of Slavery* and his 1850 *Review of Webster's Speech on Slavery* "at his own expense."[16] Phillips printed five thousand copies of both titles to donate to the AASS and the Massachusetts Anti-Slavery Society (MASS), which put the profits from sales into other projects.

Phillips, the scion of a wealthy Boston family, could afford such generosity. This was not true of Jonathan Walker, a working-class abolitionist known as "the man with the branded hand." In July 1844, Walker attempted to sail seven runaway slaves from Florida to the British West Indies. He was sentenced to a heavy fine and the pillory and his hand was branded with a double S for "slave stealer."[17] In the summer of 1845, Walker published a brief account of the episode, *The Branded Hand: Trial and Imprisonment of Jonathan Walker, at Pensacola, Florida, for Aiding Slaves to Escape from Bondage*. He covered the cost of printing the work, which he then sold at meetings across the North. "The sums received from the liberality of . . . friends, and what I have been able to collect from the sale of my book and otherwise, have nearly enabled me to meet the expense of publication," he wrote in February 1846.[18] The itinerant sale of *The Branded Hand* and his 1846 *A Brief View of American Chattelized Humanity, and Its Supports* (also self-published) enabled Walker to promote the antislavery cause while providing him with a (modest) source of income: "The last year I have disposed of four or five thousand Anti-Slavery publications; and have no doubt but I have done much more for the cause by that means than by any other. It has also been the main pecuniary support of myself and large family, though the profits were small. The urgent demands on my purse brings me considerably in arrears."[19] In early 1848, Walker lived in "extreme destitution."[20] Daniel Drayton's experience was similar, though even more tragic. Having participated in the escape of seventy-seven enslaved men, women, and children on board the *Pearl* in April 1848, Drayton, another working-class man with antislavery sympathies, was sentenced to an enormous fine. He also served a prison sentence that left him traumatized. In 1853, Drayton published the *Personal Memoir of Daniel Drayton*, written with the help of Hildreth. He sold copies on his subsequent travels, despite his failing health. In late 1853, the *Liberator* did not expect him to live long. With no hope of remission and with just twelve dollars to his name, Drayton took his own life in 1857.[21]

The publishing histories of Walker and Drayton's narratives do not differ radically from those of slave narratives dating from the 1840s. Many formerly enslaved authors, including the most celebrated, lived precarious, uncertain, itinerant lives. They penned or dictated their stories for personal as well as political reasons: they needed ready money to redeem relatives "yet in the land of bondage" or to support "a numerous family."[22] Walker's narrative has much in common with Douglass's, in terms of themes as well as publishing history. Both *The Branded Hand* and the *Narrative of the Life of Frederick Douglass, an American Slave* came out in the summer of 1845 and were "Published at the Anti-Slavery Office," as the title page indicates. Both were distributed by means of direct sales by the author and indirect sales via institutional antislavery networks. An advertisement in the *Liberator* establishes a link between the two narratives: "CAPT. WALKER'S NARRATIVE is now ready for sale at the Anti-Slavery Office. This story, and that of Douglass, containing most vivid and faithful pictures of *slavery as it is*, should be circulated throughout the length and breadth of the country."[23] White abolitionist Maria Weston Chapman did the same in her preface to *The Branded Hand*: "The narrative of Frederick Douglass gives a picture of the condition of a slave in the land that [the Founding Fathers'] folly and their fear betrayed. That of Jonathan Walker shows the condition of the freeman whose lot is cast in the same land, little more than half a century only after the perpetration of that treason to humanity."[24] The similarities led J. Noel Heermance to categorize the texts by Walker and Drayton as "parallel 'white' narratives." "So fruitful and popular were the slave narratives," Heermance argues, "that the Abolitionist press found itself extending the genre and publishing narratives of the harsh South as experienced by white men."[25] In fact, slave narratives did not precede and inspire white narratives. Rather, both were part of an older literary tradition, that of personal narratives written by outcasts or people in marginalized groups.

The genre of autobiographies by marginal figures, forming a countertradition to memoirs by illustrious men, has been studied by Mechal Sobel, Ann Fabian, and Karen A. Weyler. "In the eighteenth and nineteenth centuries, thousands of individuals, most of them of the middling sort or poor, including many at the margins, were enjoined or volunteered to write narratives of their lives," Sobel writes.[26] While Fabian calls such texts "paupers' tales" or "plebeian narratives," Weyler's concept of "outsider authorship" seems a better fit for the sheer range of author profiles.[27] Whether they were mechanics, murderers, beggars, war prisoners, captives, impressed seamen, refugees, or enslaved men and women, the authors all lived lives scarred by poverty, isolation, and violence—for some permanently, for others in the course of a single event such as a kidnap, prison sentence, or escape. Their lives were out of the ordinary, colorful, and often tragic. Most such narratives have been forgotten, though the typical structure of their titles resonates with modern readers: *The Narrative of Robert Adams, an American Sailor, Who Was Wrecked on the Western Coast of Africa, in the Year 1810* (1817); William B. Lighton's *Narrative of the Life and Sufferings of a Young British Captive* (1836); Pierre Séroude's *History of a Fugitive from Cayenne* (1857); and so on. Many of the narratives were first-person accounts by people far removed from the written word, let alone print culture. This is why they frequently include the words "written by himself/herself" on the title page, often seen as a defining feature of slave narratives but found equally in personal narratives by a variety of outsider authors. The personal nature of the texts was underpinned by the way they were printed and distributed. "Some were published ... by the writers themselves, who sometimes marketed them as well," Sobel notes.[28] Authors traveling from town to town and village to village could sometimes sell several thousand copies of their narrative, earning their own keep on the next leg of their journey.

Slave narratives belonged to this written culture of marginality. Within antebellum reform culture, their closest relatives were the autobiographies John W. Crowley calls "temperance narratives."[29] Accounts by former alcoholics also bear many similarities to those by formerly enslaved men and women, as the example of Charles T. Woodman reveals. The *Narrative of Charles T. Wood-man, a Reformed Inebriate, Written by Himself* was printed in Boston in 1843. Its title echoes the structure of slave narrative titles. The epigraph, "Truth is strange—stranger than fiction," was taken from Lord Byron's *Don Juan* (1819); the quotation already felt like a "stale adage" by the 1840s, due in part to its widespread use in antislavery publications.[30] It cropped up in the preface to Peter Wheeler's narrative in 1839 and was later used as a chapter heading for Brown's 1853 novel *Clotel* and as the title of Josiah Henson's 1858 slave narrative *Truth Stranger than Fiction*.[31] The publication address, No. 66 Cornhill, locates Woodman's narrative in the heart of reformist Boston. Douglass and Brown's narratives bear the address of the MASS office at No. 25 Cornhill. Woodman's preface also shared some of the features of outsider narratives, such as the rejection of sophisticated discourse in favor of "'a plain unvarnished' narra-tive." An amateur author, Woodman apologized for "the lack of polish in his style," reminding his readers that he had "never devoted a day's study to gram-mar in his life," in much the same way that Douglass reminded his audiences that he "never had a day's schooling in my life."[32]

There was, in Crowley's terms, an "ideological congruence" between tem-perance and abolition: alcoholics were metaphorically "enslaved" by drink.[33] Highlighting the commonalities between the two types of texts helps locate slave narratives, particularly those dating from the 1840s, in a range of writing practices that were already long established by the time Douglass came to publish his *Narrative* and extended beyond the narrow framework of the abo-lition movement to which the corpus is often restricted. Slave narratives occa-sionally showed features of temperance narratives. Jermain W. Loguen's 1859 *The Rev. J. W. Loguen, as a Slave and as a Freeman: A Narrative of Real Life* presents the harmful effects of alcohol on Loguen's enslaver, Manasseth Logue, and his wife, who were whiskey distillers as well as slave owners: "Had he been a manufacturer and vender only, it had been better for his character, habits, property and family. But unhappily, he and his wife were large consumers also, and sank together into intemperance. Their original virtues, if they had any, were lost, and they were very drunken, passionate, brutal and cruel."[34] The narrative dwells on the figure of the master with a taste for the demon drink, illustrating the various stages of the repentant alcoholic's journey like a didac-tic fable, from excess (Logue attacks Loguen in a drunken rage) to retribution (the Logue family distillery burns down) and redemption (the couple stop drinking as a result of the fire). Chapter 8 of *The Rev. J. W. Loguen, as a Slave and as a Freeman* is a narrative within the narrative, bringing together two seemingly distinct social issues—alcoholism and slavery—that were in fact closely connected in the minds of antebellum reformers.

Another major characteristic of outsider narratives was the fact that authors typically traveled widely so as to distribute copies of their pamphlet or book across a broad geographical area. In the context of reform movements, itinerancy was generally conditioned by the "lecture system" that arose in the 1830s and 1840s: a given organization would employ agents to preach abolition, temperance, prison reform, or any other cause across a given region. Douglass and Brown were hired as MASS agents in 1841 and 1847, respectively. Becoming "professional fugitives" enabled them to sell their narratives at antislavery meetings across the United States and Britain.[35] Orality and print often worked in tandem in antebellum America. Rather than belonging to separate social and cultural worlds, they were "different parts of an overall system of cultural expression" in which authors of slave narratives commonly participated.[36]

An itinerant lifestyle was not always a matter of choice, however. Some formerly enslaved men and women moved out of necessity, because they feared recapture or wished to escape a hostile environment. "Mobility," Eric Gardner observes, "was not necessarily a good thing."[37] Rhondda Robinson Thomas has usefully pointed to the problematic nature of slave narrative anthologies that focus on a specific state or city, pinning lives typified by itinerancy down to a single point on the map. Thomas H. Jones's narrative, for instance, features in the anthology *North Carolina Slave Narratives*, though Jones's history reached far beyond the state borders.[38] The title pages of the various editions of his narrative give us an idea of his journeys. First published in Boston in 1850, *The Experience of Thomas Jones, Who Was a Slave for Forty-Three Years* was reprinted in St. John, New Brunswick, in 1853; Springfield and Worcester, Massachusetts, in 1857 and 1859; and then again in Boston in 1862. Like many African Americans, Jones was forced into (temporary) exile in Canada after the adoption of the Fugitive Slave Act of 1850. There, he published an edition of his narrative and gave antislavery lectures throughout New Brunswick and Nova Scotia, at which he sold locally printed copies of his book. Returning to the United States to attempt to redeem his eldest son from slavery, he traveled across New England and published several further editions of his *Experience* until 1885.[39] Itinerancy was an important dimension of the lives of formerly enslaved men like Jones; peddling books on the road was a way of keeping their heads above water in financial terms.

The situation was not markedly different for freeborn Black authors, who occupied a marginal position in mainstream publishing, as the following chapter shows. Achieving good sales depended to a considerable extent on the author's ability to travel. Harriet E. Wilson's *Our Nig; or, Sketches from the Life of a Free Black* (1859) provides a case in point. The novel, inspired by the author's own experiences, recounts the life of Frado, a freeborn Black woman treated like a slave by the New England family who take her in. Wilson took up her pen less out of burning literary ambition than to earn a living. "Deserted by kindred, disabled by failing health," she wrote in her preface, "I am forced to some experiment which shall aid me in maintaining myself and child without extinguishing this feeble life." In the appendix, a friend of Wilson's recorded her extreme poverty: "Her health is again failing, and she has felt herself obliged to resort to another method of procuring her bread—that of writing an Autobiography."[40] Gardner's research on the reception history of *Our Nig* indicates that its failure can be attributed in part to the author's relative lack of mobility. Wilson sold copies of her book (alongside bottles of hair tonic) door-to-door, barely venturing outside her home county of Hillsborough, New Hampshire—which is hardly surprising, given her poor health. Her book was not reviewed in the press and failed to achieve a readership in Boston, where it was printed.[41]

As a poor Black woman with failing health, Wilson was an outsider in multiple ways. Weyler's book on outsider authorship emphasizes the strategies for empowerment that print gave formerly enslaved individuals, indentured servants, women, mechanics, and impressed seamen. But it should be kept in mind that these people often faced major obstacles in their own lives that hindered their efforts to distribute their books: authorship in early America was not intrinsically empowering. Formerly enslaved men such as Douglass and Brown were mobile and well connected to institutional antislavery networks. They were able to overcome difficulties and put copies of their narratives in the hands of tens of thousands of readers. Other, more isolated men and women—Black, Wilson, Edmond Kelley, John Thompson, William Hayden, and William Green to name but a few—had to make do with limited local distribution. Their narratives are now barely read and their names largely forgotten. Book history grants them the visibility they did not enjoy in their lifetime.

The Transatlantic Journeys of the *Narrative of the Life of Frederick Douglass, an American Slave*

The publishing history of the *Narrative of the Life of Frederick Douglass* covers a relatively long period. The book first came out in Boston in May 1845 (fig. 6) and was still on sale in 1854, when Douglass was about to publish his second autobiography, *My Bondage and My Freedom* (1855). The *Narrative*'s publishing history also covers a wide geographic area, from Boston to rural Ireland via Virginia, London, and Paris.[42] This can be explained in part by Douglass's own mobility and personal involvement in the process of publishing and distributing his book internationally. After four years traveling throughout the

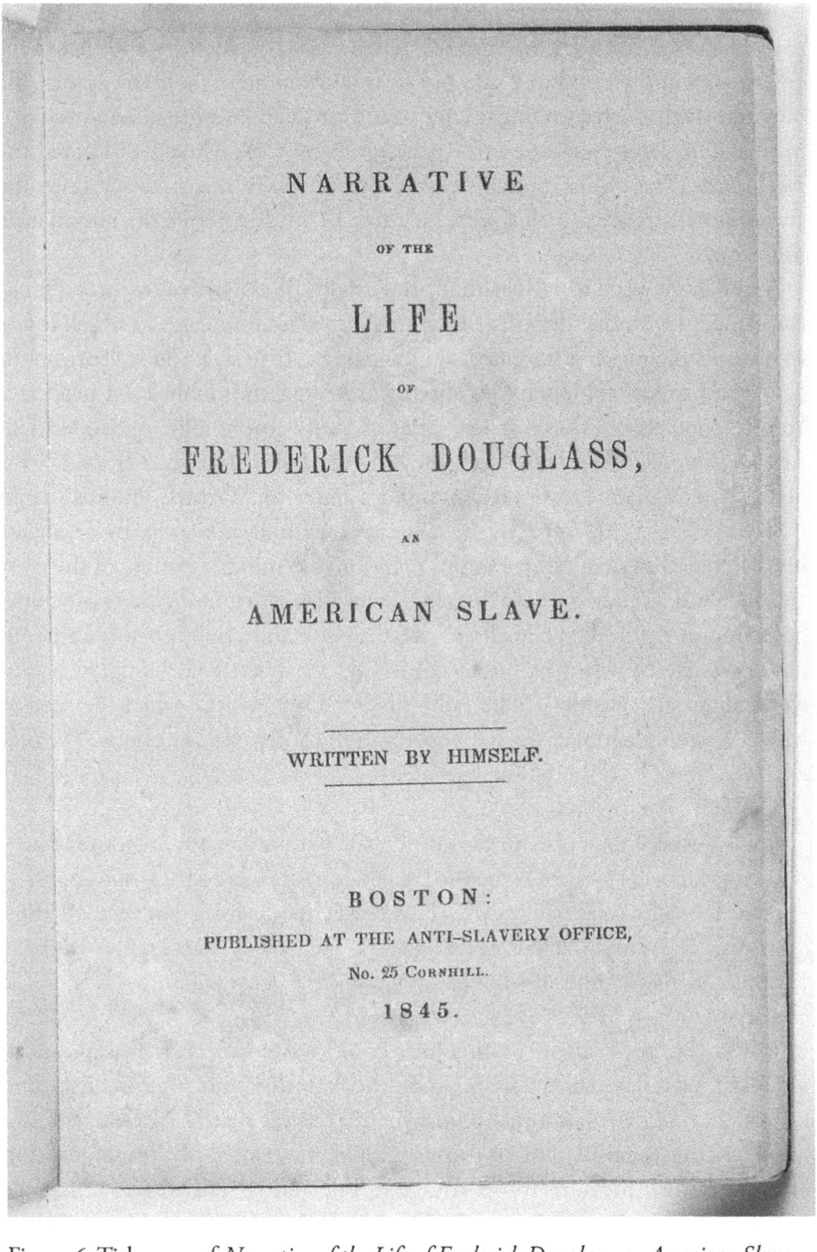

NARRATIVE

OF THE

LIFE

OF

FREDERICK DOUGLASS,

AN

AMERICAN SLAVE.

WRITTEN BY HIMSELF.

BOSTON:
PUBLISHED AT THE ANTI-SLAVERY OFFICE,
No. 25 CORNHILL.

1845.

Figure 6. Title page of *Narrative of the Life of Frederick Douglass, an American Slave*
(Courtesy of American Antiquarian Society)

North as a salaried antislavery lecturer, Douglass set out for Britain in August 1845. He was at risk after his narrative revealed his true identity and that of his enslavers, and preferred to be an ocean away from any potential captors. He only returned nineteen months later once British abolitionists had purchased his freedom. Douglass settled in Rochester, New York, where he founded the *North Star*. The publication history of the *Narrative* maps closely onto the author's own travels. In this sense, it must be read in terms of transatlantic itinerancy.

Surprisingly little is known about the origins of the *Narrative*, how Douglass came up with the idea of writing it, and the circumstances in which it was written. As biographers have noted, Douglass has little to say in his correspondence and later autobiographies about the writing and publication process.[43] Yet the paratext does offer a few clues as to its chronology. As students of African American literature well know, Douglass's narrative is fronted by a preface by William Lloyd Garrison and a letter by Wendell Phillips, dated 1 May and 22 April, respectively, and closes with an appendix by Douglass himself, dated 28 April 1845. Phillips mentions attending a reading of the *Narrative* a few days previously. It therefore seems likely that Douglass finished the book in mid-April, then consulted with Garrison and Phillips.[44] It is harder to pin down exactly when he began writing. In October 1844, Douglass was at work on an article titled "The Folly of Our Opponents," which he sent to Maria Weston Chapman for publication in the antislavery gift book *The Liberty Bell*, along with the following note:

> It was intended for a place in the Liberty Bell, but my literary advantages have been so limited, that I am ill prepared to decide what is, and what is not, appropriate for such a collection. I looked exceedingly strange in my own eyes, as I sat writing. The thought of writing for a book!—and only six years since a fugitive from a Southern cornfield—caused a singular jingle in my mind.[45]

It seems the experience of "writing for a book" was not altogether unpleasant. Douglass must have started working on the *Narrative* soon after contributing his article. The MASS annual report for 1845 states that "Mr. Douglass lectured with his usual assiduity (excepting when interrupted by the composition of his narrative) previous to his voyage to England."[46] This suggests that the bulk of the narrative was written in December 1844 and January 1845, a quiet period in Douglass's otherwise hectic schedule, spent mainly at home in Lynn, Massachusetts; in the *Narrative* itself, Douglass makes a brief allusion to writing his book "seated by my own table, in the enjoyment of freedom and the happiness of home."[47] In late February, he was already thinking past publication:

"Douglass, who is now writing out his story, thinks of relaxing by a voyage," Phillips wrote to British abolitionist Elizabeth Pease.[48] A second month-long interruption between mid-March and mid-April must be when he put the finishing touches on his manuscript.[49]

Phillips's intriguing remark about Douglass "read[ing] . . . [his] memoirs" to him points to the continuities between Douglass's lectures and his autobiographical narrative.[50] Indeed, the writing of the *Narrative* should not be uncoupled from the countless lectures that Douglass had been delivering as a MASS agent since 1841, which were still ongoing in the opening months of 1845. Even before Douglass decided to pen an autobiography, his lectures were shaping the material that was to form the *Narrative*. At meetings he tried out various ways of recounting his experiences and judged the impact of various episodes by audience reactions. The lectures, as Robert S. Levine points out, "served as a kind of writing workshop for the *Narrative* to come"—and the narrative can be seen as the result of a collaborative process involving the input of thousands of audience members who cheered, applauded, or even booed Douglass.[51] It is perhaps not surprising that Douglass was in the end able to write the 125-page text in just a few months, as he had in fact been preparing himself for it for several years.

The paratext also sheds light on Garrison and Phillips's input. In his preface, Garrison writes that "Mr. DOUGLASS has very properly chosen to write his own Narrative, in his own style, and according to the best of his ability, rather than to employ some one else. It is, therefore, entirely his own production."[52] There is no reason to doubt Garrison's words. Garrison and Phillips only saw the manuscript once it was complete, shortly before publication; Phillips suggests that he did not even "see" it but rather "heard" it, and the same may have been true of Garrison. The two white abolitionists doubtless suggested a few improvements and corrections—Douglass frequently misspelled words, and a few months earlier he had asked Chapman to "[correct] any mistakes" she might find in his *Liberty Bell* article—but their changes must have been largely cosmetic.[53] Of course, Garrison's preface and Phillips's letter significantly reshaped the form of the *Narrative*, a Black text now sealed in a "white envelope," to borrow John Sekora's term. Many contemporaries seemed to see Garrison's preface as a cumbersome and unnecessary addition. "I think it is a pity Garrison wrote a preface," Lydia Maria Child confided in a letter to a friend. "It will create a prejudice in many minds, at the outset. They had better have let him tell his own story, in his own simple manly way."[54] Written in what one reviewer of the *Narrative*, Margaret Fuller, called Garrison's "usual over emphatic style," the preface seemed to jar with the author's own sober prose.[55] Modern anthologies of African American literature have sometimes excised the white-written preface and letter, thereby "emancipating the *Narrative* from the paratext that, since the book's first publication, [has] continued to transact a form of white superiority."[56] Yet Douglass may well have asked the two men to provide the texts in full awareness that the presence of two leading white activists in the front matter of his book would bring it legitimacy and visibility. Simply put, the "white envelope" can be read in the case of Douglass—and the other narratives discussed in this chapter—as deliberate author-led publishing strategy. As Beth A. McCoy rightly notes, leaving it out strips the *Narrative* of "its appearance as the textual object it was in its time."[57]

That Garrison and Phillips prefaced Douglass's *Narrative* does not mean that it was published specifically in the service of a white-led antislavery organization. As I have just emphasized, Douglass did write and publish his narrative in the context of institutional antislavery, yet neither the AASS nor the MASS controlled the publication or circulation of the book in the way the AASS had controlled the publication and circulation of the *Narrative of James Williams*. Douglass does not feature in the minutes of the MASS executive committee, and the annual report mentions the publication only briefly.[58] It is not at all certain that "the MASS subsidized [the *Narrative*'s] publication," as Garrison's biographer claims.[59] Jonathan Walker's *The Branded Hand*, which also bears the words "Published at the Anti-Slavery Office" and the MASS address on its title page, was self-financed, as I have mentioned previously. Likewise, Goodell's self-financed *Slavery and Antislavery* has the name of an agent of the AFASS—William Harned—on its title page. Harned, Goodell explained, "was willing to sell my book on commission, and, for convenience, he lent me his name on the title page of that edition, as is customary when a publishing author has no business place of his own in the city."[60] Garrison himself emphasized Douglass's agency in the publication process when he wrote in late June 1845, "Our anti-slavery friends will be pleased to learn that the first edition of the Narrative of Frederick Douglass has nearly all been disposed of, and that *the author has a cheap edition in progress of publication*."[61] Whereas Williams did not participate in the distribution of the narrative bearing his name, Douglass played a leading role at every stage in the *Narrative*'s publication history. Unlike Williams, he had penned his own story and he felt intimately involved in the fate of his book. His life and material comfort—and those of his loved ones—depended on how well it sold. For Douglass, publishing his narrative was a more personal, less institutional undertaking than Williams's venture with the AASS. As he makes clear in *My Bondage and My Freedom*, Douglass set pen to paper not because he was asked to by white abolitionists—Phillips famously advised him to "throw the MS. into the fire" for fear it might lead to his recapture and reenslavement—but because people doubted if I had ever been a slave. They said I did not talk like a slave, look like a slave, nor act like a slave, and that they believed I had never been south of Mason and Dixon's line. . . . I resolved to dispel all doubt, at no distant day, by such a revelation of facts as could not be made by any other than a genuine fugitive.

In a little less than four years, therefore, after becoming a public lecturer, I was induced to write out the leading facts connected with my experience in slavery, giving names of persons, places, and dates—thus putting it in the power of any who doubted, to ascertain the truth or falsehood of my story of being a fugitive slave.[62]

While the AASS's earlier attempt at publicizing the life story of a fugitive slave was propagandistic in nature, Douglass's decision to publish his narrative was primarily an individual and pragmatic one. Of course, the role of the MASS was far from negligible. The society had been paying Douglass as a lecturer on the antislavery circuit, providing him in effect with the occasion for self-presentation. Paratextual elements such as the address of the MASS office and the white-authored preface and letter functioned as endorsements of the narrative. The officers of the MASS must also have put Douglass in contact with his printers, Moses A. Dow and Leonard Jackson. Located at 14 Devonshire Street, Dow and Jackson's "Anti-Slavery Press" had been printing antislavery materials for the MASS since the late 1830s.[63] Yet the raison d'être of the *Narrative of the Life of Frederick Douglass* was in no way similar to that of the *Narrative of James Williams*, and neither were its modes of publication and circulation.[64]

The publication of the *Narrative* was immediately followed by a lecture tour that took Douglass from Massachusetts to New York and gave him the opportunity to promote the book. Between 1 July and 16 August—the day he left for Liverpool aboard the *Cambria*—Douglass gave daily lectures, each time in a different place. According to Gregory P. Lampe, "He carried copies of the *Narrative* with him and sold them at the end of his lectures." He would also visit the offices of local newspapers and give editors copies of his book "in hopes that they would favorably review it, promote its sale and, at the same time, publicize his lectures."[65] The *Narrative of the Life of Frederick Douglass* circulated by means of what Raymond Williams calls "artisanal" exchange—that is, without middlemen: the producer sold the fruits of his labor directly to the consumer.[66] The economist Karl Polanyi's concept of "embeddedness," which Leon Jackson applies to the antebellum literary field, further illuminates the nature of the exchange. The act of purchasing from the author at an antislavery meeting became an act of charity; the economic dimension of the exchange—money for a book—was strongly embedded in its social dimension.[67] Far from being the object of a disembodied transaction, Douglass's book created a link between the orator and his audience. Most slave narratives published in the 1840s were distributed, at least in part, within this charitable economy model. The embodied character of the myriad interpersonal transactions that led to the transatlantic dissemination of the *Narrative* survives to this day in the form of copies signed by the author. The Schomburg Center for Research in Black Culture holds a copy of the "third English edition" printed by Joseph Barker in 1846 and inscribed to a woman named Huldah B. Gilson: "From her sincere Friend. / Frederick Douglass / Lynn. Mass / 29 April 1847" (fig. 7). Douglass had just returned from England, apparently with a cargo of books left unsold. He must have sold the copy to Gilson (or given it to her, if "sincere Friend" is to be construed as more than a polite formula) during one of the several meetings that were organized at the end of April and beginning of May 1847 to welcome him back to his native country.

While emphasizing that Douglass played an essential role in the dissemination of the *Narrative*, I do not claim that he sold thousands of copies unaided. Although there was no plan of systematic dissemination in the case of Douglass, American and British abolitionists—at least for those who supported the Garrisonian brand of abolitionism to which Douglass himself then subscribed—used their own formal and informal networks to circulate the book. The *Narrative* was regularly advertised in leading antislavery newspapers such as the *Liberator*, the *National Anti-Slavery Standard*, and the *Anti-Slavery Bugle*; it was for sale at antislavery offices in New York, Boston, and Philadelphia; it could be purchased at the National Anti-Slavery Bazaar that took place in Faneuil Hall, Boston, in December 1845; it was personally distributed by white and Black abolitionist women such as Jane Elizabeth Hitchcock and Betsey Mix Cowles in Ohio and Lydia Mott and Mary E. Miles (Bibb's wife-to-be) in upstate New York; it rubbed covers with books on capital punishment at the office of Charles and John M. Spear's *Prisoner's Friend*; and reform bookstores— Bela Marsh in Boston, Finch & Weed in New York, Barnaby & Whinery in Salem, Ohio—had copies on their shelves.[68] In short, the effective circulation of Douglass's *Narrative* was less the result of a concerted institutional effort than of a series of individual initiatives. The book was mailed, sold, lent, or passed around by fellow abolitionists like this anonymous "friend to liberty," who declared in the pages of the *Liberator*:

> Before reading the preceding article in the Olive Branch [an attack against Douglass], I had bought one copy of the "Narrative of Frederick Douglass, written by himself," which I lend to my neighbors; but since I read that article, I have purchased *one dozen copies* more, to spread abroad in the community, that they

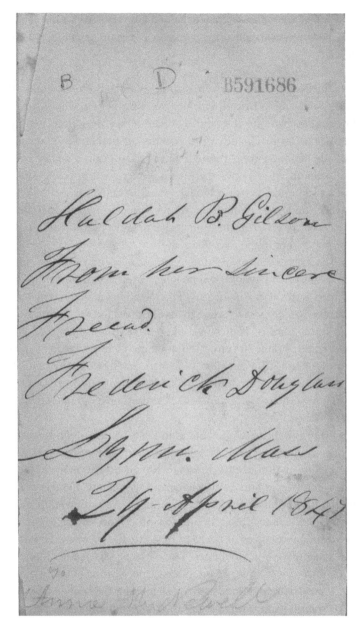

Figure 7. Inscribed copy of *Narrative of the Life of Frederick Douglass, an American Slave* (Courtesy of Manuscripts, Archives and Rare Books Division, Schomburg Center for Research in Black Culture, New York Public Library, Astor, Lenox and Tilden Foundations)

can see how a "*miserable negro*" can write, and for them to see what a noble soul he possesses, notwithstanding slavery laid her iron grasp upon him in his most early life.[69]

Copies of the Boston edition also crossed the Atlantic. Boston abolitionist Samuel May Jr. sent one to Bristol reformer Mary Carpenter, who in turn lent it to fellow abolitionist John B. Estlin.[70] Whether they were circulated by Douglass himself or by Black and white activists on both sides of the Atlantic, copies of the *Narrative* went through what Jackson calls a deeply embedded authorial economy. The books themselves "functioned to create and sustain powerful social bonds" between Douglass and his audiences on the one hand, and between supporters of abolition on the other.[71] Among other antislavery texts, the *Narrative* served as the cement that held the transatlantic abolitionist community together in the mid-1840s.

Initiatives such as that of the aforementioned "friend to liberty" proved all the more useful when Douglass was no longer present to promote his narrative in the United States after August 1845. The MASS made sure it remained available in his absence. The society seems to have been behind the "fourth edition"— "in cheap form," that is, bound in paper—printed in early 1846.[72] However, these later editions came in runs of no more than a few hundred copies, a far cry from the AASS print runs for Williams's narrative, in the tens of thousands.[73] White abolitionist leaders maintained their support for Douglass's narrative, but without the grand-scale distribution program set up for the *Narrative of James Williams*.

Upon his return to the United States in 1847, Douglass got to work on his second major publishing initiative, the *North Star*. The project met with hostility from white abolitionists in Boston, who saw no advantage in the launch of another competing antislavery newspaper.[74] Though Douglass was kept busy by the new publication and the polemics surrounding it, he still made time for the narrative that brought him to fame. Upon leaving Massachusetts, he packed unbound copies of the 1847 Boston edition, which he had bound with stiff green covers in Rochester. The cover of this 1848 edition proudly gave "the *North Star* Office" as the place of publication. Only a handful of copies of the *North Star* edition survive, suggesting that only a few were ever bound. Yet it both makes visible Douglass's itinerancy and testifies to his active involvement in the book production process.

In parallel, copies were still being sold by antislavery societies. An edition dated 1849 was available from the AASS office in New York, demonstrating the Garrisonians' ongoing interest in the text in spite of increasing tensions with its author.[75] Only in the early 1850s did their relationship break down completely. In May 1851, Douglass announced that he no longer subscribed to the AASS's proslavery interpretation of the U.S. Constitution. "The Constitution," he famously said in his 1852 Fifth of July oration, "is a GLORIOUS LIBERTY DOCUMENT" that should serve as the springboard for antislavery activism.[76] Douglass simultaneously came to embrace political action as an abolitionist tactic, which the Garrisonians rejected. Under the circumstances, Garrison's followers wondered whether it was still acceptable to help circulate Douglass's book. Abby Kelley Foster and Stephen S. Foster had been selling the *Narrative* on their lecture tours since the summer of 1845, among other antislavery publications such as Phillips's *The Constitution a Pro-Slavery Compact* (1844) and *Can Abolitionists Vote or Take Office under the United States Constitution?* (1845).[77] On 9 August 1851, Abby consulted with her husband: "How many Douglass have you on hand? There is no compromise of principle in selling that work, of course, but I doubt the policy of giving any man who stands as he does particular prominence. Therefore I shall not be in favor of selling any more than we have on hand."[78] Although the *Narrative* had nothing objectionable to it, it could obviously not be sold alongside pamphlets denouncing the Constitution as a "pro-slavery compact" any longer.[79] Authors of slave narratives who were part of the abolitionist community were also enmeshed in its politics.[80] While Douglass enjoyed a greater degree of autonomy than others, the publication and circulation of his narrative were still contingent on the dynamics of institutional antislavery.

Copies of Douglass's *Narrative* also circulated in the South, though more sporadically than the *Narrative of James Williams*. In 1849, Methodist preacher Jarvis C. Bacon was arrested in Virginia and charged with circulating two "incendiary" publications—Douglass's *Narrative* and "an abolition address delivered at Cincinnati." The arrest was part of a sustained legal and propaganda campaign designed to hamper and ultimately expel northern antislavery missionaries from the South. Bacon, the counsel argued, had not sought to incite the enslaved to rebellion but "merely loaned the books to two [white] persons, at their request."[81] Whatever his intentions, he escaped with a fine. Two years later, he had no choice but to leave in a hurry "when local authorities posted a one-thousand-dollar reward for him, dead or alive, following the murder of a white man by fugitive slaves near Bacon's church."[82] He returned to his native Ohio. As Dickson D. Bruce Jr. notes, the case is testimony "both to the book's [southern] circulation and to its power to frighten slaveholders."[83] It also reveals how dangerous it was to distribute slave narratives in the South in the 1840s.

A year before Bacon was charged with circulating antislavery publications, a certain Mr. Gover, a citizen of Hartford County, Maryland, and a former slave owner, was tried for mailing a copy of Douglass's narrative to Colonel W. B. Stephenson, a member of the state legislature. This time, the counsel pleaded senility. "It was shown . . . that Mr. Gover was naturally of strong intellect—that, within a few days past, the infirmities of advanced age (about 80 years) had almost totally destroyed his memory and reasoning faculties— and that the once vigorous intellect of the man had become as that of a child—that his impaired mind was most evident upon the subject of Slavery, to the great annoyance of his numerous and respectable relatives."[84] It is tempting to see the counsel's case as a means of excusing a deliberate act by a slave owner converted to antislavery by Douglass's narrative. Gover had freed his slaves shortly before: reading Douglass may have prompted him to act. The narrative's circulation in the South could thus lead to concrete changes on the ground. Interestingly, the copy Gover sent to Stephenson was not the Boston edition. Accounts of the trial described the work as "a pamphlet, printed in Philadelphia, containing the life of Frederick Douglass, a runaway negro slave."[85] This was *Extracts from the Narrative of Frederick Douglass*, a pamphlet with a run of ten thousand copies printed by the Pennsylvania abolitionist Edward M. Davis (the son-in-law of abolitionist Lucretia Mott) for distribution to "those who are not willing to be identified with the active Abolitionists."[86] The pamphlet was distributed at no cost. Davis clearly had in mind readers in the upper South, particularly the adjoining states of Maryland and Delaware, where slavery was falling out of favor and reading carefully selected extracts of Douglass's narrative might prove beneficial.[87] In 1845 Davis's pamphlet had also fallen into the hands of A. C. C. Thompson, the author of a well-known attack on Douglass's narrative in the *Delaware Republican*: "It is with considerable regret that I find myself measurably compelled to appear before the public; but my attention has lately been arrested by a pamphlet which has been freely circulated in Wilmington [Delaware] and elsewhere, with the following superscription:—*Extract from a Narrative of Frederick Douglass, an American Slave, written by himself.*"[88] Thompson's virulent rejection of Douglass's "falsehoods" in fact demonstrated that the people of Wilmington were interested in his narrative. This distribution method was similar to that implemented for the *Narrative of James Williams*, published by the AASS in a newspaper-like "cheap" edition for circulation in the South. The publication of the *Extracts*, however, did not follow any systematic plan; it was a one-off, individual initiative.

The people of Maryland had their own reasons for wanting to read the *Narrative*: Douglass, after all, was a local celebrity. "We have most cheering intelligence from Virginia and Maryland, of the demand for anti-slavery publications," Philadelphia abolitionist Mary Grew wrote to Maria Weston Chapman.

"Frederick Douglass' narrative is doing a good work in the latter State."[89] A Baltimore correspondent for an Albany, New York, newspaper confirmed that "Frederick Douglass's Narrative is now circulating and being read in this city, and five hundred copies are still wanted here. They would be read with avidity, and do much good. And thus Garrison, who is proscribed here in person, would be heard in Baltimore, in the burning language of his Preface to the Narrative."[90] Some 16 percent of Baltimore's population were free Black men and women; the southern, urban readership of the *Narrative* must have included African Americans, some of whom would have known Douglass under his former name of Frederick Bailey.[91] "Despite severe Maryland laws against dissemination of abolitionist literature," Dickson J. Preston concludes, Douglass's *Narrative* "was widely circulated in the state."[92]

Narrative of the Life of Frederick Douglass, of course, was much more widely circulated in Britain and Ireland. Even before the *Cambria* docked in Liverpool in late August 1845, Douglass began planning the distribution of his book outside the United States.[93] Douglass's traveling companion James N. Buffum had been refused first-class tickets: the two abolitionists were assigned to steerage below decks. This did not prevent Douglass from mingling with the other passengers and circulating "a number of copies of his narrative," as he later recounted in several letters and speeches: "We had anti-slavery singing and pro-slavery grumbling; and at the same time that Governor Hammond's Letters were being read, my Narrative was being circulated."[94] Douglass also accepted an invitation from Captain Charles Judkins to give a speech. Proslavery passengers, displeased that a fugitive slave was being given such a platform, booed Douglass and accused him of misrepresenting slavery. A riot nearly broke out, and the captain was forced to intervene.[95] The well-known episode is a reminder that Douglass brought his narrative to public attention in circumstances that were sometimes difficult or even downright dangerous. Despite his fame, in many people's view, Douglass remained a subversive who should be silenced at all costs.

Once Douglass arrived in Ireland, where he was due to spend the first part of his stay, he immediately had the narrative reprinted, as his income was mainly derived from book sales.[96] On Wendell Phillips's advice, he turned to the Dublin printer Richard D. Webb, asked a few weeks previously by the British abolitionist George Thompson whether he would be "reprinting the adventures of Douglass."[97] In Ireland as in the United States, Douglass enjoyed the support of the Garrisonians but remained the main driving force behind the narrative's publication and distribution. Webb was fervently pro-Garrison and a committed, progressive Quaker. He and his partner Richard Chapman had printed many works in support of philanthropic, social, and political causes, including temperance, help for victims of the Great Famine, and the abolition of slavery.[98] "No more devoted, faithful, and steadfast friend of the American slave can easily be found, on either side of the water, than Mr. Webb," Garrison wrote in an article praising Webb's launch of a new periodical in 1852, the *Anti-Slavery Advocate*.[99] Webb printed two thousand copies of Douglass's narrative in September 1845.[100] He detailed the conditions in a letter to his friend Elizabeth Pease:

> I am supplying the paper & binding at cost prices and he has I believe some money with him which may perhaps enable him to pay for them—and I can wait for the printing till he has sold Books enough to pay for it. The sale of 700 copies at 2/6 will pay for the whole & leave him if he sells the rest a profit of nearly £180. He has been at no expense in Dublin—nor will he be at any in Cork—nor in Belfast to both of which he is invited.[101]

As the letter shows, the Irish editions of the *Narrative* were self-financed. Webb did, however, point out that Douglass could expect a quick return on his investment, especially as his living costs would be low.

Douglass wasted no time. "My Narrative is just published," he wrote to Garrison in late September, "and I have sold one hundred copies in this city."[102] His works circulated across Britain and Ireland by broadly the same mechanisms as in the United States. Douglass distributed copies wherever he went, as indicated by Joseph Sturge's speech to a large crowd at a chapel in Finsbury, London, on 22 May 1846: "Frederick Douglass has left a wife and four children in America, and I wish to state that he has published a little book, entitled *The Narrative of Frederick Douglass*, which may be had at the door, and by the sale of which he and his wife and children are supported."[103] The women and men who listened to Douglass, who applauded him and laughed at his sarcastic remarks against his former enslaver, could purchase the "little book" directly from its author once the lecture was over. Hence the need for Douglass to keep a constant supply of books on hand. "Well all my Books went last night at one blow. I want more[.] I want more," he wrote to Webb from Belfast in December 1845.[104] Nine months later, interest in the *Narrative* had not flagged. "F. D. sold, on the spot, a considerable number of his Narrative," Garrison commented after a spirited meeting in Sheffield.[105] Meanwhile, Webb had had a second edition of two thousand copies printed.[106] He recommended that copies be kept "out of the booksellers hands" and that Douglass sell them "as much as possible after his lectures as he goes from place to place." Booksellers, he warned, "require a large discount and it is extremely tedious waiting for a settlement from them."[107] Offering his book for direct sale rather than through booksellers allowed Douglass to maximize his gains and reap immediate (and much needed) profits. In Britain and Ireland as in the United States, the *Narrative* was also sold "among private friends . . . for Douglass's benefit."[108] Well-connected families such as the Estlins in Bristol and the Jenningses in Cork bought copies in bulk from Webb and distributed them locally.[109] "I remit the money to Mr. Webb . . . as soon as I have disposed of 50 books," John B. Estlin explained.[110] Douglass was very much aware that the dissemination of his book depended on these informal antislavery networks. "The Books go off grandly," he rejoiced in December 1845. "A very kind quaker lady a Mrs. Wakefield I believe her name is has taken the sale of them in hand[.] They must go in such hands."[111]

The third British edition—a copy of which Douglass signed for Huldah B. Gilson on his return to the United States—was published in Wortley, near Leeds, under the imprint of Joseph Barker, who did much to bring American slave narratives to England. This "cheap" edition, which came out in the fall of 1846 in a run of five thousand copies, was the last one Douglass ordered himself, though Gerald Fulkerson points out that Douglass was in fact too busy speaking at public meetings to closely supervise the publication.[112] Barker, according to Webb, "lost by it."[113] Several further editions were published after Douglass left Britain, in all likelihood without his approval. No fewer than four London editions came out between 1847 and 1852. The first was published in 1847 by R. Yorke Clarke, the successor to Harvey & Darton, who had printed the first editions of Moses Roper's narrative. He was followed in 1851 by H. G. Collins, while the last two, both dating from 1852, were the work of G. Kershaw & Son and Somers & Isaac.[114] It is perhaps not surprising that new editions were printed in 1852, which also saw the publication of Harriet Beecher Stowe's *Uncle Tom's Cabin*, a runaway success in England and the United States alike. In the absence of an international copyright agreement before the 1891 Chace Act, Stowe's novel was published in multiple unauthorized editions in England.[115] Douglass's narrative was no safer from transatlantic piracy.

Douglass played an active role in the production of the two Dublin editions—*too* active, as far as the printer was concerned, and the two men were soon at loggerheads. Relations between Douglass and Webb broke down fast. On 16 September 1845, Webb was full of praise for Douglass, fresh off the ship: "Douglass is a marvellous fine fellow—full of talent, sense, and quick wittedness."[116] Two weeks later, his opinion was quite different: "Frederick is tricky, huffish, haughty, & I think selfish."[117] While he acknowledged that Douglass was a man of charisma and eloquence, Webb thought his swift rise to international fame had gone to his head; his comments were often paternalistic in nature. The strained relationship between the two men marked an early stage in Douglass's gradual estrangement from Garrisonianism between 1845 and 1851.

The tensions arose in the context of the *Narrative*'s publication in Dublin, making them a major chapter in the book's publication history.

The first clash came over a portrait of Douglass for the frontispiece of the first Dublin edition. After part of the run had already been sold, the decision was taken to include Douglass's portrait facing the title page, as in the Boston edition (figs. 8 and 9). Douglass sat for several days for Bessie Bell, a distant relation of the Irish abolitionist James Haughton, and the resulting miniature was sent to the London engraver Henry Adlard.[118] "The result was a good likeness and as I am told a very good specimen of art," Webb later informed Maria Weston Chapman.[119] Though he had not yet seen Douglass in person, John B. Estlin concurred: "I much prefer it . . . to that in the Boston edition which has a scornful, contemptuous look."[120] Douglass himself found the engraving detestable. "I am displeased with it not because I wish to be, but because I can[']t help it," he wrote to Webb in mid-January 1846.[121] As Julia Lee notes, in the Boston portrait, Douglass appears "somber and resolute, his lips grimly set. His arms are crossed and his hands closed into fists." In the Dublin portrait, by contrast, Douglass's determined—rather than "scornful"—expression has given way to a "curious half-smile." Douglass is "stiffly posed, with an elongated face and nose, prominent cheekbones, stylized hair, and truncated bust."[122] The portrait, Robert S. Levine adds, "presents Douglass, out of character, as a sort of meek-looking British dandy—and relatively light-complected besides."[123] Douglass refused to use this whitewashed image of himself in the second Dublin edition. While in Glasgow, he had a local engraver, Joseph Swan, execute another portrait, copied from the Boston edition. "It has its faults," Douglass concluded, "but I'll try no more—it must answer."[124] A less-than-charitable Webb confided to a U.S. correspondent that he found the newly commissioned engraving "*diabolical*, neither more nor less," adding, "This delights me exceedingly after the thankless trouble I had about the other."[125] In a *North Star* review of British Quaker Wilson Armistead's *A Tribute for the Negro* (1848), where the Dublin portrait reappeared, Douglass made explicit the reasons for his dislike of the Adlard engraving, ironically noting that "it has a much more kindly and amiable expression, than is generally thought to characterize the face of a fugitive slave." He went on:

> Negroes can never have impartial portraits, at the hands of white artists. . . . Artists, like all other white persons have adopted a theory respecting the distinctive features of negro physio[g]nomy. . . . They associate with the negro face, high cheek bones, distended nostril, depressed nose, thick lips, and retreating foreheads. This theory impressed strongly upon the mind of an artist exercises a powerful influence over his pencil, and very naturally leads him to distort and exaggerate those peculiarities, even when they scarcely exist in the original.[126]

It seems clear why Douglass came to prefer photography, seeing it as guaranteeing a degree of objectivity. The frontispiece portrait in *My Bondage and My Freedom* was engraved from a daguerreotype.[127]

A second paratextual element sparked further strife between Douglass and Webb. Two Irish clergymen who had enjoyed the *Narrative*, Thomas Drew and Isaac Nelson, furnished Douglass with letters of praise that he wished to append to the book. Webb replied that "testimonials from ministers were not usual in this country unless the book was of a purely religious or sectarian character."[128] Douglass was taken aback. "Pardon me if I venture to say you have trifled with me in regard to getting letters from clergymen," he wrote back. "You were the first to suggest and advise it,—and now that I have taken the advice you are the first to condemn, and oppose it."[129] Webb denied ever making such a recommendation, but the archives back up Douglass's record of events: in December 1845, he wrote to Webb that "getting letters from such persons as you name is a wise suggestion and I have already adopted measures to obtain them."[130] There must have been a misunderstanding between the author and his printer. The two men were communicating by post—Douglass only stayed in Dublin for a little more than a month—which no doubt complicated matters.[131] Douglass's forthright character and Webb's ambivalence toward him cannot have helped. In addition to the letters from Drew and Nelson, the second Dublin edition included Douglass's response to A. C. C. Thompson's attack on his narrative, "Falsehood Refuted," which Webb described to a fellow abolitionist as "clever but swaggering."[132] Levine reads the paratext of the Dublin editions as a site of emancipation, where Douglass "take[s] back" a narrative initially written in Garrison's shadow; notably, Douglass wrote his own preface, relegating the white-authored prefatory materials to second place.[133] Yet the paratext was also a site of struggle, where Douglass had to impose his will on a white abolitionist who intended to keep the editorial upper hand. Seen in this light, it provides a typical example of the "gray" envelope, to borrow Frances Smith Foster's revision of Sekora's "black message/white envelope" paradigm.[134]

The integrity of the narrative itself came under threat. One passage was censored, or at least altered, between the first and second Dublin editions. As I have pointed out previously, Bristol abolitionist John B. Estlin had read the *Narrative* thanks to a copy of the first American edition sent by his Boston friend Samuel May Jr. Estlin found Douglass's text a powerful testimony against slavery and helped distribute it across southern England, but he was ill at ease with a passage in chapter 10 in which Douglass recounted how Caroline, an enslaved woman, was used by the notorious "slave breaker" Edward Covey as a "breeder."[135] "The horrid part of the '*slave breeding*' iniquities of Slavery is too important a feature to be left out of view in communicating

Figure 8. Frontispiece portrait to the first Boston edition of *Narrative of the Life of Frederick Douglass, an American Slave* (Courtesy of American Antiquarian Society)

Figure 9. Frontispiece portrait to the first Dublin edition of *Narrative of the Life of Frederick Douglass, an American Slave* (Courtesy of Stuart A. Rose Manuscript, Archives, and Rare Book Library, Emory University)

information on the subject," he wrote to Webb in November 1845, "but I should have been very glad had F. D. not described so minutely as he has done, Covey's proceedings with his purchased breeder. . . . The minutia following,—that he hired a married man, shut him up with the woman every night for a year, & that the result was twins, are *unnecessary* and disgusting." Estlin made the same case for decency as William Jay did about Charles Ball's narrative a decade earlier. The sexually explicit episode and the level of detail were liable to hinder the book's uptake among British readers. "I could not circulate it among my friends, & especially among ladies, (young ones particularly,) until I had erased all the paragraph after the statement that Covey intended the woman he bought for a '*breeder.*'" "These particulars," he added, "will be offensive to English taste."[136] As Audrey A. Fisch documents, Estlin scribbled the passage out in the copy he gave his twenty-five-year-old daughter Mary Anne, no doubt stoking her curiosity.[137] This may seem like a somewhat pointless act given the abundance of graphically violent scenes in the *Narrative*, starting with the beating of Aunt Hester in chapter 1, but it shows how seriously Estlin took his role as British mediator of American antislavery—and as arbiter of "English taste" and gender norms. He suggested that Webb omit the passage "in any future edition" of the *Narrative*.[138]

Webb categorically opposed Estlin's request at first, arguing that readers should be told the whole story, however shocking. May agreed that removing the passage was not desirable, though he admitted to having torn an image of a half-naked enslaved woman undergoing violent corporal punishment from his copy of Walker's *The Branded Hand*.[139] Estlin did not give up, insisting that English sensibilities should be taken into account: "I should grieve to think that even the most objectionable evils in American Slavery might not be *sufficiently* presented to the English nation in a manner inoffensive to delicacy, & refined feeling," he wrote to Webb.[140] Rather than simply omitting the offending passage, Estlin suggested an "alteration," which eventually made its way into the second Dublin edition.[141] The passage was abridged and reworded, as a comparison of the two texts demonstrates:

Dublin, 1845

The facts in the case are these: Mr. Covey was a poor man; he was just commencing in life; he was only able to buy one slave; and, shocking as is the fact, he bought her, as he said, for *a breeder*. This woman was named Caroline. Mr. Covey bought her from Mr. Thomas Lowe, about six miles from St. Michael's. **She was a large able-bodied woman, about twenty years old. She had already given birth to one child, which proved her to be just what he wanted. After buying** her, he hired a married man of Mr. Samuel Harrison, to live with him one year; and him he used to fasten up with her every night! The result was that, at the end of the year, the miserable woman gave birth to twins. At this result Mr. Covey seemed to be highly pleased, both with the man and the wretched woman. Such was his joy, and that of his wife, that nothing they could do for Caroline during her confinement was too good, or too hard to be done. The children were regarded as being quite an addition to his wealth.[142]

Dublin, 1846

The facts in the case are these: Mr. Covey was a poor man; he was just commencing in life; he was only able to buy one slave; and, shocking as is the fact, he bought her, as he said, for *a breeder*. This woman was named Caroline. Mr. Covey bought her from Mr. Thomas Lowe, about six miles from St. Michael's. *To complete the wickedness of this transaction, Covey hired of Mr. Samuel Harrison a married slave, who was torn from his own wife, and compelled to live as the husband of this wretched woman. Eventually she gave birth to twins, and such was the joy of Covey and his wife, that nothing they could do for Caroline during her confinement was too good, or too hard to be done.* The children were regarded as being quite an addition to his wealth.[143]

Various changes were made to Douglass's text. The description of Caroline as "a large able-bodied woman" disappears in the second edition, as if her powerful physique contradicted Estlin's ideal of sweet, fragile femininity; nor is the reader informed that Caroline has "already given birth to one child."[144] Guided by his strict moral code, Estlin places both protagonists within appropriate bonds of matrimony and fidelity. His version focuses more than Douglass's on the fact that Samuel Harrison's slave (whose name is Bill Smith, we learn in *My Bondage and My Freedom*) was a married man "torn" from his legally wedded wife.[145] Though Bill and Caroline are forced into a relationship, in the second edition they are framed as a proper couple: Bill is described as Caroline's "husband." In short, Estlin strives to bring a modicum of morality to a system in which it is completely alien, to the point of creating a contradiction in terms. The reworded passage points to the lack of respect for marital bonds between the enslaved while simultaneously inventing a marriage of sorts between Bill and Caroline. Estlin also omits the most explicit sexual reference—"and him he used to fasten up with her every night!"—in an act of outright censorship. Douglass's indignation, indicated by the exclamation mark, is watered down.

Estlin had his way. "The 2nd Dublin edition is now out," he wrote to May in April 1846, "& Mr. Webb has adopted an alteration I suggested, which renders the objectionable passage such as might be read *aloud*, without concealing the important & iniquitous facts detailed."[146] Had Douglass even been consulted? There is no indication he was. The revision is not mentioned in any of his correspondence, and he may even have sold copies of the second edition unaware of the change. In *My Bondage and My Freedom*, he seems to adopt a rhetorical stance close to Estlin's, concluding the episode with a sentence not found in the *Narrative*, "But I will pursue this revolting subject no further."[147] Yet Douglass does not abandon Bill and Caroline to their fate. The two individuals, described as helpless victims in the second Dublin edition of the *Narrative*, recover a degree of agency in another well-known episode of Douglass's autobiography—the fight against Covey. Where Douglass resisted Covey alone in the *Narrative*, Bill and Caroline join him in *Bondage* by refusing to help Covey. Douglass concludes, "We were all in open rebellion, that morning."[148]

Just as he had resisted Covey, Douglass sought—with varying degrees of success—to resist the white abolitionists who set out to reshape the *Narrative* in both text and paratext to make the book more "palatable" to English tastes. As has been shown, the struggle for editorial control led to tensions between Douglass and abolitionists in Britain and Ireland. One final link in the publishing chain further raised Webb's hackles: Douglass's profits from sales. The topic cropped up regularly in his correspondence: "If he go on as he has begun in Ireland, through Great Britain he will pocket 2500 dollars in twelve months time"; "Of £52 his book cost (for paper & printing 2000, & binding 500) about £30 is cleared off by gifts & sales. . . . He has great reason to be satisfied with poor Ireland"; "He makes 200 percent or nearly that on every copy"; and so on.[149] Webb had agreed to republish the *Narrative* but seemed uncomfortable with the money Douglass was making in Britain and Ireland. Nor did he look kindly on the "direct contributions" certain British abolitionists gave Douglass.[150] These earnings led Douglass to grow in confidence and independence and to detach from Webb and the other Garrisonians, such as Estlin and Maria Weston Chapman, who wanted to keep him under their control both in Britain and the United States. Relations between Webb and Douglass grew increasingly strained as the accounts linked to the *Narrative*'s publication grew more tangled.[151] After a brief truce, Douglass informed Webb he wished to be sent the remaining copies of his book and close his accounts. Webb suspected Douglass was in touch with a cheaper printer for the third edition, which proved to be the case.[152] This was the bitter conclusion to Douglass and Webb's personal and professional relationship.

How much did Douglass eventually earn from itinerant sales of his narrative in Britain and Ireland? Webb's estimation—"he will pocket 2500 dollars in twelve months time"—proved right on the mark. "The sale of his book has bought him a comfortable house in Lynn with ¾ acre of ground," Phillips wrote in a letter of August 1847, adding, "it cost him $2500."[153] This did not include $2,500 paid to him directly by British abolitionists for the purchase of a printing press to launch the *North Star*. Douglass himself differentiated between the latter sum, acquired "without any personal effort on my part," and income earned from his tireless efforts to promote his books.[154] Not only did Douglass promote his narrative at event after event, but he also had to keep on top of its complex distribution logistics: Would he have enough copies to sell in Belfast? Would the copies ordered express from Dublin arrive on time? Why didn't Webb have all the first edition copies bound at the same time? These were questions white authors published by mainstream publishers did not have to worry about. Moreover, Douglass's audiences did not see his book sales as a particularly valuable income stream. When invited to comment on a speech by Douglass in 1846, the Congregationalist minister John Campbell described him as a poverty-stricken figure earning a meager living from the "poor profits of his publication, the sketch of his life."[155] Countering scholars who call the *Narrative* an "international bestseller," Sarah Meer has usefully compared its sales with those of *Uncle Tom's Cabin*. The *Narrative*, she writes, "took five years of promotion to sell 30,000 copies in the 1840s: its hard-won English, Irish, and Scottish readers were wooed by Douglass himself during an energetic lecture tour. *Uncle Tom's Cabin* managed similar returns within weeks and made its way across the Atlantic without assistance; perhaps half a million copies had been sold . . . in Britain and its colonies by 1853."[156] Stowe's popularity and success were of an altogether different nature from Douglass's.

Ten years after the *Narrative* and three years after *Uncle Tom's Cabin*, Douglass published his second autobiography, *My Bondage and My Freedom*. The editorial context had changed, as the following chapter demonstrates, and the book came out with a trade publisher. *Bondage* was far longer than the *Narrative* and made the earlier work somewhat obsolete, while indirectly prolonging its dissemination in the numerous quotations carried over into it. It marked the end of the *Narrative* in the antebellum literary landscape, overtaken by its augmented version—at least until the late twentieth century, when *Bondage* lost its place to the *Narrative* in the American literary canon.

Reprinting and Recycling the *Narrative of William W. Brown, a Fugitive Slave*

It is hard to evaluate how much the authors of slave narratives knew about earlier accounts. Scholars tend to present *Narrative of the Life of Frederick Douglass* as the culmination of a literary tradition of which Douglass himself had full knowledge. "What great slave narrative informed Douglass's?" Henry Louis

Gates Jr. asks in the introduction to his 1987 anthology *The Classic Slave Narratives*. "Although it is obvious that Douglass read widely, and avidly devoured those narratives published by other ex-slaves between 1831 and 1845, was he revising another classic slave narrative, one whose form and themes he could appropriate and 'rewrite' in that profound art of grounding that creates a literary tradition?"[157] In fact, Douglass's pre-1845 writings never refer to slave narratives published prior to his own *Narrative*, even allusively. It should also be borne in mind that Douglass was only fully active in the antislavery struggle from 1841 onward, when he was hired as a MASS agent. It is by no means certain that he held a central enough role in the abolition movement to access accounts published in the 1830s, particularly Williams's account, which had been withdrawn from circulation in late 1838. Clearly, Douglass could have read the accounts by Williams, Ball, and Equiano some years after publication; he later reviewed Bibb's and Henry Box Brown's narratives in the *North Star*.[158] Asking how and where readers accessed such narratives calls for a consideration of the "slave narrative" as something other than a fixed genre category into which aspiring slave narrators dipped for inspiration.

It can be stated with certainty that Douglass's narrative was a touchstone for William Wells Brown—a model to follow and from which to diverge. Douglass and Brown knew each other, they followed each other round on the antislavery lecture circuit, and both were involved in the Colored Conventions movement. They shared the same political and intellectual milieu. White abolitionists often compared Brown to Douglass; Brown was generally held to be less charismatic but easier to get along with. "He is very intelligent & easy, full of anecdote, and staunch to his colour," Webb wrote in 1849. "I have no doubt he will make his way. He is not so great a man than Douglass—but neither is he so haughty and impatient."[159] "I do not know that his intellectual power is equal to that of Douglass, but he is of a much higher cast of character," another abolitionist added.[160] Brown took inspiration from Douglass's publication and distribution strategies for his own narrative. The publication history of the *Narrative of William W. Brown, a Fugitive Slave* offers many parallels with the *Narrative of the Life of Frederick Douglass*.

The most immediately apparent similarity is in the paratext. The *Narrative of William W. Brown* was, like Douglass's account, introduced by two white abolitionists, Joseph C. Hathaway, president of the Western New York Anti-Slavery Society (for which Brown had worked from 1843 to 1847), and Edmund Quincy, a leading member of Boston society. In his brief "Letter from Edmund Quincy, Esq.," Quincy pointed to the qualities of the narrative and what set it apart from Douglass's account. "It presents a different phase of the infernal slave-system from that portrayed in the admirable story of Mr. Douglass," he wrote, "and gives us a glimpse of its hideous cruelties in other portions of its domain."[161] He mentioned that he had only made minor changes to the text, at Brown's behest. While white sponsors intervening in texts by Black authors are often read as intrusive, in this instance it was clearly done at Brown's request, as Brown knew what Quincy could bring to the narrative. Quincy's correspondence sheds some light on the exchanges between the two men. In a letter to abolitionist Caroline Weston, Maria Weston Chapman's sister, Quincy writes that he received the "corpulent roll of MS." in mid-June 1847 but only had time to read it on 1 July. "It was so good that I could not lay it down until dinner-time," he enthused. Brown happened to choose that day to visit the house. Quincy suggested "one or two alterations & additions" and each wrote a part of the paratext—Brown a dedication to Wells Brown, the Ohio Quaker who took him in after he ran away, and Quincy the aforementioned letter. "The title-page was the hardest thing to hit," Quincy wrote to Weston. "He [Brown] wished to have something different from Douglass's, & yet to be simple & without affectation. We settled at last, subject to further advisement, on this. 'Personal Narrative of William W. Brown, a Fugitive Slave.'"[162] The term "personal"—which does not feature in the title of any book-length antebellum slave narrative—was eventually dropped. The choice of the adjective "fugitive" rather than "American" was the main element setting the title of Brown's narrative apart.

Like Douglass's narrative, Brown's bore the words "Published at the Anti-Slavery Office" and the MASS address on the title page, which would tend to suggest that the society helped fund its publication, as Claire Parfait and Marie-Jeanne Rossignol point out.[163] They have, however, demonstrated that Brown financed the publication himself. It was a significant investment: Brown had to pay $144 up front for two thousand copies with paper covers, a further $152 for a thousand copies bound in cambric, and $30 for the engraved portrait—a total of $326.[164] It is thus not exactly accurate to state that "the [MASS] agreed to print the work and to do it in-house, assuring its speedy, controlled production."[165] The first edition run bears the printer's name on the reverse of the title page, Andrews & Prentiss, then at 11 Devonshire Street, a few doors down from Dow & Jackson, who printed Douglass's narrative. Like Dow and Jackson, Samuel G. Andrews and Henry J. Prentiss were independent printers with close links to the MASS, printing material for the society and its members throughout the 1840s and 1850s, including annual reports, gift books such as the *Liberty Bell*, posters, pamphlets, and books by Black and white authors such as Brown, Phillips, and William Cooper Nell. "Prentiss is a fine fellow, a good abolitionist, and will take pleasure in serving you," Oliver Johnson informed Maria Weston Chapman in 1844.[166] Joseph Andrews, who engraved

Brown's portrait from a daguerreotype by Lorenzo Chase, had previously worked for Phillips.[167] The MASS likely put Brown in touch with the printers and engraver and may even have handled their exchanges. Yet it remains open to question whether *Narrative of William W. Brown* was, in the words of Brown's most recent biographer, "an autobiography issuing through the publishing infrastructure of a tightly run white organization": this would be an apter description of Williams's narrative.[168] That is not to deny Brown's obvious links to institutional antislavery. They were, however, looser than has often been claimed, and Brown had more agency in producing his narrative than is generally assumed. This explains his real investment, financial and emotional, in every stage of its publication history.

The first edition of the *Narrative of William W. Brown* came out in late July 1847. Brown immediately took charge of distribution. Like Douglass, he sent copies to antislavery journals and sold the work at antislavery meetings.[169] Reviews of public lectures in the press offer glimpses of the artisanal distribution process, which was somewhat labor-intensive in that it involved selling single copies but offered a maximum return on his initial investment. The average manufacturing cost per copy was under eleven cents; it sold at 25 cents with paper covers and 35 or 37½ cents with a cambric cover. Brown sold "some fifteen or twenty copies of his Narrative" in Upton, Massachusetts, after a two-hour lecture during which "he held the large audience in almost breathless silence."[170] "It is gratifying to see young and old crowd around friend Brown for his books," declared a campaigner in Northboro, Massachusetts.[171] As a recent MASS recruit, Brown benefited from a status and salary that facilitated the dissemination of the book. He spoke to audiences in their thousands at numerous annual antislavery society conventions in Massachusetts, New York, New Hampshire, and Pennsylvania.[172] The *Narrative* was simultaneously being disseminated within the wider antislavery network. Unsurprisingly, it was available from the MASS book depository in Boston, the AASS office in New York, Jane Elizabeth Hitchcock and Betsey Mix Cowles in Ohio, and Bela Marsh's bookstore and the *Prisoner's Friend* office in Boston, alongside Douglass's narrative.[173] The *Narrative of William W. Brown* could also be acquired from storekeepers like Richard Plummer, a member of the Essex County Anti-Slavery Society and secretary of the Washington Temperance Society, who stocked copies in his ironmongery in Newburyport, Massachusetts.[174] Books were often readily available in such stores at that time. One Dover, New Hampshire, hairdresser sold "an assortment of ANTI-SLAVERY BOOKS" that included Bibb's narrative.[175]

The *Narrative of William W. Brown* circulated for the most part among abolitionist audiences. Almost all reviews of the book appeared in antislavery and religious newspapers. Yet Brown was able to publish no fewer than four editions in two years, reworking his text more or less extensively each time. The first run of three thousand copies sold out in six months, and Brown brought out a further two thousand in February 1848.[176] Sure of his readership, he had his *Narrative* stereotyped by George A. Curtis at the New England Type and Stereotype Foundry. This was again a significant investment, the plates costing between seventy-five and eighty dollars, but a shrewd one in the longer term.[177] The second "enlarged" edition was some thirty pages longer: Brown had added three full-page engravings, an essay on the "American slave-trade" first published in the *Liberty Bell* of the same year, the lyrics of Margaret Lucy Shands Bailey's "The Blind Slave Boy"—which also appeared in Brown's 1848 songbook *The Anti-Slavery Harp*—and a lengthy appendix featuring extracts from southern newspapers as evidence of the violence visited on the enslaved. This motley paratext, combining writing by Brown with other authors and incorporating music, polemics, and journalism, heralded the "patchwork aesthetic" that scholars have identified as typical of Brown.[178] The second edition again sold out in six months. In October 1848, Brown ordered three thousand copies for the third edition.[179] He replaced Hathaway's preface with one of his own, including a letter from his former enslaver, Enoch Price, who had been sent a copy; like Thompson's letter to Douglass two years previously, Price's letter to Brown partially confirmed the facts of the *Narrative* in an attempt to discredit it. A fourth "complete" edition of Brown's narrative was eventually published in the spring of 1849, shortly before Brown left for Europe.[180] The title page boasted that the four Boston editions had reached a total print run of ten thousand copies. "No anti-slavery work has met with a more rapid sale in this country, than this narrative," declared Brown, a master self-promoter.[181] A new twelfth chapter to the narrative suggested that he was in the process of moving away from autobiography: its focus was not on Brown himself but on formerly enslaved people living in Canada whose Tennessee enslavers had failed to recapture them. The fourth edition was published by Bela Marsh, who owned a "social reform bookstore" close to the MASS office. Marsh published numerous antislavery books and several slave narratives, including the *Narratives of the Sufferings of Lewis and Milton Clarke* (1846) and the *Narrative of Henry Watson, a Fugitive Slave* (1848). His store also sold the narratives by Douglass, Bibb, and Box Brown.[182] The commercial reporting agency R. G. Dun & Company described Marsh as "a fine old gentleman: has always been in the Book & Stationery bus[iness]. . . . His store is well kn[own] here as the Depository for all kinds of Anti-Slavery, Hydropathic, Phrenological, Physiological, Comeouter and Transcendental Publications. Perf[ectly] honest & g[ood] for his contracts."[183] Little more is known about Marsh,

whose name rarely features in scholarship on slave narratives. Yet he was instrumental in making many of them public.

This brief overview of the four American editions indicates that it would be
useful to publish scholarly editions of the *Narrative of William W. Brown* and
other slave narratives that take into account textual and paratextual variants, as
Christopher Mulvey has done digitally for the four versions of Brown's novel
Clotel, which he constantly revised and reworked.[184] Many slave narratives
share similar (para)textual instability, reflecting their specific publishing circumstances. Their itinerant authors faced changing audiences in a range of
geographical regions at a time when their own career of professional activism
was in its infancy: every trip, every event, could trigger a modification to the
narrative. The abolition movement was likewise constantly shifting as friend-
ships and allegiances were formed or broken, calling for changes to the books it
supported—or for a wholly new book, in the case of Douglass's *My Bondage
and My Freedom*. Levine's claim that Douglass "conceived of his autobiography
as a work in progress in need of regular updating and rearticulation" is true of
a number of slave narrative authors.[185] The narratives by Douglass, Brown,
Bibb, Truth, Jones, and Box Brown all came out in numerous editions that
testify to their multiple contexts of publication and republication. This is what
makes book history a necessary tool in understanding and interpreting them.

Brown sold ten thousand copies of his *Narrative* in two years, an impressive
figure considering that "the work only circulated through specific, restricted
channels, outside the mainstream book economy."[186] Yet reversing the perspective reveals that this kind of information distribution circuit was in fact
highly efficient and long-lasting. Where a trade publisher would stop promoting and printing a book when the public seemed to begin to lose interest,
Brown—with the support of abolitionists—kept selling his *Narrative* as long
as he could, introducing it to new audiences. Trade distribution did not necessarily translate into higher sales. Once the *Narrative* had been widely distributed across the North, Brown took another leaf out of Douglass's book and
crossed the Atlantic. His main reason for traveling was to attend the International Peace Congress in Paris in August 1849, but he decided to stay in England after the passage of the 1850 Fugitive Slave Act. He only returned to the
United States five years later, once British abolitionists had purchased his freedom from Price. For Brown, 1849–54—a period covered in part in *Three Years
in Europe* (1852)—was a time of intellectual ferment: he was constantly writing
and promoting his works, including his autobiography.

Word of the *Narrative of William W. Brown* reached Britain before its author.
Samuel May Jr. sent John B. Estlin two copies of the second edition—"Having
heard us often speaking of yourselves and other Transatlantic friends, he [Brown]

requested me to inscribe the names of a few in copies of his book, & forward them as tokens of his respect"—and William Lloyd Garrison mentioned it on several occasions in his letters to Elizabeth Pease.[187] Setting sail for Liverpool on 18 July, Brown took some copies to sell on board the *Canada*, which caused none of the fuss Douglass's shipboard lecture had done four years previously on the *Cambria*. Most importantly, Brown carried with him the stereotype plates of the *Narrative*.[188] Over the previous decade, stereotype technology had let the AASS print and distribute antislavery literature on a grand scale. It now granted Brown a degree of freedom, letting him print copies cheaply as and when needed. Brown, Jeffrey Makala argues, "was intimately connected to the set of plates to his *Narrative* as both a foundation of selfhood and as a means of independence and liberation."[189] On docking, Brown hurried to Dublin, as Douglass had done. "I am about to print an edition of his Narrative from the stereotype plates," Webb wrote to a friend in early August, "& I hope to be able to do the job to his satisfaction, & that he will be easier to deal with than Douglass was who appeared to be eaten up with suspicion."[190] The printer's fears soon proved groundless. The business relationship between the two men had its ups and downs—Webb had to press Brown for several late payments—but overall it was less stormy than with Douglass. On 16 August, after the inaugural event of Brown's European lecture tour, Webb announced the forthcoming publication to the Dublin audience, should they wish to order a copy.[191]

The first British edition, published in late August 1849, bore the words "ELEVENTH THOUSAND" on the title page, suggesting it consisted of a thousand copies added to the ten thousand already printed in the United States. This is confirmed by Webb's registers, now in the National Library of Ireland.[192] The paratext was redesigned for British readers to include several testimonials by white activists Garrison and May and Black campaigners John T. Hilton and Isaac H. Snowden, as well as a section of "Opinions of the American Press" featuring praise for Brown's narrative, described as "an interesting narrative" and "a thrilling tale."[193] The work was also preceded by a "Note to the Present Edition," which drew in part on the Dublin edition of Douglass's narrative, a copy of which Webb may have given to Brown. In September 1845, Douglass had written:

In May last the present Narrative was published in Boston, U. S., and when I sailed for England in September, about 4,500 copies had been sold. This rapid sale may be accounted for by the fact of my being a fugitive slave, and from the circumstance that for the last four years I have been engaged in travelling as a lecturing agent of the American Anti-slavery Society, by which means I became extensively known in our country.[194]

In August 1849, Brown wrote:

> The present Narrative was first published in Boston, (U. S.) in July, 1847, and
> eight thousand copies were sold in less than eighteen months from the time of
> its publication. This rapid sale may be attributed to the circumstance, that for
> three years preceding its publication, I had been employed as a lecturing agent
> by the American Anti-slavery Society; and I was thus very generally known
> throughout the Free States of the great Republic.[195]

This was not Brown's only borrowing: his account was renamed *Narrative of
William W. Brown, an American Slave* (instead of *a Fugitive Slave*). The new
title made sense in the British context, but considering Brown's extensive pla-
giarism throughout his literary career—he was, in Geoffrey Sanborn's phras-
ing, "the most original artist of nonoriginality in American literary history"—
the comparison with Douglass is inescapable.[196]

One aspect of the British edition of Brown's narrative did set it apart from
Douglass's. The *Narrative of William W. Brown* was printed by Webb but came
out with the London publisher Charles Gilpin, who did as much as Webb and
Joseph Barker to bring American slave narratives to British readers. Quaker-
born Gilpin was the nephew of Joseph Sturge, the founder of the British and
Foreign Anti-Slavery Society. In the early 1840s, he had "opened a bookseller's
and publisher's business in Bishopsgate-street, where he made for himself a
large connexion."[197] Gilpin was also a frequent speaker on behalf of the Peace
Society and met Brown at the Paris Peace Congress.[198] As a bookseller, Gilpin
published and reprinted many slave narratives: he was behind the London
edition of *The Life of Josiah Henson* (1849) in 1851, and he published the first
editions of the *Narrative of the Life of Moses Grandy* (1843) and James W. C.
Pennington's *The Fugitive Blacksmith* (1849).[199] Publishing Brown's narrative
was to prove the first step in a long-standing business relationship. Gilpin also
published *A Description of William Wells Brown's Original Panoramic Views of
the Scenes in the Life of an American Slave* (1850) and *Three Years in Europe*. By
joining forces with a trade publisher, Brown was able to access more regular,
systematic distribution for his book across Britain; unlike Douglass's narrative,
Brown's is recorded in the trade periodical *The Publishers' Circular*.[200] Brown
had serious literary ambitions and doubtless wanted to see his book reach
audiences beyond reform circles. He wrote of putting it "into the booksellers'
hands" when Webb had sought to keep Douglass's narrative "out of" their
hands.[201]

Brown did not give up on his own efforts to distribute the book. He kept
on selling copies wherever his lecture tour took him. At a meeting in the

London suburb of Croydon, he sold no fewer than fifty copies of the *Narrative* in a single evening.[202] Like Douglass, Brown was dependent on book sales for income, as he had no society affiliation in Britain. As Garrison had explained to Pease, "Mr. Brown does not go out officially from any anti-slavery society, simply because he prefers to stand alone responsible for what he may say and do. . . . Nor does he go out to be a pecuniary burden or to make himself an unwelcome guest to any one; but he hopes, that, by the sale of his Narrative, . . . he shall be able to meet such expenses as may arise beyond what the hospitality of friends may cover."[203] One episode in *Three Years in Europe* points to Brown's precarious finances. He was due to attend a public meeting in Worcester where he hoped to sell the *Narrative* but found himself stuck in London, penniless, exhausted, hungry, with no idea where to turn for help: "In vain I wandered from street to street, with the hope that I might meet some one who would lend me money enough to get to Worcester." Providentially, a friend who had sold some copies of the book to his immediate circle came to Brown's home with the proceeds, and Brown was able to set out for Worcester.[204] The *Narrative of William W. Brown* had impressive print runs, but this should not overshadow the harsh realities of its distribution. The editions came thick and fast, their title pages giving ever higher figures: the year 1850 saw "TWELFTH THOUSAND" and "Thirteenth Thousand" editions, followed by the "FOURTEENTH THOUSAND" in 1851. The latter was lightly revised and retitled *Illustrated Edition of the Life and Escape of Wm. Wells Brown from American Slavery*. This "eighth English edition" (in fact the fourth English edition after four American ones) cost one shilling compared to two shillings and six pence for the previous editions, making it a "cheap" edition liable to boost sales. This edition was not noticeably more illustrated than the previous ones. It merely added three generic images to the paper covers and title page, alongside the three original engravings. The term "illustrated" was intended above all to give an aging work a new lease of life.

Brown soon published a new book, *Three Years in Europe*, which pushed the *Narrative of William W. Brown* into the background. The publication of his travelogue saw a new turn in the critical discourse on Brown's literary output, apparent in May's opinion: "W. W. B. . . . very generously sent a considerable number of his handsome & very agreeable book—(think of a Chattel Slave become the Author of so clever & handsome a volume!)—to friends here—to myself, among the number, a beautiful copy."[205] Whereas earlier critics had somewhat dismissively referred to the *Narrative* as "a thin duodecimo" and "the little book of Wm. Wells Brown," May emphasized the attractiveness of *Three Years in Europe*.[206] He drew an implicit contrast between the sober autobiography—"a plain, unvarnished tale," according to one American critic—and the sophisticated, cosmopolitan travelogue, recording Brown's social encounters with the European aristocracy and intelligentsia, including Harriet Martineau, Victor Hugo, Alexis de Tocqueville, the Duchess of Sunderland, and Charles Dickens.[207] May also underlined the work's fine literary quality, as did many critics: "Though he never had a day's schooling in his life, he has produced a literary work not unworthy of a highly-educated gentleman," in the words of the *Eclectic Review*.[208] Not even the most laudatory reviews of the *Narrative* made similar judgments. This does not mean that Brown did not think of the *Narrative* as a work of literature: that he had the manuscript read by Quincy, a well-known man of letters, rather than by Garrison, suggests he harbored literary ambitions.[209] Yet Brown's *Narrative* was generally regarded by its readers as a modest volume that would prove useful in the fight for abolition. It was valued as a documentary record rather than as a work of literary merit.

The publication of *Three Years in Europe* seems to have made Brown a genuine "Author" in the eyes of critics. The term was only used occasionally in reviews of the *Narrative*. It cropped up more frequently in reviews of *Three Years in Europe* and of *Clotel* the following year: "A fugitive slave successfully turning author . . . is a surprising event even in this age of wonders," the *Liberator* wrote.[210] The title page of *The Black Man* (1863) described Brown as "AUTHOR OF 'CLOTELLE,' 'SKETCHES OF PLACES AND PEOPLE ABROAD,' 'MIRALDA, OR THE BEAUTIFUL QUADROON,' ETC."[211] Wasn't Brown also the author of the *Narrative of William W. Brown*? His biographer William Edward Farrison claims Brown first described himself as a professional author on his marriage certificate in 1860.[212] A close study of the original editions of the *Narrative* indicates that Brown in fact readily used the term as early as 1847. A copy of the first edition at the New-York Historical Society is inscribed "R. H. Conklin, from his sincere friend the author"; a damaged copy at the Wisconsin Historical Society contains the words "Respects of the *auth[or]*." Brown seems to have begun to think of himself as an author—not just as a producer of texts, but as a creator of literary content—as soon as the *Narrative* was published. To be recognized as such by others, however, he had to prove his worth in nobler genres such as travel writing and novels.

The final British edition of the *Narrative* came out the same year as *Clotel*. It was published by William Tegg without Brown's approval, and what profits there may have been escaped him.[213] Once again, the wave of enthusiasm from British readers for *Uncle Tom* explains why a trade publisher brought out a new edition at this relatively late juncture. Tegg was not a man of scruples: just a few months before, he had published a British edition of W. L. G. Smith's proslavery *Life at the South; or, "Uncle Tom's Cabin" as It Is* (1852). The content was of less importance than the opportunity for sales.

What was happening to the *Narrative of William W. Brown* back in the United States during this period? Since Brown took the stereotype plates with him, the most recent American publisher, Bela Marsh, could only bring out a new edition if he was willing to typeset the entire work afresh. The copies printed before Brown's departure remained on sale until the stock ran out. Tracking the narrative in the antislavery press, it is clear that it gradually fell from view; the MASS offices stopped selling it in February 1850 and the AASS in May of the same year.[214] In August, Stephen S. Foster was still able to send his wife twenty copies.[215] Nearly a year later, he wrote to her that "there are none of Brown's Nar. or the Harp to be had."[216] The *Narrative of William W. Brown* and *The Anti-Slavery Harp* were out of print.

Yet Brown's later writings drew heavily on the *Narrative*, a mode of self-quotation typical of his authorial practice. While other slave narratives circulated in antislavery newspapers, almanacs, and pamphlets, playing into the antebellum culture of reprinting, Brown's narrative "circulated" in his own oeuvre. The opening chapter of *Biography of an American Bondman* (1856), a book attributed to Brown's daughter Josephine but likely written by Brown himself, is a case in point. It quotes the *Narrative* word for word, with just a few minor changes in typography and style.

Narrative of William W. Brown, 1847

Nothing was said to Randall by the overseer, for more than a week. One morning, however, while the hands were at work in the field, he came into it, accompanied by three friends of his, Thompson, Woodbridge and Jones. They came up to where Randall was at work, and Cook ordered him to leave his work, and go with them to the barn. He refused to go; whereupon he was attacked by the overseer and his companions, when he turned upon them, and laid them, one after another, prostrate on the ground. Woodbridge drew out his pistol, and fired at him, and brought him to the ground by a pistol ball. The others rushed upon him with their clubs, and beat him over the head and face, until they succeeded in tying him.[217]

Biography of an American Bondman, 1856

Nothing was said to Randall by the overseer; for more than a week. One morning, however, while the hands were at work in the field, he came into it, accompanied by three friends of his,—Thompson, Woodbridge, and Jones. They came up to where Randall was at work, and Cook ordered him to leave ~~his work;~~ and go with them to the barn. He refused to go; whereupon he was attacked by the overseer and his companions, when he turned upon them, and laid them; one after another; prostrate ~~on the ground~~ **before him**. Woodbridge drew out his pistol; and fired at him, and brought him to the ground ~~by a pistol ball~~. The others rushed upon him with their clubs, and beat him over the head and face; until they succeeded in tying him.[218]

Twenty-nine percent of the book consists of quotations from Brown's previously published works, including the *Narrative*, and 34 percent later reappeared under his name. It is "extremely likely," Sanborn concludes, "that William Wells Brown wrote or pieced together most of *Biography of an American Bondman* and that he put Josephine's name on the title page for the sake of creating a fresh, saleable context for his much recycled life history."[219] Brown likewise recycled episodes from his autobiography in his fiction and history writing. The passage of the *Narrative* where Brown helps the slave trader James Walker becomes a comic episode in *Clotel*, where Brown's role is played by the fictional Pompey and the slave trader is renamed Dick Walker. The section "A Man without a Name" in *The Black Man* is similarly "a fictionalized account of Brown's own life."[220] Several of Brown's books open with (auto)biographical sections that draw on his life story: *Clotel* begins with a "Narrative of the Life and Escape of William Wells Brown" of some fifty pages, written by Brown himself in the third person and interspersed with lengthy quotations from the *Narrative*; *Three Years in Europe* begins with William Farmer's "Memoir of William Wells Brown," while Brown's *The Rising Son* (1874) is preceded by Alonzo Moore's "Memoir of the Author." When a text like *Clotel* was revised and republished in three separate formats— as a book, a dime novel, and newspaper serial—the borrowings from the *Narrative* proliferated. In 1859, Brown published another autobiographical narrative, the thirty-six-page *Memoir of William Wells Brown, an American Bondman*.

Throughout his literary career, Brown incorporated episodes from his own life into his writings, layering various versions to the point of confusion and contradiction. While he tended to rewrite and adapt the *Narrative* rather than simply quote it, the later texts nonetheless acted as biographical relays once the initial narrative had fallen from view. In 1884, Brown's obituary in the *Boston Evening Transcript* listed his works:

> As a prolific writer, commanding a clear intellect and facile pen, he undoubtedly did much useful work. His compositions include "Three Years in Europe," a record of travel; "Clotelle; or, the President's Daughter," a narrative of slave life in the Southern States; "The Black Man," "The Negro in the Rebellion," "Sketches of Places and People Abroad," and two dramas, entitled "Dough Face" and "The Escape; or Leap for Freedom."[221]

Once again, the *Narrative of William W. Brown* did not make the list. It is unclear whether it was a mere oversight or whether the journalist had genuinely never heard of it. Either way, the details of Brown's life story survived in his other titles. Brown's autobiographical urge can thus be understood as the urge to build a record in as many ways and formats as he could—biography, novel, history, books, pamphlets, newsprint—of a life he knew would otherwise be forgotten.

Other Narratives, Other Trajectories: Henry Bibb, Leonard Black, Sojourner Truth

The publication histories of the *Narrative of the Life of Frederick Douglass* and the *Narrative of William W. Brown* have much in common. This does not mean that all slave narratives printed at the same period followed the same pattern. Henry Bibb's narrative was supported by another branch of the abolition movement; Leonard Black's failed to reach an audience beyond its region of publication; Sojourner Truth distributed her work by similar channels to Douglass and Brown but at a later date, when antislavery discourse was gaining in legitimacy and other methods of publication were within reach. The closing section of this chapter turns to a study of these alternative trajectories.

As Douglass's case has shown, slave narrative authors involved in the abolition movement were affected by ideological quarrels in which they themselves took part. When Bibb published his *Narrative of the Life and Adventures of Henry Bibb, an American Slave*, he had long since nailed his colors to the mast. In 1844–45, he lectured and campaigned for the Liberty Party ticket in Michigan and Ohio; in 1848, he delivered a well-received speech at the founding meeting of the Free Soil Party in Buffalo, New York; in 1849, the year his *Narrative* came out, he spoke at a Free Soil convention in Ohio.[222] In a word, Bibb had clearly come down on the side of political abolitionism, at a time when Douglass was just beginning to approach it. As a result, he was roundly rejected by the Garrison camp. "Bibb has identified himself with Anti Garrisonianism," Wendell Phillips wrote to Elizabeth Pease. "He has allowed himself to be a tool in the hands of priests & Liberty Party men. . . . I put no confidence in him."[223] As such, when Bibb set out to publish his autobiography, he could not expect any support from Phillips, Quincy, or Webb. Though Bibb was a well-known activist, he was nonetheless an outsider in the field of authorship, with limited financial resources. He wrote to political abolitionist Gerrit Smith of his hopes of overcoming such difficulties: "I am now laboring to publish the Narrative of my life; and of my bereaved wife and child who are still left to linger out their days in hopeless bondage. I have no means of doing this of myself, but the work is thought to be so worthey of aid, and so well calculated without note or comment to push forward the Anti-Slavery cause that I doubt not that I shall get *help*."[224]

In the end, Bibb received support from the AFASS, which was in favor of political campaigning against slavery. The AFASS, often overlooked compared to the AASS and the MASS, played an equally significant role in distributing slave narratives in the 1840s. The *Liberty Almanac*, published by the AFASS from 1847 to 1852, gives some idea of the books and pamphlets available from its "Anti-Slavery Depository, Publication Office, and Free Reading Room," located successively at 5 Spruce Street, 22 Spruce Street, and 61 John Street, New York. It sold several of the slave narratives published in the period, and the AFASS made every effort to stock new titles as soon as they came out, as the following table shows.

The AFASS helped distribute Bibb's narrative, but more importantly, it lent Bibb the money he needed to publish the book in the first place. The society's minute book indicates for 9 May 1849, "A letter to the Com. from H. Bibb . . . was read, in which he asks for a loan of $250 to enable him to publish his History &c. A letter to the Cor. Sec. from Rev. L. C. Matlack, stating his views of Mr. Bibb's work, was also read. Resolved, That the Treasr of the G. Fund be authorized to loan H. Bibb two hundred and fifty dollars . . . taking security on the stereotype plates and cuts of his History."[225] This financial backing proved crucial; the narrative may never have been published without it. It was, however, only a loan, and the society was not the official publisher. Like many

Slave narratives available for sale from AFASS, 1847–1852

Author	1847	1848	1849	1850	1851	1852
Frederick Douglass	[?]	37½¢ (b)	30¢ (p)	—	—	25¢ (p)
Lewis and Milton Clarke	[?]	37½¢ (b)	25¢ (p)	25¢ (p)	25¢ (p)	25¢ (p)
William Wells Brown	—	37½¢ (b)	25¢ (p)	25¢ (p)	25¢ (p)	—
Henry Watson	—	—	12½¢ (p)	12½¢ (p)	12½¢ (p)	12½¢ (p)
Henry Bibb	—	—	—	50¢ (b)	50¢ (b)	50¢ (b)
Thomas H. Jones	—	—	—	—	—	12½¢ (p)

Note: (b) = bound volumes; (p) = pamphlets.

other nineteenth-century African American authors, Bibb self-published his book, as indicated by the words "Published by the Author" on the title page. He was also responsible for some of its distribution. Bibb had done the groundwork: in January 1849, Black abolitionist George Weir Jr. informed readers of the *North Star* that citizens of Buffalo, where Bibb had recently lectured, had resolved that "as a token of our appreciation of so valuable a work, (should it be published,) containing, as it will, a complete history of his life during twenty-five years' experiences of slavery, we pledge ourselves to become subscribers thereto, and also to use all proper means to have its circulation widely extended wherever our influence may reach."[226] Selling copies on his travels let Bibb repay his loan gradually. "I have succeed very well in selling my Book & can begin to see my way clear," he wrote in March 1850 to Lewis Tappan, a founding member of the AFASS.[227] Two days later, he sent the executive committee twenty-five dollars.[228] At least three editions were published between 1849 and 1850, suggesting sales must have been brisk.

Bibb was granted the loan thanks to the support of Lucius C. Matlack. Matlack was part of a group of abolitionists who had withdrawn from the Methodist Episcopal Church, deeming it too timid in its condemnation of slavery, and joined the Wesleyan Methodist Connection instead. The Wesleyans had close links with the AFASS, whose religious orientation contrasted with Garrisonian anticlericalism; some Wesleyans were influential within the society.[229] Bibb's *Narrative* was not published under the AFASS imprint, but it did bear discreet traces of the church-oriented abolitionism behind its publication. The introduction was written by Matlack, and the book printed by Luther Lee, another Wesleyan minister who served on the executive board of the AFASS. The address on the title page, 5 Spruce Street, New York, was home to the office and book depository of the AFASS and the Wesleyan Methodist Connection's official organ, the *True Wesleyan*. This is where one of the earliest announcements of the *Narrative* is found: "This fugitive brother, so long and favorably known to the Christian community, has in press, to be issued next week, a thrilling narrative of his adventures as a slave. It will contain some 200 pages, large duodecimo size, tastefully bound and illustrated by plates, with a fine engraving of himself. Price, 75 cts. To be had at No. 5 Spruce-st., for cash, by the quantity, at 25 per cent. discount."[230] The *True Wesleyan* repeatedly promoted the narrative throughout 1849. Four years later, the book was still on sale at the office of the Syracuse, New York, *Wesleyan*.[231] The Wesleyans also helped distribute Bibb's *Narrative* below the Mason-Dixon line. As Stanley Harrold notes, they were the first to support antislavery missionaries in the South. Among the books and tracts circulated there by the Wesleyan Methodist Connection, the AMA, and the American Baptist Free

Missionary Society were copies of *Narrative of the Life of Frederick Douglass*, as previously noted, and copies of *Narrative of the Life and Adventures of Henry Bibb*.[232]

At the same time, the narrative was passed around by readers close to political abolitionism. "I have just read your deeply interesting Narrative. I would that every reader in the nation and in the world might read it," Gerrit Smith wrote to Bibb soon after publication; in 1853, Tappan sent copies to Louis Alexis Chamerovzow, later secretary of the British and Foreign Anti-Slavery Society, while the fine copy with gilt ornaments now held by the New-York Historical Society bears the signature of James G. Birney, the Liberty Party candidate for the presidential elections of 1840 and 1844.[233] Though he complained he received the book long after publication, the soon-to-be political abolitionist Douglass positively reviewed the book in the *North Star*, calling it "a most valuable acquisition to the anti-slavery cause."[234] The Garrisonians did not boycott Bibb's narrative, which made no specific reference to his allegiances. The *Narrative* was sold at all the usual outlets—the AASS book depository in New York, the MASS office in Boston, the Pennsylvania Anti-Slavery Society office in Philadelphia, and Bela Marsh's Boston bookstore.[235] Reviewing the *Narrative* in the *Liberator*, Garrison was just as generous as Douglass. "Henry Bibb, the well-known fugitive slave, has just published, in elegant style and with sundry pictorial illustrations, a Narrative of his Life and Adventures, written by himself, and remarkably well-written too," he announced. "Of all the narratives that have been published, no one exceeds this in thrilling interest."[236]

The title of the *Liberator*'s review—"More Slave Narratives"—offers a rare example of the term "slave narrative" being used in the antebellum era. As I explained in the introduction, the label that we commonly use today to refer to the genre gained currency in the twentieth century. Still, Garrison's fortuitous use of the term identifies Bibb's publication as a new chapter in the establishment of a recognizable corpus of narratives by formerly enslaved men and women published in book form. To the extent that such developments can be clearly dated, the year 1849 is when a growing awareness of slave narratives as a new literary genre emerged. Matlack's introduction to the *Narrative* states, "Naturally and necessarily, the enemy of literature, [slavery] has become the prolific theme of much that is ... thrilling in narrative. ... Startling incidents authenticated, far excelling fiction in their touching pathos, from the pen of self-emancipated slaves, do now exhibit slavery in such revolting aspects, as to secure the execrations of all good men, and become a monument more enduring than marble, in testimony strong as sacred writ against it."[237] Bibb's own preface demonstrated he was familiar with the works of his predecessors: "It may be asked why I have written this work, when there has been so much already written and published of the same character from other fugitives?"[238] A few weeks later, Ephraim Peabody published his famous article "Narratives of Fugitive Slaves" in the *Christian Examiner*. "AMERICA," he declared, "has the mournful honor of adding a new department to the literature of civilization,—the autobiographies of escaped slaves."[239] Theodore Parker followed Peabody in the summer of 1849 with his lecture "The American Scholar," describing "the Lives of Fugitive Slaves" as a "wholly indigenous and original" form of literary production.[240] The topos of celebrating a new, typically American literary form crossed the Atlantic; most slave narratives being reprinted by a handful of individuals, most notably Webb and Gilpin, British readers felt the books were all of a family. "A new species of literature has sprung up in the United States, and is making its appearance in this country," wrote a contributor to the *Anti-Slavery Reporter* in October 1849. "Slaves who have escaped from the horrors of American bondage are telling their own tales, with an ability and pathos which, while they surprise, at the same time convince us that our coloured brethren, whatever may be the shade of their complexion, possess rare abilities."[241]

Along with other narratives that came out at the same time, Bibb's narrative was a catalyst in establishing slave narratives as a distinct literary genre. Only abolitionists fully involved in institutional antislavery networks, however, were in a position to create rapprochements between the various narratives and identify them as a single genre, which they referred to in a number of ways—"slave narratives," "autobiographies of escaped slaves," "Lives of Fugitive Slaves," and so on. Even Peabody, whose essay was supposed to be a review of the narratives of Henry Watson, Lewis and Milton Clarke, William Wells Brown, Frederick Douglass, and Josiah Henson, only in fact mentioned the last two, as if he had been unable to read the others. There cannot have been many people at the crossover of the various publishing trajectories of such narratives and in a position to read many of them. Some narratives circulated on such a small local scale that even Garrison and Douglass never came across them.

Such was the fate of the narratives by Leonard Black, William Hayden, Edmond Kelley, William Green, and John Thompson, among others. All were formerly enslaved men who wrote an autobiography. Their narratives are often overlooked precisely because they do not fit the typical slave narrative mold. Some are exceptionally short, like the twenty-three-page *Narrative of Events in the Life of William Green* (1853). Others lack the "white envelope" that usually framed the "black message," like *The Life of John Thompson, a Fugitive Slave* (1856). Others still, like Kelley's *A Family Redeemed from Bondage* (1851), are unusual in their structure. Their relative neglect by scholars is also due to their conditions of publication, circulation, and reception. Published in short print runs by authors on the fringes of the abolition movement, they remained outside, or just inside, the sphere of institutional antislavery. The narratives circulated locally, among the author's friends, neighbors, and community. Many were never intended to be read any further afield. This seems to have been the case for Leonard Black's 1847 narrative.

The Life and Sufferings of Leonard Black, a Fugitive from Slavery, Written by Himself echoes the "classic" slave narratives penned by Douglass and Brown, not least by its title. Its structure is broadly similar to better-known narratives. Two chapters focus on Black's life in slavery in the South, one on his escape, two on his life as a free man in the North, and the last consists of a ringing denunciation of slavery. The book opens with an introduction by Black himself and a "notice" by a certain A. M. Macy guaranteeing the narrative's authenticity. The main difference between Black's narrative and those by Douglass and Brown is its length—just sixty-three pages, compared to more than one hundred for the narratives that now form part of the canon. One critic described Black's account as "a minor example of the literary genre known as the slave narrative."[242] The "minor" nature of *The Life and Sufferings of Leonard Black* has played into its marginalization: it does not feature in any of the major slave narrative anthologies. Its publication history may also explain why it was, and is, disregarded by critics. Black's narrative was not published in New York, Boston, or Philadelphia—the three great centers of antislavery activity—but in New Bedford, Massachusetts. To be sure, New Bedford was not an "unexpected place" on the map of American abolitionism, to borrow Eric Gardner's term. It had "a widely spread fame as an Anti-Slavery town."[243] It took in hundreds of runaway slaves in the antebellum period, some of whom settled there permanently, and several Black abolitionists well known for their autobiographical narratives, including Douglass and Jacobs, spent time there.[244] Still, New Bedford was a small town, not a major publishing center.

Instead of a publisher's imprint, Black's title page bears the words "Press of Benjamin Lindsey." Lindsey was the proprietor and editor of one of the town's newspapers, the *New Bedford Mercury*.[245] He did not call himself an abolitionist and he was known to criticize antislavery propaganda campaigns such as the Great Postal Campaign of 1835, which he thought was ill-judged and liable to increase the oppression of the enslaved rather than help emancipate them.[246] The *New Bedford Mercury*, Kathryn Grover writes, was "an antislavery but not an abolitionist-leaning newspaper."[247] Lindsey sympathized with the African American population of New Bedford: for a time, he hired the fugitive William

Henry Johnson to deliver the *Mercury* to subscribers.[248] But in printing *The Life and Sufferings of Leonard Black*, Lindsey was merely acting as a book and job printer, and he probably paid no more attention to Black's narrative than he did to the dozens of pamphlets, speeches, directories, and other ephemera he printed. His name tops the list of works published in New Bedford from 1840 to 1859 by some distance.[249] A number of such "minor" narratives were printed by job printers in small- to medium-sized towns like Syracuse, New York; New Bedford and Worcester, Massachusetts; and New Haven, Connecticut. The same year as Black brought out his narrative, Andrew Jackson printed the *Narrative and Writings of Andrew Jackson, of Kentucky* on the press of the Syracuse *Star*.[250]

The same system had been used a decade previously to publish the first edition of Charles Ball's narrative in Lewistown, Pennsylvania. Black, like Ball, was assisted in publishing his narrative by local white citizens, visible on the margins of the text. Lindsey was one. The author of the "notice," Andrew M. Macy, was a resident of Nantucket, where Douglass had given his first antislavery lecture to a white public a few years earlier. Black's narrative was printed in New Bedford, but he was a preacher in Nantucket, as his narrative makes clear.[251] There he met Macy, an abolitionist who had joined the struggle to integrate public schools on the island.[252] Macy ran a bookstore and it seems likely that he shared his expertise in book production and distribution with Black.[253] Another nameless contributor helped at an earlier stage: a "friend of the author," Macy wrote, had reworked the text "to fit it for the press."[254]

Where Ball had played a minor role in the publication of his own narrative, Black was a more enterprising figure. "I have published this account of my life and sufferings," he explained in the introduction, "with the hope that I might realize a sufficient sum from its sale, to enable me to procure a greater degree of education, thereby increasing my usefulness as a preacher."[255] He foregrounded the book's earning potential, suggesting its political message was of secondary importance. Black's thrilling experiences as an enslaved man who had escaped slavery justified telling his life story, but the book was not framed as an abolitionist polemic. Its structure reflects its ambiguous genre attribution. There is a surprising lack of transition between the first five chapters, in which Black gives an at times harrowing account of his "life and sufferings," and the sixth, a critique of slavery that gives the impression of having been tagged on almost as an afterthought. The closing chapter opens, "I will now say something of slavery. I shall say nothing but what I know to be true"—as if the preceding chapters had not broached the topic at all.[256] *The Life and Sufferings of Leonard Black* was primarily what Bryan Sinche calls a "supplicant text," that is, "a publication that announces its author's need for economic support and is offered in exchange for that support." For Black and other authors of "minor" slave narratives, print was more about increasing their earnings than fighting for a cause. Sinche focuses on *The Light and Truth of Slavery: Aaron's History* (ca. 1840s), "a self-published, heavily plagiarized supplicant text that is only nominally concerned with slavery."[257] A further example is *A Narrative of the Life of Rev. Noah Davis, a Colored Man* (1859). "The object of the writer, in preparing this account of himself," Davis writes in his "notice to the public," is "to RAISE SUFFICIENT MEANS TO FREE HIS LAST TWO CHILDREN FROM SLAVERY."[258] Davis "reached for the uppercase," Augusta Rohrbach notes, "to ensure that the reader recognized the economic factors prompting his tale."[259] His narrative, which was published in Baltimore, was not conceived as a critique of slavery. Tellingly, the words "slave" and "slavery" do not appear in the title. Black did denounce slavery in no uncertain terms, calling it a "cruel system" and revealing its horrors—like Ball's and Williams's, his narrative contains a "cat-hauling" scene—but his main motivating factor for penning his narrative was financial.

Most of these narratives circulated on a small local scale. Not a single reference to *The Life and Sufferings of Leonard Black* or its author is to be found in the antislavery press; the narrative was not available from the antislavery book depositories in Boston, New York, and Philadelphia, nor did the best-known antislavery activists, Black or white, mention it in their correspondence. It would likely have been possible to buy a copy from the New Bedford Anti-Slavery Society office or Macy's bookstore. If Black traveled, he left no traces. Unlike Douglass, Brown, Bibb, and Truth, Black seems to have led a rather sedentary life as a free man, limiting the circulation of his narrative. Without an institutional framework to promote it, his little self-published book soon dropped out of sight. Today, it is largely forgotten.

It would be inaccurate to associate a particular publishing model with a given decade: the artisanal model of the 1840s survived into the 1850s and beyond. Even after *Uncle Tom's Cabin* came out in 1852 and trade publishers began to take an interest in antislavery literature, many formerly enslaved men and women still used the same methods of publication and distribution as Black. In 1859, G. W. Offley ordered a thousand copies of his twenty-four-page *Narrative of the Life and Labors of the Rev. G. W. Offley, a Colored Man* from two printers in Hartford, Connecticut. Newton Case and James Lockwood gave Offley credit, and he repaid his debt of $23.44 from his sales. He made two $5 payments in July and August 1859, then paid the balance in January 1860.[260] Like Lindsey, Case and Lockwood printed everything from dictionaries and Bibles to schoolbooks, official documents—and self-published pamphlets. Their decision to give Offley credit and to print the *Life of James*

Mars, a Slave Born and Sold in Connecticut in 1864 suggests they had some sympathy for the two impoverished African Americans hoping to earn a living from their books. "The question is sometimes asked me if I have not any means of support," the elderly Mars wrote in a later edition of his *Life*. "The fact is, I have nothing but what I have saved within the last three years. I have spent a portion of that time with my book about the country."[261]

The case of Sojourner Truth is particularly interesting, as the publication history of the *Narrative of Sojourner Truth* overlaps with *Uncle Tom*. Her narrative, first published in 1850, was written with the help of an amanuensis, Olive Gilbert. A little-known white abolitionist, Gilbert was a member of the Northampton Association of Education and Industry, a utopian community founded in Massachusetts in 1842. Truth met her in Northampton, where they worked together on the narrative in the latter half of the 1840s.[262] Garrison, a regular visitor to Northampton, played an active role in ensuring its publication. He wrote a brief (anonymous) preface to the narrative and acted as go-between for Truth and her printer, James Brown Yerrinton, who printed the *Liberator* with his son for many years.[263] Like Douglass and Brown, Truth had her *Narrative* printed by a man with ties to Garrisonian institutional antislavery. Yerrinton was himself a committed antislavery activist. "Your work on the *Liberator* has not been a mere mechanical performance," Garrison wrote to him soon after the newspaper was discontinued in 1865. "You have mingled with it the liveliest interest in the welfare of the paper, in the principles it has inculcated, in the humane and godlike object it has aimed to achieve. . . . You were an abolitionist from the start."[264] Truth's ties to institutional antislavery were strengthened by excerpts from Theodore D. Weld's *American Slavery as It Is* appended to her work. As chapter 1 demonstrated, the AASS had published Weld's antislavery compendium in 1839 to bury the *Narrative of James Williams* scandal and restate the truth of the antislavery argument. Coming full circle, Truth used Weld's work a decade later to bolster the veracity of her own account.

Though Truth was close to Garrison and the AASS, she self-published her narrative, as indicated by the words "Printed for the Author" on the title page. Yerrinton gave her credit, as Case and Lockwood were to do for Offley some years later. Truth alludes to the financial arrangement in her correspondence. "Will you please inform me How much I am now indebted to Yerrington for the printing," she asked Garrison in a letter dated August 1851. "Please send Mr Yerrington's bill in full & all receipts upon it—I wish to know precisely how the matter stands." The letter sheds light on the complex logistics of distribution, handled by Truth herself. "I have sold but few books during the summer," she went on, "but now the way seems opened for me to do better at the conventions which are now being held—Will you please forward to me care of *John Skinner Ravenna* [Ohio] 600 of the books. My last box cost me $7.00 It was nearly half full of paper & shavings—Don't send so much next time I don't like to pay transportation on it."[265] Lost and damaged books, costly and delayed deliveries, and forced reliance on numerous middlemen were all hurdles faced by itinerant authors distributing their own works.

Truth traveled thousands of miles across the North throughout the 1850s, attending multiple antislavery conventions and public meetings where she sold her books. Her travels were initially supported by Garrison and the British abolitionist George Thompson, who invited Truth to join them for a lecture tour in central and western New York in 1851. In a letter to Garrison written during the Civil War, Truth looked back at her poverty at that point: "I had been publishing my Narrative and owed for the whole edition. A great debt for me! Every cent I could obtain went to pay it. You said to me 'I am going with George Thompson on a lecturing tour. Come with us and you will have a good chance to dispose of your book.' I replied that I had no money. You generously offered to bear my expenses."[266] Press accounts of that tour and of subsequent ones were unanimous in their praise. "This uneducated woman spoke for a short time in her peculiar manner, and was most kindly received by the audience, who pressed around her to purchase her books," the *Liberator* wrote after a lecture in Union Village, New York. Augusta, Ohio, gave her an even warmer welcome: "The meeting was completely captivated by her, they bought a good number of her books." Four years later, Truth sold many copies of her *Narrative* in Boston: "She certainly did very well with her book, for the abolitionists bought it like fun."[267] Like other African American activists, Truth sometimes spoke in what P. Gabrielle Foreman calls "Black contexts," where demand for her *Narrative* was equally high.[268] "A respectable audience of coloured people assembled at their church, in Anthony-st., last evening to listen to an address from a woman of their race, named Sojourner Truth," the *New York Daily Tribune* reported. "After her address she did a considerable business in the way of selling the first part of her life, done up in some 120 pages, 12mo., to support the remainder."[269] Free Black communities, one historian points out, "provided the core audience for antislavery crusaders like Sojourner Truth"—and likewise they composed part of the readership for slave narratives.[270] The *Narrative of Sojourner Truth* was mainly read in reform circles, but it did extend beyond white and Black antislavery activists to other social movements, particularly women's rights. "I sold a good many books at the Convention and have thus far been greatly prospered," Truth was pleased to report after the Woman's Rights Convention in Akron, Ohio, in May 1851, where she gave one of her most famous speeches.[271] Sales via institutional antislavery channels seem to have been rather slender in comparison with face-to-face sales at such events. The *Liberator* contains just one brief item in 1850 hailing the publication and an announcement printed over several weeks from April to June informing readers the book was on sale at the MASS office.[272]

Truth's success was all the more striking for being the narrative of a woman enslaved in New York, a northern state where slavery had been abolished more than two decades previously.[273] From this angle, it was closer to the narratives by Chloe Spear (enslaved in Massachusetts), Peter Wheeler (New Jersey and New York), and James Mars (Connecticut) than those by Douglass, Brown, and Bibb. While the paratext firmly anchored the account in second-wave abolitionism, the *Narrative of Sojourner Truth* might have seemed at odds with recent events in the sectional crisis of the 1850s; this is very clear in comparison with Solomon Northup's *Twelve Years a Slave* (1853), a book that dramatized the precarious nature of Black freedom in the age of the Fugitive Slave Law. Furthermore, much of the *Narrative* focused not on slavery but rather on Truth's religious experience and spiritual journey in the context of the Second Great Awakening. A "strikingly spiritual" text, the *Narrative* "ends, not with indictment, but with the Christian forgiveness of a slaveholder," Nell Irvin Painter notes.[274] The *Narrative of Sojourner Truth* owed its success less to its topicality than to the reputation of its charismatic author and her own efforts in publishing and distributing the book—what Augusta Rohrbach calls her "keen sense of the publishing market."[275] Truth used a set of stereotype plates produced for the second edition to reprint copies at regular intervals, in 1853, 1855, and 1857, always using the same publishing strategy.[276] Every edition printed in Boston and New York was marked "Printed for the Author" or "Published for the Author." After *Uncle Tom*, Truth could have had her text reprinted by a trade publisher like John P. Jewett, who published Harriet Beecher Stowe's novel and many other antislavery texts, as the next chapter will show. After all, Truth knew enough about the publishing landscape to ask Stowe for a new introduction, which she prefixed to the 1855 edition of the *Narrative*.[277] But publishing with a trade publisher would have meant giving up a degree of autonomy, losing income—or at least having to wait for it—and risking losing control of her narrative and the image she wanted to promote in print.

In April 1863, the *Atlantic Monthly* printed Stowe's well-known article "Sojourner Truth, the Libyan Sibyl." The white novelist looked back at her meeting with Truth some ten years earlier. Her portrait was full of the romantic racialism found in abundance in *Uncle Tom's Cabin*. Stowe's literary Truth, Margaret Washington writes, was "an oddity, speaking in a droll, thick, almost incomprehensible dialect, uttering queer homilies and phrases, and expressing herself with gullibility and foolish reciprocity."[278] Moreover, Stowe got fundamental details of Truth's biography wrong, writing for instance that she was born in Africa. Three months later, Truth replied to Stowe via a letter to James Redpath, the abolitionist editor of the Boston *Commonwealth*. Her tone was polite but firm. "The history which Mrs. Stowe wrote about me, is not quite correct," she declared. "There is one place where she speaks of me as coming from Africa. My grandmother and my husband's mother came from Africa, but I did not; she must have misunderstood me, but you will find in my book a correct history." "I will send you six copies today," she added. "You will find them correct, they are Sojourner herself."[279] Truth took back control of her own story, exhibiting her book as the embodiment of a truth all too readily misrepresented by a novelist with little care for accuracy and blinded by her own prejudice. Truth's "little pamphlet" had become an extension of her selfhood: her book, she said, was herself.[280] By keeping control of its publication and circulation, Truth kept control of her life, her life story, and her own posterity. She understood that "the book's true power lies in its ability to produce memories and thus history."[281]

CHAPTER THREE

"Quite a Sensation"

Slave Narratives in the Age of Uncle Tom

H ISTORIANS OFTEN DESCRIBE the 1850s as a "crisis decade." Book-
ended by the compromise of 1850 and the execution of John Brown
in December 1859, the period was marked by an increasingly intense
sectional crisis linked to the proliferation of violent conflicts on the question
of slavery, ever more radical stances within the pro- and antislavery camps, and
the wider social reach of the debate, which now extended beyond a minority
of determined activists to involve all Americans. Until the late 1840s, abolitionism remained an unpopular doctrine among a majority of white northerners. "The followers of Garrison and Phillips were few," antislavery novelist
John Townsend Trowbridge recollected in his memoirs. "Society looked upon
them as dangerous fanatics, and the very name of *abolitionist* was covered
with an opprobrium that clung to it long after the course of political events
had justified their moral convictions." Because it turned the North into "a
hunting-ground for escaping human chattels," the Fugitive Slave Law of 1850
roused "a spirit of resistance in thousands who had hitherto remained indifferent, or timidly submissive, to the encroachments" of slavery.[1] The new law
made it a crime to aid a runaway slave in any way or attempt to hinder their
recapture, increased the number of federal agents authorized to deliver extra-
dition certificates for fugitives, and provided for greater financial reward for
agents who ordered the repatriation of supposed fugitives to the South. The
Fugitive Slave Law was a threat not only to formerly enslaved people who had
managed to flee North but also to freeborn Black men and women who were
at greater risk of abduction. It was at odds with the fundamental liberties of all
northerners, who could be forced into participating in the recapture of fugitives.[2] The adoption of the law helped legitimize the use of violence within the
abolition movement, particularly among Black activists. Faced with an ever-
more aggressive Slave Power, antislavery could not remain a wholly pacifist

movement focused on so-called moral suasion. The 1850s saw many outbreaks of violence, from attempted (and sometimes successful) fugitive slave rescues in the North to Bleeding Kansas in the West and John Brown's 1859 raid on Harpers Ferry, Virginia, in the South. At the same time, political abolitionism grew in importance as new parties such as the Republican and Radical Abolition Parties were founded to restrict slavery or abolish it outright, and leading figures like Frederick Douglass were taking new ideological directions. The days when it was hoped slavery could be abolished by the power of the pen were over. Antislavery campaigners from all sides still used newspapers, books, and pamphlets to spread their message and convince readers of the necessity and urgency of their cause. But they now wielded real weapons alongside pens and paper.

Yet the Fugitive Slave Law sparked one of the most popular texts of American antislavery, Harriet Beecher Stowe's novel *Uncle Tom's Cabin; or, Life among the Lowly*, serialized in the *National Era* from June 1851 and published in book form in 1852. Like many northerners, Stowe was outraged at what she called "this miserable wicked fugitive slave business."[3] She chose fiction to speak out against slavery, drawing on several slave narratives in the process. The book soon became a best seller, and its success helped reshape the publishing landscape. While most antislavery literature had tended to be published and distributed outside trade publishing circuits, some publishers began to produce novels, essays, and narratives that critiqued slavery. Some did so based on their own beliefs, others because there was money to be made out of it, and many on both grounds. A number of slave narratives were brought out by trade publishers in the 1850s. The circumstances of publication differed from the narratives of previous decades, and so did the texts. In the decade before the Civil War, Manisha Sinha writes, slave narratives took "a romanticist turn."[4] From Solomon Northup's *Twelve Years a Slave* (1853), the narrative of a free Black New Yorker who was kidnapped and then enslaved in Louisiana, to *Running a Thousand Miles for Freedom* (1860), an account of the incredible escape of Ellen and William Craft—she disguised as a white man and he as her Black servant—the narratives of formerly enslaved men and women became more thrilling and novelistic than ever. Whereas Douglass had remained silent on his means of escape, even in his second autobiography *My Bondage and My Freedom* (1855), the Crafts' escape North was central to their narrative; whereas Douglass was born in slavery, Northup was a free man who should never have been enslaved and who was fortunate to escape. Trade publishers played a role in "sensationalizing" slave narratives, as the 1858 edition of Charles Ball's account with the new title *Fifty Years in Chains* shows. For Douglass, by now a high-profile Black intellectual and journalist, access to trade publishing afforded a degree of independence from the Garrisonian networks that had helped in publishing his *Narrative* and which he now wished to keep at arm's length. This chapter discusses the publishing history of *Twelve Years a Slave, My Bondage and My Freedom,* and *Fifty Years in Chains,* and concludes with a study of Harriet Jacobs's *Incidents in the Life of a Slave Girl,* published on the eve of the Civil War in 1861. It was slated for publication with a trade publisher but was eventually self-published, pointing to the ongoing difficulties encountered by a formerly enslaved woman on the path to publication. The discourse of formerly enslaved individuals remained deeply polemical and subversive in the early 1860s, and only a handful of mainstream publishing figures were willing to broadcast it.

"The Servile Publishers of That Day": Antislavery and the Book Trade

The United States developed a national book trade system in the first half of the nineteenth century. As previous chapters demonstrated, evangelical organizations pioneered new forms of mass production and distribution, which were then picked up by the trade publishing sector. New technologies in typesetting such as stereotype and electrotype, paper production, binding, and image reproduction let trade publishing—an ever-larger and more competitive sector—produce far more books at far less cost.[5] The emergent railroad and canal network led to the "transportation revolution" and more trade, which benefited publishers. Books printed in the urban centers of the Northeast could now be sent across much of a vast and constantly expanding territory. Despite slowdowns due to the Panics of 1837 and 1857, the publishing sector continued consolidating until the Civil War. As Michael Winship writes, at the end of the eighteenth century, the American book trade had been "comprised largely of small, unspecialized shops employing a few craftspeople of varying skill, producing books and other printed matter for local consumption." By the 1850s, "a well-organized national book trade existed, centered primarily in New York, Philadelphia, and Boston, with an effective distribution network reaching across the nation. The trade included a number of specialized firms, many of considerable size, dedicated to a particular branch of book manufacture and distribution."[6]

A handful of major publishers soon came to dominate this new context, including Carey & Lea in Philadelphia, Ticknor & Fields in Boston, and Harper & Brothers in New York. The latter opened their vast, seven-floor premises in 1855, unusually bringing every step in production and sales under one roof.[7] These publishers offered diverse catalogs and developed tools to regulate the profession and unite its membership. The 1830s saw the launch of the first trade periodicals, such as *Norton's Literary Gazette and Publishers' Circular* and the *Literary World*. The book trade also adopted informal cooperation agreements such as the (more or less widely followed) "courtesy of the trade," by which the first publisher to announce an edition of a foreign work had exclusive rights to produce it in the United States for some months.[8] America now had its own publishing industry, with its own stakeholders, outlets, and practices. The Association of New York Publishers honored the flourishing industry with a grand banquet at the Crystal Palace in September 1855.[9]

Many authors were invited to the banquet, including Washington Irving, William Cullen Bryant, and Nathaniel Parker Willis, to celebrate the emergence of a truly American literature. As Ezra Greenspan points out, however, "The guest list was overwhelmingly white, Anglo-Saxon, and Protestant." The organizers "overlooked the black author most likely to be invited, Frederick Douglass, whose *My Bondage and My Freedom* was issued the month before by a trade publisher and was currently receiving unusual publicity and registering strong sales."[10] His absence reflects the marginal position of African Americans in the publishing industry and in American literary culture more broadly. "Black publishing houses and presses were relatively rare, short-lived, and had limited circulation," Ronald J. Zboray and Mary Saracino Zboray write. "Social networks that provided entrées to publishers were less extensive for African Americans than for whites."[11] African American authors, whether or not they had experienced slavery, were "authors of a strange race," as one of them wrote, and generally published in nonmainstream circuits.[12] Many Black texts were self-published—slave narratives as well as spiritual autobiographies, travelogues, and essays. The words "Published by the Author" or similar expressions appear on the title pages of *The Life and Religious Experience of Jarena Lee, a Coloured Lady* (1836), *A Narrative of the Life and Travels, of Mrs. Nancy Prince* (1850), and Martin R. Delany's *The Condition, Elevation, Emigration, and Destiny of the Colored People of the United States* (1852). Other books with only the printer's name were similarly financed and distributed by their authors, such as William Cooper Nell's *Services of Colored Americans, in the Wars of 1776 and 1812* (1851).[13] Two of the best-known African American novels of the age—William Wells Brown's *Clotel* (1853) and Frank J. Webb's *The Garies and Their Friends* (1857)—were printed in Britain. A third—Hannah Crafts's *The Bondwoman's Narrative*, dating from the late 1850s or early 1860s—remained a manuscript until it was rediscovered in the twentieth century.[14] In the United States, the periodical remained the most accessible format for aspiring African American authors. As Eric Gardner notes, "The exclusionary practices of 'mainstream' white print culture regularly made the nineteenth-century Black press the best—and often the *only*—outlet for many Black authors."[15] Though antebellum Black periodicals found it hard to survive, titles like *Freedom's Journal*, the

Colored American, the *Anti-Slavery Herald*, the *Anglo-African Magazine*, the *Weekly Anglo-African*, and Douglass's newspapers gave many African American writers and intellectuals a platform in print.

Publishing in the Black press was not without limits, though, as the case of Martin R. Delany demonstrates. His novel *Blake; or, The Huts of America* was serialized in the *Anglo-African Magazine* in 1859–60 and in the *Weekly Anglo-African* in 1861–62. Both periodicals were launched by the African American journalist and activist Thomas Hamilton, the latter later taken over by his brother Robert.[16] The limited resources and lack of experience of the Hamilton brothers meant Delany was disappointed by how his novel appeared in the pages of the *Anglo-African Magazine*. "The three chapters published in the first number of the Magazine, were full of errors, in consequence of the hurried manner in which it was got out," he complained in a letter to William Lloyd Garrison. Nor did serial publication in periodicals pay well. Delany hoped for profits that would help finance his new project of establishing an African American–led settlement in the Niger region of Africa, prompting him to write to Garrison to appeal for help contacting mainstream publishers. "I am anxious to get a good publishing house to take it, as I know I could make a penny by it, and the chances for a negro in this department are so small, that unless some disinterested competent persons would indirectly aid in such a step, I almost despair of any chance."[17] Whether Garrison would not or could not help Delany, or whether no publisher would take on a novel whose hero, Henry Blake, escapes slavery and then plans a hemispheric slave rebellion, *Blake* was never published as a book in Delany's lifetime. In the words of textual scholar Jerome McGann, the work "caught the attention of almost no one for nearly one hundred years after its publication."[18]

The vast majority of slave narrative authors never attempted to approach a trade publisher. Their narratives were often published spontaneously, to defend a sullied reputation or to earn a living, by formerly enslaved men and women who had sometimes barely escaped slavery and had no intention of selling their narrative to readers outside their immediate circle. It is unlikely that Douglass set out to find a commercial publisher when it came to publishing his own *Narrative* in 1845. His main motivation was publishing quickly to legitimize his position, and he therefore turned to the print networks of institutional antislavery, while handling much of the editorial process himself. Douglass would probably never have found a trade publisher on his own. Antislavery literature, by Black and white authors alike, was almost unanimously rejected by publishers in the 1830s and 1840s—or at the very least, they used "extreme caution" for fear of alienating southern readers.[19] Richard Hildreth's *The Slave* (1836) is a case in point.

In the mid-1830s, Hildreth, a young historian and sometime editor of the
Boston *Atlas*, spent over a year on a Florida plantation, where he wrote what
is now regarded as the first antislavery novel—a fictive first-person account of
life in bondage titled *The Slave; or, Memoirs of Archy Moore*. Having returned
to the North in 1836, Hildreth sought a publisher for his book but could not
find one either in Boston or New York. "No bookseller dared to publish anything of the sort," he later explained, "and so complete was the reign of terror,
that printers were almost afraid to set up the types."[20] As Leonard L. Richards
has documented, the emergence of interracial immediatism in the early 1830s
sparked a wave of antiabolitionist violence that peaked in the middle of the
decade, with mobs and race riots being instigated by "gentlemen of property
and standing."[21] In 1836, the *Liberator* also warned of a "reign of terror" across
the North.[22] In the end, Hildreth had no choice but to have the book printed
at his own expense. Only the name of John H. Eastburn, a friend of Hildreth's, founder of the *Atlas* and city printer of Boston, appeared on the title
page.[23] Hildreth himself did not acknowledge authorship of the novel at first:
The Slave came out anonymously. Its circulation, he noted, "was almost
entirely among professed Abolitionists. The work was unknown both to the
critics and to the booksellers."[24] The one paper that gave it some attention in
the months following its publication was the *Liberator*, which reprinted a
number of extracts, reviews, and letters from enthusiastic readers. Copies
could be purchased at the book depository of the Massachusetts Anti-Slavery
Society (MASS); most of them had been sold by mid-1837.[25] A few editions
were published throughout the 1840s by various antislavery societies and
minor reform-oriented publishers, but even as it grew in popularity, the novel
failed to reach "the great reading public."[26]

Most trade publishers avoided anything that smacked of antislavery, turning down manuscripts or excising sections that they deemed too subversive.
Harper & Brothers, for instance, went out of their way to conciliate their
southern readership. In 1835, a South Carolina newspaper objected to a book
just published by the New York firm, Andrew Reed and James Matheson's *A
Narrative of the Visit to the American Churches, by the Deputation from the Congregational Union of England and Wales*, because it contained "incendiary"
matter.[27] Indeed, Reed and Matheson, two British Congregationalist ministers
who had recently toured the United States, expressed strong antislavery sentiments in the second volume of the book:

> Yes, the slave must go free! Slavery now has a legal existence only in America.
> But America is the very place, of all others, where it cannot, must not be toler-
> ated. . . . Much evil may be; but this cannot be! What, slavery, in the last home

of liberty! The vilest despotism in the presence of boasted equality! The deepest oppression of man, where the rights of man are professedly most honoured! No, this cannot continue. Slavery and Liberty cannot exist together; either slavery must die, or liberty must die.[28]

Having been alerted to these statements, Harper & Brothers immediately wrote to the editor of the newspaper, claiming that they had not suspected anything "improper" and had agreed to publish the work without examining it carefully. To prove their good faith, they added that on several occasions they had rejected potentially profitable manuscripts precisely on account of their "objectionable" politics with respect to slavery. They had just decided against bringing out an American edition of a book of travels first published in London by social reformer Edward S. Abdy—"we were told . . . that Mr. Abdy was an abolitionist," they wrote, "and we would have nothing to do with him."[29] Reflecting on this episode a decade later, a member of the MASS stated that Abdy's *Journal of a Residence and Tour in the United States of North America* "was *tabooed* in consequence of [the author's] anti-slavery fidelity, and put under the ban of the servile publishers of that day."[30] Again, in 1836, Harper & Brothers inadvertently republished *Tales of the Woods and Fields* by British popular writer Anne Marsh-Caldwell, a work that referred in a footnote to the "dreadful cruelties" inflicted on the enslaved in the "abominable regions" of the American South.[31] Harper & Brothers apologized to the Charleston bookseller who had pointed out the passage and made clear that they "uniformly decline publishing works calculated to interfere in any way with southern rights and southern institutions."[32] A new expurgated edition of *Tales of the Woods and Fields* was soon printed. Alongside the three British works was one by a French author, Gustave de Beaumont, who traveled with his friend Alexis de Tocqueville across the United States in 1831–32. His novel *Marie; or, Slavery in the United States* (1835), harshly critical of "prejudice against race," was never published in book form in antebellum America, Garrison noted, "owing to the subserviency of northern publishers to southern slaveholders."[33] Instead, it was partially serialized in the *Liberator* in July and August 1845. The antislavery press was the sole outlet available for some authors, white and Black alike.

Bookstores initially proved no more welcoming than publishers. "Booksellers, like other people, are afraid of, and do not love Abolitionists," the *National Anti-Slavery Standard* declared in 1846.[34] Black intellectual Hosea Easton described the antebellum bookstore as one among many other sites of white supremacy: he noted that a majority of "popular book stores, in commercial towns and cities," had their "show-windows" lined with "cuts and placards descriptive of the negroe's deformity."[35] Booksellers' hostility to abolition prompted antislavery societies to set up book depositories on their premises. Some antislavery bookstores were, however, founded in the antebellum period, the best known by the Black abolitionist David Ruggles, head of the New York Vigilance Committee, who assisted Douglass when he first arrived in New York in 1838. In 1834, Ruggles opened the country's first Black-owned bookstore at 67 Lespenard Street. It sold "Anti-Slavery publications of every description," including Lydia Maria Child's *The Oasis* (1834), *Address of the New York Young Men's Anti-Slavery Society, to Their Fellow-Citizens* (1834), and the *Productions of Mrs. Maria W. Stewart* (1835).[36] Ruggles's bookstore was more than just a commercial space: it had been established as a political space for antislavery activism, a literary space for Black authorship and writing, and a social space to incorporate white and Black New Yorkers in a dialog on slavery and abolition.[37] Ruggles would undoubtedly have sold slave narratives had his store survived, but tragically it was destroyed by arsonists a little more than a year after opening. In the 1830s, running an antislavery bookstore was potentially deadly.[38] Finch & Weed's antislavery bookstore, also in New York, was equally short-lived. A short walk from the American Anti-Slavery Society (AASS) office, the newspaperman Myron Finch and Thomas Allen Weed, a former Oberlin College student, sold "an extensive assortment of Anti-Slavery publications, consisting of the prominent works published by the A. S. Societies from their commencement."[39] When the store opened in 1845, its selection included works such as Lysander Spooner's *The Unconstitutionality of Slavery*, George Bourne's *A Condensed Anti-Slavery Bible Argument*, and *Narrative of the Life of Frederick Douglass*, all published in 1845.[40] Finch & Weed also acted as agents for the *True American*, a newspaper printed in Lexington, Kentucky, by Cassius M. Clay, a former plantation owner and enslaver turned abolitionist.[41] The business failed to turn enough of a profit, and the debts piled up until it was forced to close.

Publishers and booksellers changed their attitudes to antislavery literature in the 1850s after *Uncle Tom's Cabin*. Stowe's novel was a runaway best seller, selling more than three hundred thousand copies in the first year, at a time when sales of more than ten thousand meant "a decided hit."[42] The novel was reviewed in all the major newspapers; some critics were lavish in their praise, others highly critical. It generated dozens of spin-offs, such as stage adaptations, songs, board games, card games, silverware, dolls, and postcards featuring characters from the story. Some twenty different editions were published in Britain, and eleven French translations came out in 1852 and 1853. Many pro-slavery authors countered Stowe with their own works of fiction, like Mary H. Eastman and her *Aunt Phillis's Cabin; or, Southern Life as It Is* (1852). John P.

Jewett promoted his publication of *Uncle Tom's Cabin* with an advertising campaign on an unprecedented scale, reflecting new business practices in the age of the industrial book.[43] There was a potentially lucrative market for tell-all novels about the grim realities of slavery, a hitherto taboo topic.

Donald E. Liedel describes the post–*Uncle Tom* years as "the golden age of the antislavery novel."[44] Few people nowadays read the countless novels of the 1850s set on southern plantations, such as Mary Hayden Pike's *Ida May: A Story of Things Actual and Possible* (1854), Samuel Mosheim Schmucker's *The Planter's Victim: or, Incidents of American Slavery* (1855), and Francis Colburn Adams's *Our World: or, The Slaveholder's Daughter* (1855). Some did sell well in their day, but none made their mark on literary history. As well as bearing a political message, many such novels set out to meet the public craving for more books like *Uncle Tom's Cabin*. The tales of sadistic masters, "tragic mulattoes," and free northerners kidnapped into slavery were intended to stir indignation—and to titillate. Most of these novels were published by enterprising young publishers who had not acquired a sizable southern market and hoped to cultivate the new mass market in the North. Long-established firms such as George P. Putnam in New York and Ticknor & Fields in Boston usually did not publish antislavery novels, though the latter did issue some works by respected antislavery authors Lydia Maria Child, John Greenleaf Whittier, and James Russell Lowell. Harper & Brothers not only avoided publishing any book tinged with antislavery sentiment but offered readers an extensive list of southern regional novels.[45]

Many publishers who brought out *Uncle Tom*–style novels also published other types of books against slavery, including slave narratives. The sincerity of a publisher's antislavery beliefs can often be measured by the variety of genres they published, from novels to autobiographies and polemical writings. Stowe's publisher, John P. Jewett, is a prime example.[46] Based in Boston, Jewett was one of the rare commercial publishers who in the 1850s showed a consistent (and not entirely profit-driven) interest in abolitionist literature of all kinds. Besides *Uncle Tom's Cabin*, his list included editions of three speeches by antislavery politician Charles Sumner, a book by Garrisonian abolitionist Giles B. Stebbins denouncing colonization as "a scheme of wholesale expatriation unparalleled in its atrocity and wickedness," the first volume of the antislavery gift book *Autographs for Freedom*, an edition of the slave narrative of Josiah Henson, and the "Juvenile Anti-Slavery Toy Books" series designed specifically for children—among other titles by William Wells Brown, Richard Hildreth, and William Jay.[47] That a thriving commercial publisher was actively involved in the production of such books allowed for their extensive distribution in the North and Northwest—the company had a branch in Cleveland, Ohio—but also legitimized a literature otherwise decried as "inflammatory." Writing to Sumner about the speech against the Kansas–Nebraska Act the senator had delivered in Congress on 21 February 1854, Jewett asked: "How would it do for me to print an *elegant* edition of it on choice paper large type, & *gilt edges?*" Barely a week later, Jewett sent Sumner copies of the work titled *The Landmark of Freedom.* "I hope you will consider the garb worthy of the contents," he wrote. "I want Southern Senators to see it, & to . . . know from them if a speech can be printed in that style in slavery[']s dominions?"[48] Printed on fine paper with gilt edges, Sumner's words gained an authority and prestige that they did not have in Congress, where Sumner was generally booed by proslavery opponents. Jewett was willing to lose money in the process. "We got it up for other reasons than to make money," he wrote about the pamphlet.[49]

Jewett may have sparked the fashion for antislavery fiction, but he published no further novels in the *Uncle Tom* vein. The rival Boston firm of Phillips, Sampson did publish many novels in the 1850s drawing on themes and motifs popularized by Stowe, including Pike's *Ida May* and *Caste: A Story of Republican Equality* (1856) and Trowbridge's *Neighbor Jackwood* (1857). To promote *Ida May*, the melodramatic tale of a white girl kidnapped on her fifth birthday and sold into slavery, Phillips, Sampson set up a major advertising campaign designed to keep readers on the edge of their seats. The firm deliberately pushed back the publication date for the hotly anticipated novel, sent newspaper offices extracts from the proofs, and kept the author's identity secret—she was thought to be Stowe for a while. All these strategies, now widely used, were relatively new developments in the 1850s.[50] Phillips, Sampson may have been trying to make up for their past blunder in turning down *Uncle Tom's Cabin* on the grounds that a novel published serially in an antislavery newspaper had no chance of selling as a book. The business did eventually give Stowe a home, publishing her 1856 *Dred: A Tale of the Great Dismal Swamp.* Phillips, Sampson's somewhat opportunistic move (and resentment at losing a highly successful author) likely explains Jewett's bitter tone in a letter to Sumner: "She [Stowe] has gone to Phillips & Sampson, a pro slavery concern."[51]

Mainstream trade publishers who brought out antislavery literature included, last but not least, Derby & Miller, who became Miller, Orton & Mulligan in 1854.[52] I will return to this firm, which published (or copublished) no fewer than three slave narratives—Northup's *Twelve Years a Slave*, Douglass's *My Bondage and My Freedom*, and Peter Still's *The Kidnapped and the Ransomed* (1856)—alongside essays, novels, and collective biographies with abolitionist leanings. Held up by Liedel as one of the most vibrant publishers on the antislavery scene, Derby & Miller had a sufficiently extensive output to include a special section of "Anti-Slavery Books" in its catalogs.[53]

Many contemporaries commented on the sudden surge in the publication of antislavery literature. Stowe was naturally very pleased with the development. "A few years ago there was no anti-slavery literature," she wrote in the New York *Independent*, "and a book devoted to this subject could scarce find a publisher who dared issue it, and it lay under the ban of public opinion when issued. Now, every publisher and every press pours out anti-slavery books of every form and description, lectures, novels, tracts, biographies."[54] This context explains why older antislavery works, including slave narratives, were now being reprinted, even when they had gone unnoticed in previous decades. A new, enlarged edition of Hildreth's *The Slave*, for instance, came out under the imprint of several publishers in the 1850s. It was first published in 1852 under the title *The White Slave; or, Memoirs of a Fugitive*; Miller, Orton & Mulligan brought out their own version in 1856 as *Archy Moore, the White Slave; or, Memoirs of a Fugitive*. The revamped novel brought Hildreth his long-awaited success, not only in the United States but also in Great Britain and France, where a staggering number of editions and translations were issued in quick succession. As white abolitionist J. Miller McKim pointed out, "Books on the subject of emancipation were read formerly almost only by Abolitionists, and were for sale only at Anti-Slavery depositories." Now they were "read by all classes in the United States."[55] The new higher profile of antislavery authors irked some, such as George R. Graham, the conservative editor of *Graham's Magazine*, now remembered for its racist attacks on *Uncle Tom's Cabin* and the novels it inspired. "The *strong, money-making side for a publisher now, is the antislavery side*," he thundered in his magazine.[56] In fact, publishing proslavery novels proved just as lucrative. Eastman's *Aunt Phillis's Cabin* sold eighteen thousand copies in a month. Published in 1854, Mary Virginia Terhune's *Alone* passed through ten American editions by 1855.[57] According to Nina Baym, many more pro- than antislavery novels were reviewed in magazines.[58]

It is therefore important not to overstate the popularity of antislavery literature as a broad category. The impression Americans in the 1850s had of an abundance of books on slavery was largely created by the huge success of a handful of works, first and foremost *Uncle Tom's Cabin*, driven by a powerful media marketing campaign and the novel's various afterlives. The same titles— *Uncle Tom's Cabin*, *Ida May*, and *The White Slave*—tend to crop up in account after account. While the early 1850s did witness what Liedel calls a "vogue of Uncle Tom literature"—and what contemporaries referred to as "Uncle Tomi- tudes" or (Graham's term) "Uncle Tom-Foolery"—many antislavery writers whose works bore no relation to *Uncle Tom* still found it difficult to get their manuscripts into print.[59] Sentimental antislavery novels sold well, abolitionist tracts and treaties much less so. Having recently relocated from Maryland to

Philadelphia, where he hoped his sons would be protected from "the common prejudices of slave society," John Dixon Long, a minister of the Methodist Episcopal Church, decided to commit his views on slavery to writing. The "city of brotherly love," however, was far from the abolitionist haven of his imaginings. "I found prevailing a vast deal of pro-slavery sentiment," he later wrote. "When my manuscript was ready, no publisher . . . that I approached would undertake its publication." Like Hildreth twenty years before, Long self-published *Pictures of Slavery in Church and State* (1857), a book whose introduction ended with the rallying cry: "May the blessing of Christ rest on the antislavery cause!"[60] At the exact same time, Hinton Rowan Helper, a native of North Carolina, failed to secure a northern (let alone a southern) publisher for his own manuscript, in which he blamed slavery for hindering the economic and cultural progress of the South while limiting the opportunities of nonslaveholding whites (humanitarian concerns were absent from Helper's criticism of slavery). *The Impending Crisis of the South* was eventually issued in 1857 by an obscure New York book agent and at the author's risk.[61] Three years later, Louisa May Alcott saw one of her antislavery short stories rejected by the *Atlantic Monthly*. "The dear South must not be offended," she commented ironically in her diary.[62] Abolition always was a radical doctrine that few book trade professionals would endorse. Publishers such as Harper & Brothers—now HarperCollins—might well have to publicly acknowledge their responsibility in promoting slavery in the not-too-distant future, as other institutions—universities and the press for instance—have already started doing. As two scholars have recently argued, "We need the book publishers who have been responsible for promulgating ideas of white supremacy to acknowledge their role in creating the social world of today."[63]

The Business of *Twelve Years a Slave*

Twelve Years a Slave, the narrative of Solomon Northup, was the first slave narrative issued under the imprint of a trade publisher—namely, Derby & Miller. James C. Derby had started as a bookstore owner in Auburn, New York, in 1840 before branching out as a publisher of books in 1844. His firm largely contributed to the town's prosperity, consuming the products of the paper mill and selling books profitably and on a large scale. The books Derby and his partner Norman C. Miller issued were both timely and popular. Derby was quick to seize the moment of intense public interest in a subject, Madeleine B. Stern writes, publishing appropriate books at the time of the death of national heroes or during presidential elections. Some of his hits included Samuel G. Goodrich's *History of All Nations* (1850) and Fanny Fern's *Fern Leaves from Fanny's Portfolio* (1853), which sold between seventy and eighty thousand copies in its first year.[64] According to R. G. Dun & Company, Derby was a "v[ery] shrewd & sagacious" entrepreneur. In 1851, his firm was doing "a first rate bus[iness] better than ever & mak[in]g money."[65]

Derby started publishing books on the subject of slavery in 1852. Derby & Miller were instrumental in bringing out texts that were highly critical of slavery, such as *The Higher Law* (1852) by the antislavery advocate and Underground Railroad supporter William Hosmer, also based in Auburn. "The abolition of slavery is demanded by common sense," Hosmer argued. "Slavery is not simply wicked—it does not accomplish its ends by merely unjustifiable means. It evinces everywhere extreme imbecility. In whatever light we view it, it is a thoroughly contemptible arrangement."[66] Printing such content was in itself a form of political activism, heralded as such by abolitionists. In 1855, the *Radical Abolitionist* drew the attention of readers to "the enterprise and manly independence of the publishers, Messrs. MILLER, ORTON AND MULLIGAN [successors to Derby & Miller], who advertise, among other valuable books, a variety of Anti-Slavery publications—in cheering contrast to the craven class who suppress or expurgate whatever is offensive to slaveholders."[67] That said, Derby & Miller began publishing antislavery texts just as sales of *Uncle Tom's Cabin* really started to take off, and it might be wondered if the company would have gone down the same road had Stowe's novel not shown them the way. The bulk of its antislavery output—in fact, just some ten or so titles—consisted not of essays like *The Higher Law*, but of novels and biographies, including the three aforementioned slave narratives, alongside lives of Thomas Jefferson, Napoleon Bonaparte, and Empress Joséphine; Derby & Miller's list was perhaps less the product of firmly rooted convictions than of the "Biographical Mania" that gripped nineteenth-century America.[68] In a word, Derby does not seem to have been an activist publisher of the Jewett stamp. A native of upstate New York, a hotbed of religious and reform activity, Derby may have had antislavery sympathies, but he was no radical abolitionist. It was above all his nose for opportunity that led him to publish *Twelve Years a Slave*, *My Bondage and My Freedom*, and *The Kidnapped and the Ransomed*—three books he rightly judged would attract a large readership, given that *Uncle Tom* fever showed no signs of cooling. During the Civil War, Derby reunited with his former partner. Derby & Miller's new list was made up entirely of proRepublican pamphlets and books. "Mr. Derby is of course a *Union Man*; and thinks *Secession* is a grave sin," one of his authors wrote in 1861. Yet Derby also arranged with another trade publisher, J. B. Lippincott, to issue an edition of Augusta Jane Evans's 1864 arch-Confederate novel *Macaria; or, Altars of Sacrifice*, which according to Melissa J. Homestead demonstrates his "political and commercial opportunism." Derby likely did not publish the novel under his own name because he wanted to avoid accusations of Confederate sympathies, but he did not wish to forsake a potentially profitable publishing venture either.[69]

Unlike the narratives by Douglass and Brown, *Twelve Years a Slave* is not the story of a man who was born enslaved but of a freeborn Black man kidnapped into slavery. This sets it apart from previous slave narratives. Northup was born in 1808 to a father emancipated after the death of his enslaver, and he lived in the state of New York as a free man for more than thirty years. In the late 1830s, he was living in Saratoga Springs with his family, earning a living by various means; he was a talented violinist and occasionally played in local hotels. In 1841, two men claiming to be connected with a circus company then in Washington, DC, offered him a job as a musician. They traveled together to Washington, where Northup was drugged, kidnapped, and sold to the slave trader James H. Birch, then forcibly transported to Louisiana and auctioned off. As several historians have shown, free African Americans were regularly abducted in antebellum America: the phenomenon is sometimes described as a Reverse Underground Railroad.[70] Only after twelve years of slavery did Northup manage to contact the family who once enslaved his father, the white Northups, and was he able to regain his freedom.

The extraordinary story of Northup's kidnapping, enslavement, and rescue grabbed the headlines of northern newspapers. The Washington correspondent for the *New York Daily Times* was the first reporter to broadcast it on 20 January 1853. He was also the first to draw a parallel between Northup and Uncle Tom, noting that both the real man and the fictional character had been enslaved in the Red River region of Louisiana. Northup's condition during the nine years he was in the hands of the cruel Edwin Epps "was of a character nearly approaching that described by Mrs. STOWE, as the condition of 'Uncle Tom' while in that region."[71] On 21 January, Northup returned to his wife, Anne, and his children. Events then moved fast: *Twelve Years a Slave* came out just six months later. Without taking the time to recover from his ordeal, Northup began making appearances on the antislavery circuit, lecturing alongside Douglass and Jermain W. Loguen in Troy, New York, on 1 February. He also attended receptions held in his honor. This is probably where he met David Wilson, who served as his amanuensis. Wilson had no ties to the abolition movement. A lawyer by training, he had turned to writing and published several books on history and local events. Wilson's *The Life of Jane McCrea* (1853) recounted the story of a young woman who was murdered and scalped by Native Americans near Saratoga during the Revolutionary War; her body had been exhumed and reburied in 1852. *Henrietta Robinson* (1855) was about the highly publicized trial of a supposedly demented woman known as "the veiled murderess" in Troy in 1855. Like for his other works, Wilson took inspiration for *Twelve Years a Slave* from a local event covered widely in the press, turning it into a dramatic tale of suspense. The idea was not so much to condemn slavery morally and politically as to give the public the sensationalist reading matter they craved. In this sense, Wilson is not dissimilar to Isaac Fisher, who claimed to have written Ball's narrative as a work of history rather than as an act of partisanship. Wilson's preface to Northup's account echoes Fisher's preface to Ball's narrative. "It is believed that the following account of his experience on Bayou Bœuf presents a correct picture of Slavery, in all its lights and shadows, as it now exists in that locality," he wrote. "Unbiased . . . by any prepossessions or prejudices, the only object of the editor has been to give a faithful history of Solomon Northup's life, as he received it from his lips."[72] One 1837 critic wrote that *Slavery in the United States* was "written by a gentleman . . . who is not, we believe, an avowed abolitionist." The same was true of Wilson: "I believe he never was suspected of being an Abolitionist—he may be anti-slavery—somewhat conservative," wrote John Thomson, a friend of the white Northups.[73] Wilson never returned to the subject of slavery.[74]

Sam Worley rightly argues that "Wilson seems to have primarily seen Northup's adventures as . . . an opportunity to tell and sell a particularly sensationalistic tale."[75] The fact that Wilson was not himself an abolitionist does not, however, make him a neutral figure. Given that his aim was to grab the public's attention, Wilson had every reason to foreground certain aspects of Northup's story. *Twelve Years a Slave* contains lengthy descriptive passages that edge the slave narrative toward the travelogue or novel, overshadowing its biographical dimension. Speaking through Wilson, Northup paints a picture of plantations, the people who lived on them, and their farming practices and customs. He dwells on the Louisiana landscapes at several points. "The bay and the sycamore, the oak and the cypress, reach a growth unparalleled, in those fertile lowlands bordering the Red River," he notes. "From every tree, moreover, hang long, large masses of moss, presenting to the eye unaccustomed to them, a striking and singular appearance."[76] The language is sometimes technical—for instance, in Northup's account of growing cotton and sugar cane: "A sugar field is hoed three times, the same as cotton, save that a greater quantity of earth is drawn to the roots. By the first of August hoeing is usually over. About the middle of September, whatever is required for seed is cut and stacked in ricks, as they are termed. In October it is ready for the mill or sugar-house, and then the general cutting begins."[77] Northup may have given Wilson an outline for these passages, but it is unlikely he dictated them word for word. Like Fisher before him, Wilson may have drawn on other sources to flesh out his text with descriptions liable to appeal to northern readers keen to learn about far-flung places. At a time when the South was still largely inaccessible to the rising domestic tourist trade, slave narratives offered a glimpse of unfamiliar lands. This is particularly true of the novelistic narratives of the 1850s.[78]

Yet the armchair traveler reading the book fundamentally owed the experience to Northup, who acted as a proxy for northern readers. Every effort was made to channel his voice directly to the reader. Wilson's name did not feature on the title page, and he played down his role in the preface. The narrative is written in the first person. While Northup's voice was indeed mediated by Wilson, *Twelve Years a Slave* creates "the illusion of an accurate, firsthand account of slavery in the Deep South."[79] It was easy to feel empathy for Northup: he was born free and unjustly enslaved, and as such was doubtless worthier of interest for a majority of white northerners than a plantation-born slave. The Fugitive Slave Law had exacerbated northern resentment against proslavery southerners, who stood accused of threatening the freedom of all citizens, white and Black, and no longer just the enslaved. Novels like *Ida May* echoed such fears, taking them to extremes by including "white slave" characters. As early as 1848, William H. Brisbane's *Amanda: A Tale for the Times* featured a dark-complexioned young girl kidnapped by a man who eventually convinces her she was born a slave and adopted by a white northern family.[80] Derby & Miller were attuned to the political relevance and novelistic potential of the abduction of free northerners when they published *Twelve Years a Slave* and, three years later, copublished (as Miller, Orton & Mulligan) *The Kidnapped and the Ransomed* by Peter Still, a freeborn African American who was kidnapped as a child and spent forty years in slavery.[81]

The publication of *Twelve Years a Slave* was in tune not only with contemporary politics but also with the latest literary trends. Derby & Miller and Wilson shaped the text and paratext to put readers in mind of *Uncle Tom's Cabin*. *Twelve Years a Slave* is dedicated to "Harriet Beecher Stowe: whose name, throughout the world, is identified with the great reform." Northup had in fact only recently encountered *Uncle Tom's Cabin* for the first time—it came out while he was still enslaved—and it seems likely that the dedication was included at the urging of the publishers or of Wilson himself, all equally aware of what Stowe's name would mean to potential readers. The dedication also presents *Twelve Years a Slave* as "another key to *Uncle Tom's Cabin*"—a reference to Stowe's *A Key to Uncle Tom's Cabin*, published in April 1853, two months before Northup's book. In response to those who accused her of overstating the horrors of slavery, Stowe's compendium provided documentation that attested to the veracity of the depiction of slavery in the novel. Much of the chapter on abductions of free African Americans was based on Northup's experiences; Stowe included extracts from the January article in the *New York Daily Times*.[82] The opportunity was too good for Derby & Miller to miss. The narrative itself contains a number of more or less explicit references to *Uncle Tom's Cabin*—for instance, when Northup says he did not have "the Christian fortitude of a certain well-known Uncle Tom."[83]

Robert B. Stepto has argued that the rapprochement of Stowe and Northup should not be seen as a form of literary pillage. He sees a clear difference between Northup's narrative and the "shamelessly entrepreneurial" publications based on *Uncle Tom's Cabin* whose white authors sought to "steal Stowe's thunder." Northup did not poach on Stowe's success; rather, Northup and Stowe "shared the antislavery thunder of the 1850s."[84] Stepto overlooks the fact that Northup was supported by a publisher—Derby remains unnamed in his essay—who, like any businessman, was driven by the hope of profiting from the books he printed. As Zora Neale Hurston bluntly put it in 1950, "Publishing houses . . . are in business to make money. They will sponsor anything that they believe will sell."[85] Derby & Miller were fully aware that *Twelve Years a Slave* was likelier to sell if it was closely associated with *Uncle Tom's Cabin*. That is not to say, as the southern press claimed, that the publication was purely money-driven: "Why should Jewett & Co. carry off all the plunder to be made out of the credulous old women of the North," the *Daily Picayune* spouted, when Derby & Miller "stood ready to do the same dirty work?"[86] Yet *Twelve Years a Slave* cannot be fully understood without taking account of the various links to *Uncle Tom's Cabin* in its publication history—all part of a well-honed marketing strategy that inevitably slanted how *Twelve Years a Slave* was read. The *Albany Evening Journal* critic titled his review "'Uncle Tom's Cabin.'—No. 2."[87] The women of the Oneida utopian community read Northup's narrative together in 1855, describing it in their daily record of events:

> Friday, Mar. 23.—Finished reading "Twelve years a Slave." It did not seem possible when first proposed, to have reading aloud in our after-dinner bees, in a room where a hundred pair of hands are busy at work, braiding and sewing. . . . We found the narrative of a Slave's experience on Red River, a good sequel to "Uncle Tom's Cabin." It did not perhaps draw as many tears, as did its predecessor when read to the same circle three years ago; but its truthfulness and its glimpses of Providential arrangements, recommend it.[88]

The editorial framing of *Twelve Years a Slave* meant Northup's narrative was inevitably read in the light of Stowe's novel.

Northup himself was not indifferent to the financial outcome of his book. His years in bondage had left him and his family in a financial quandary.[89]

Several newspaper articles refer to his monetary gains. The local press wrote that Derby & Miller offered Northup "$3,000 for the copyright of his book, which is now being prepared by a member of the bar of that county."[90] It sounds like a generous amount, yet this suggests that Northup was to have no share in the book's commercial success and would have much to lose if it sold as well as *Uncle Tom's Cabin*. Claire Parfait points out that most writers who opted for a lump sum payment—as opposed to a royalty—were pressed for money, as was Northup on his return North.[91] Other sources, however, claim that Northup also received some money on each copy sold. "A large portion of the net proceeds are secured to SOLOMON," the *New York Daily Times* noted. "Northup gets a profit on all the books sold, and by helping yourselves and neighbors to some of them, you will help him at the same time," the Syracuse, New York, *Wesleyan* added. John Thomson, the aforementioned friend of the white Northups, went even further: "I understand the profits of the entire sale of the book is to be for the benefit of 'Uncle Sol.' and his family."[92] This seems highly unlikely given the profile of Derby & Miller. Though it is hard to state exactly how much Northup made from *Twelve Years a Slave*, we know that prior to the book's release he was able to purchase real estate in Glens Falls, New York, for $275.[93]

Northup's book marked a new chapter in the history of the antebellum slave narrative. A mainstream publisher like Derby & Miller could afford to give *Twelve Years a Slave* unprecedented exposure. For the first time, a slave narrative entered the traditional mainstream publishing circuit rather than remaining restricted to the author's local community or antislavery networks. In 1856, Peter Still's amanuensis Kate E. R. Pickard would rejoice at the partnership of their local publisher—William T. Hamilton of Syracuse—with Miller, Orton, and Mulligan: "Mr. Hamilton has taken as partner in this business the Firm of Miller, Orton, & Mulligan, of Auburn—one of the best publishing houses in the state. They published Fred. Douglas' book last year, and have published several other works on Slavery. I think the arrangement will be a great help to the circulation of the book."[94] In Northup's case, Derby & Miller were the main publishers, but they joined forces with two other publishers whose names feature on the title page, Derby, Orton & Mulligan of Buffalo, New York, and Henry W. Derby of Cincinnati, Ohio. The threefold geographical reach came about thanks to partnerships between James C. Derby and George and Henry, two of his three brothers, who also worked in the book trade. Henry moved to Cincinnati in 1844 to establish what soon became one of the most reputable publishing houses in the American West. He also opened the largest bookstore west of the Appalachians. Likewise, George developed a flourishing bookstore in Buffalo and published extensively.[95] His list included at least one proslavery book, W. L. G. Smith's 1852 anti-Tom novel *Life at the South: or, "Uncle Tom's Cabin" as It Is*—a novel that, according to the *Liberator*, "contained not a single well-drawn character, not a single natural conversation, not a single skillfully-adapted incident."[96] One Miller, Orton & Mulligan catalog includes *Life at the South* and *Twelve Years a Slave* on the same page—strange bedfellows indeed.

Twelve Years a Slave was promoted on an unprecedented scale, even before publication. As early as March 1853, papers in upstate New York were noting that "a local gentleman in this county is engaged in writing the life of Sol. Northup."[97] The following month, the book was reported to be in press. *Twelve Years a Slave* was the focus of a concerted advertising campaign. In April alone, Derby & Miller placed announcements in the local press (the Auburn *Cayuga Chief*), in major urban centers (the *New York Daily Times*), the antislavery press (the *National Era, Frederick Douglass' Paper*), and trade periodicals (*Norton's Literary Gazette and Publishers' Circular, Literary World*).[98] James C. Derby was a leading innovator in book promotion, working with others to develop aggressive communication strategies that, as the new edition of Ball's narrative will show, sometimes verged on the misleading. *Putnam's Monthly* spoke out against the "machinations" of publishers ready to do anything to promote their latest sensation book—showering the press with pre-publication copies, overstating sales, making shameless use of "little epigrammatic remarks" on the lines of "The Greatest Book of Its Kind," as Jewett's tagline for *Uncle Tom's Cabin* ran, and so on. The article concluded: "This is the great blast of advertisements with which every successive book is driven forth to life; as if shot out of a prodigious wind-gun. Every book is The Greatest Book of the Age. Twenty Thousand Copies are Ordered in Advance of Publication. Fifty Thousand Copies are Sold in Two Weeks after Publication. There is a Tremendous Excitement. Everybody is Talking About It."[99]

Most of the slave narratives discussed in this chapter were promoted with major advertising campaigns. The April advertisement for *Twelve Years a Slave* was relatively low-key but nonetheless used abundant capitals and exclamation marks to draw the reader's eye. The publisher also provided a detailed list of illustrations, an effective sales argument at a time when books were "more typographic than graphic."[100] A copy cost one dollar, the standard price for a duodecimo cloth-bound book of more than three hundred pages. *Twelve Years a Slave* was a plain yet elegant object, bound in embossed brown cloth with the title stamped in gilt on the spine. Where Douglass and Brown had been wholly involved in shaping their respective narratives, the commercial nature of Northup's project sidelined him to a certain extent, particularly since the whole project was something of a rush job.

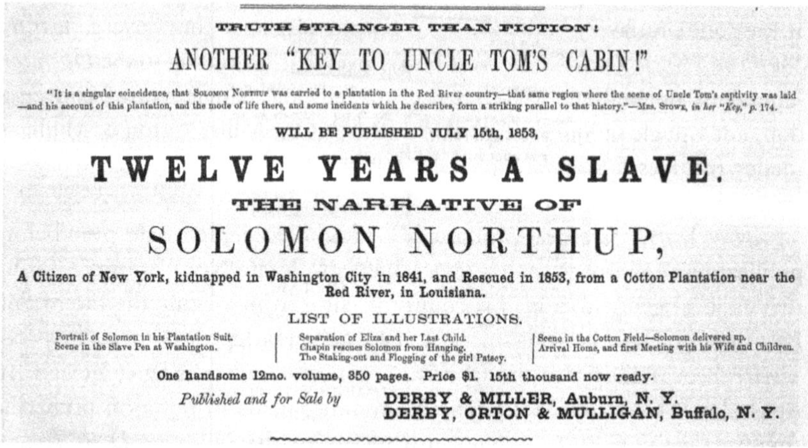

Figure 10. Advertisement for *Twelve Years a Slave*, *Norton's Literary Gazette and Publishers' Circular*, 15 August 1853, 137 (Courtesy of Fales Library and Special Collections, New York University)

Twelve Years a Slave eventually came out in July 1853. It was launched almost simultaneously by Derby & Miller in the United States and across the Atlantic by Sampson Low, a London publisher who regularly worked with American colleagues, particularly on antislavery books. Low and Jewett brought out Mary Low's *A Peep into Uncle Tom's Cabin* under their joint imprint the same year.[101] Once *Twelve Years a Slave* was on sale, Derby & Miller promoted it even harder, targeting an ever-broader range of press outlets and designing ever-more eye-catching advertisements. One of the most ostentatious took up the central third of one (large) page in the *Norton's Literary Gazette* in the summer of 1853 (fig. 10).[102] Derby & Miller once again underlined the kinship between Northup's tale and Uncle Tom. They quoted *A Key to Uncle Tom's Cabin* with a page reference to demonstrate that Stowe herself had noted the "striking parallel" between Northup's account and her novel. At the same time, Derby & Miller distanced themselves from *Uncle Tom's Cabin* as fiction by playing the reality card with the well-worn adage "TRUTH STRANGER THAN FICTION!" *Twelve Years a Slave* was both uncannily like and singularly unlike *Uncle Tom's Cabin*.

Aside from the geographical parallels, and whatever Stowe herself may have said, *Uncle Tom's Cabin* in fact had relatively little in common with the story of a free New Yorker kidnapped into slavery. That did not stop Derby & Miller from using Stowe's quote whenever they could. For instance, they included it above the dedication in most later editions of *Twelve Years a Slave* and at the top of the whole-page advertisement for the book in the September issue of the Boston magazine *Littell's Living Age*.[103] This was the crowning point of the campaign for *Twelve Years a Slave*, with a text-heavy full-page advertisement in a general interest magazine, mainly consisting of snippets from literary reviews published over the summer. The range of newspapers cited gives some idea of the book's impressive distribution, from New York to Pittsburgh via Buffalo, Syracuse, and Detroit. The book was also available in Hartford, Connecticut; Dedham, Massachusetts; and, more surprisingly, Alexandria, Virginia.[104]

Working with a trade publisher guaranteed a far more systematic presence in bookstores than had been the case for Douglass's and Brown's narratives. In Albany, New York, *Twelve Years a Slave* could be purchased from Little & Co., 53 State Street; E. H. Bender, 75 State Street; and E. H. Pease, 82 State Street.[105] Derby & Miller also took on agents to sell Northup's book "in all parts of the United States [and] Canada," a widespread practice among trade publishers.[106] *Twelve Years a Slave* was a far cry from the charitable economy principally based on individual contact between author and audience or exchange within an ideology-based community: it was a commercial undertaking, less personal, more mediated, and at least partly disconnected from institutional antislavery. It thus offers an example of the process of "social disembedding" that characterized nineteenth-century authorship according to Leon Jackson.[107] This does not mean that *Twelve Years a Slave* was not read in abolitionist circles. Though Northup apparently never joined an antislavery society himself, he peddled copies of his book across New York and New England and took part in public meetings with well-known antislavery activists; he likely thought of his own book not so much as the sensationalist biography his publishers framed it as but rather as political testimony.[108] The book was sold in some antislavery book depositories and at Bela Marsh's reform bookstore in Boston. Douglass, Abby Kelley Foster, Henry Clarke Wright, William Henry Furness, and Samuel May Jr. were among his most eminent readers.[109] "Have you seen the volume of Solomon Northup?" May asked to his British friend John B. Estlin. "It is well worth reading; doubtless, it is essentially the truth, and is destined to have a powerful effect in this country. What those poor souls suffer, who can tell, or conceive?"[110] The way the question is formulated reveals that Boston and New York abolitionists had no hand in producing the work, reading it at the same time as everyone else. For this reason, the readership for *Twelve Years a Slave* was more diverse than for the *Narrative of the Life of Frederick Douglass*, as awareness of the book was not restricted to those already familiar with the abolition movement.

Did trade publishing translate into higher sales? The publisher's figures should be considered cautiously: it was in Derby & Miller's interest to announce significant sales. Various notices in the press suggest sales of between fourteen and fifteen thousand copies in the summer of 1853, which would be remarkable but understandable given the scale of the advertising campaign and the book's hot topic.[111] The publisher and economist Henry C. Carey recorded a print run of twenty thousand copies in a book published at the end of the year.[112] Northup's account continued to sell, albeit more slowly, in 1854. Two editions marked "TWENTY-FIFTH THOUSAND" and "TWENTY-SEVENTH THOUSAND" came out that year. Sales began to fall in 1855–56: the last known edition was printed in 1856 as the "TWENTY-NINTH THOUSAND."[113] The book was a success, but its shelf life proved shorter than that of the narratives by Douglass, Brown, and Truth. Derby & Miller stopped printing new copies when demand fell, while the authors of earlier slave narratives kept working hard to distribute their books—for over seven years, in Truth's case. While Northup's and Douglass's narratives were disseminated via different channels, in the end they reached roughly equal readerships; it is generally estimated that some thirty thousand copies of the *Narrative of the Life of Frederick Douglass* were printed in the United States and Britain from 1845 to 1850.[114] Either way, it seems Derby & Miller were pleased with the outcome, as they kept publishing slave narratives. Thirty years later, Derby wrote in his memoirs: "This book was brought out by my firm, and Solomon's thrilling experiences caused quite a sensation among the reading community, the book meeting with a rapid and large sale."[115]

Northup's experience was less thoroughly positive. *Twelve Years a Slave* did earn him enough to keep his family in the months following publication; it brought him a degree of fame and ensured his personal history would be remembered for generations. However, Northup saw his identity as a free Black man partly elided with Uncle Tom, and his newfound fame did not help him achieve reparations. Congress refused to consider the many petitions to compensate Northup for his time in bondage.[116] Northup tried to keep up interest in his story by producing two plays based on *Twelve Years a Slave* in 1854 and 1855, but the venture failed, further contributing to his financial stress and embarrassment.[117] Northup dropped out of sight at some point between the late 1850s and early 1860s. To this day, it is not known when or how he died.

Old Friends, New Names: Frederick Douglass and Charles Ball Redux

The post–*Uncle Tom's Cabin* period saw the rise of a new phenomenon, as narratives printed back in the 1830s and 1840s were revisited and reprinted in new formats. These included the accounts by Douglass and Ball, which I discuss in the following pages, as well as Josiah Henson's 1849 narrative *The Life of Josiah Henson, Formerly a Slave, Now an Inhabitant of Canada*, reprinted in 1858 as

Truth Stranger than Fiction: Father Henson's Story of His Own Life.[118] The new context called for new editorial packaging. The narratives were given a new lease of life by trade publishers who brought them out of the parallel print economies. Henson's narrative, self-published in 1849, came out again a decade later under Jewett's imprint. Several of the narratives were updated and all were largely reshaped in line with new ideological, literary, and commercial imperatives.

When *My Bondage and My Freedom* came out in 1855, Douglass was in a very different place compared to ten years previously, when the *Narrative of the Life of Frederick Douglass* was first published. He had become the leading Black abolitionist, giving hundreds of speeches to enthusiastic crowds on both sides of the Atlantic; had founded his own newspaper, the *North Star*, soon renamed *Frederick Douglass' Paper*; and had broken with Garrison to form closer ties with Gerrit Smith and political abolitionism. "Who has not heard of Frederick Douglass?" one New York journalist asked rhetorically.[119] The formerly enslaved man turned international celebrity had forged a place for himself in the intellectual and political landscape of the 1850s. In these circumstances, the publication history of *Bondage and Freedom* was bound to differ significantly from that of the *Narrative*. Douglass's second autobiography was not self-published and self-distributed with the assistance of Garrisonian networks. It was brought out by Miller, Orton & Mulligan. *Frederick Douglass' Paper* had reviewed *Twelve Years a Slave* not once but twice, and Douglass knew Northup's publishers by reputation at the very least. He had been living with his family for several years in Rochester, some sixty miles north of Auburn, where Miller, Orton & Mulligan still had premises.[120] It comes as no surprise that he came to have business dealings with them.

In the mid-1850s, Douglass was busy with his journalism, however, and it seems the idea of writing another autobiography was not his originally. He suggests as much in the "Editor's Preface" to the volume, which reproduces a letter he wrote to the editor on 2 July 1855 about his doubts "when first you kindly urged me to prepare for publication a full account of my life as a slave, and my life as a freeman." There is a question mark over the identity of the editor, whom Douglass addresses as "DEAR FRIEND."[121] It is generally, and probably correctly, held to be his friend and collaborator Julia Griffiths, a British activist who met Douglass in Newcastle in 1846. Griffiths followed Douglass to the United States and worked with him until 1855, when she returned to Britain. She played an active role in abolitionist circles in Rochester for several years, leading the Rochester Ladies' Anti-Slavery Society, and helped Douglass manage the *North Star/Frederick Douglass' Paper*. She lived at the Douglass family home for some years, earning scurrilous accusations from the

Garrisonians about the exact nature of their relationship. Griffiths worked as an editor at the *North Star/Frederick Douglass' Paper*—she contributed one of its two reviews of *Twelve Years a Slave*—and in 1853 she edited the first volume of the antislavery gift book *Autographs for Freedom*, which included Douglass's novella "The Heroic Slave."[122] At least one account suggests she also edited *Bondage and Freedom*. In a volume of reminiscences published to mark Douglass's death in 1895, his Rochester friend Jane Marsh Parker pointed to his debt to Griffiths as a young journalist. Parker recalled Douglass's words: "Think what editing a paper was to me before Miss Griffiths came! I had not learned how to spell; my knowledge of the simplest rules of grammar was most defective." Douglass, Parker added, "rewrote his autobiography under [Griffiths's] supervision."[123] That Griffiths preferred to remain anonymous is understandable in the light of past hostility toward her; much of her work was done in Douglass's shadow anyway. Gerald Fulkerson is thus right to note that Griffiths "may have exerted considerable influence on the form and substance of *Bondage and Freedom*." Alex W. Black likewise suggests it should be read as "a collaborative text."[124] Griffiths's role was even more significant if she indeed persuaded Douglass to put pen to paper for his second autobiography.

In publishing *Bondage and Freedom* with a trade publisher in upstate New York, a hotbed of political abolitionism, Douglass signaled his complete break with Garrison, his followers, and their ideology. Relations between Douglass and the Garrisonians had broken down over the previous years. They could not forgive his turn to political abolitionism and his antislavery reading of the U.S. Constitution, and attacked him on the grounds of his allegedly immoral relationship with Griffiths. As Susan M. Ryan points out, "Douglass published *My Bondage and My Freedom* apart from—indeed, in defiance of—the abolitionist network that had launched his first autobiography."[125] These internal disputes are apparent in *Bondage and Freedom*. Part two of the work, "Life as a Freeman," discusses his infantilizing, condescending treatment at the hands of white MASS abolitionists in his early campaigning days. Garrisonians, Douglass writes, sought to curb his tongue, asking him to stick to a plain account of his years of slavery without venturing into analysis or criticism. "Give us the facts," John A. Collins famously said to him, "we will take care of the philosophy." Nor should his discourse seem too erudite. "'People won't believe you ever was a slave, Frederick, if you keep on this way,' said Friend [George] Foster. . . . It was said to me, 'Better have a *little* of the plantation manner of speech than not; 'tis not best that you seem too learned.'" Having discussed the "American prejudice against color," Douglass added that "the abolitionists themselves were not entirely free from it."[126] His tone was measured but the words were bound to anger their targets, given that relations were already strained. When abolitionist George Thompson praised *Bondage and Freedom* in the British press, Garrison soon snapped back:

> In the same number of *The Empire* is a panegyric upon Frederick Douglass's new volume, "My Bondage and my Freedom"—a volume remarkable, it is true, for its thrilling sketches of a slave's life and experience, and for the ability displayed in its pages, but which, in its second portion, is reeking with the virus of personal malignity towards Wendell Phillips, myself and the old organizationists [i.e., Garrisonians] generally, and full of ingratitude and baseness towards as true and disinterested friends as any man ever yet had on earth, to give him aid and encouragement.[127]

Thompson apologized, confessing he had not actually read the book. Douglass later denied his text was driven by spite.[128] Yet *Bondage and Freedom*, which he was able to write and publish outside the Garrisonians' orbit, did let him air his side of the relationship with them. The emphatically repeated "My" in the title gestures to Douglass regaining the upper hand over his own life narrative.

The entire paratext of *Bondage and Freedom* can be read as a declaration of independence. Douglass replaced Garrison's preface and Phillips's letter, included in most editions of the *Narrative*, with an introduction by the Black intellectual and activist James McCune Smith, "whom he considered without rival in terms of talent and learning."[129] Like Douglass, McCune Smith had become a campaigner with the support of the Garrisonians, and had eventually distanced himself from them and turned to political abolitionism. McCune Smith readily denounced the paternalism of white abolitionists who pushed African American men and women into the background in the struggle against slavery. "It is emphatically our battle; no one else can fight it for us," he declared at a meeting of the National Council of Colored People.[130] His paratextual presence rooted *Bondage and Freedom* in collective forms of Black activism that Douglass had long been part of, while remaining a leading figure in Garrisonian abolitionism until the late 1840s. It made explicit Douglass's "turn to a militant antislavery politics grounded in black solidarity and community."[131] Douglass presided the national Colored Convention held in Rochester in 1853; soon after *Bondage and Freedom* came out, he and McCune Smith attended the national Colored Convention held in Philadelphia, which steered the Colored Conventions movement away from the white-led antislavery movement.[132] At a time when Garrison was still advocating peaceful methods to combat slavery, the Black activists of the Colored Conventions movement now openly called for political violence.[133] Elements of this more

combative rhetoric are found in the introduction to *Bondage and Freedom*.
McCune Smith mentions the discord between Douglass and Garrison, noting
the author's "strong self-hood, which led him to measure strength with
Mr. Covey, and to wrench himself from the embrace of the Garrisonians"—
drawing a parallel between the slave breaker Edward Covey and Garrison the
abolitionist.[134] Garrison cuttingly responded, "The preface by J. McCune
Smith is, in its innuendoes, a very base production."[135] Not all white abolitionists were so intemperate. Lewis Tappan, who had long opposed Garrison
himself and, like Douglass and McCune Smith, favored electoral politics to
attack slavery, remarked on "the beauty of Dr Smith's Introduction to Douglas's Life."[136]

The publication history of *Bondage and Freedom* is intimately bound up
with another white abolitionist, Gerrit Smith. The intellectual and ideological
affinities between Smith and Douglass are well-known.[137] According to John
Stauffer, a shared "revolutionary ethos" brought them, and McCune Smith,
together in the 1850s.[138] The three men had talked in June 1855 at the inaugural
convention of the Radical Abolition Party, heir to the Liberty Party, in Syracuse, when Douglass was busy working on his manuscript. Douglass held Gerrit Smith in high esteem and dedicated *Bondage and Freedom* to him. The
dedication was particularly lavish, speaking of Douglass's "esteem for [Smith's]
character, admiration for his genius and benevolence, affection for his person,
and gratitude for his friendship." It also pointed out Smith's antislavery interpretation of the U.S. Constitution. Smith's support for the antislavery cause in
general and Douglass in particular was not just symbolic. As a wealthy philanthropist, he had repeatedly given Douglass financial support, as their correspondence makes clear. Smith thanked Douglass for his dedication with
another spontaneous financial donation, which Douglass accepted after some
polite demurring:

> It would have been quite compensation enough to know that the dedication of
> my Book afforded you pleasure. The dedication was inserted not to place you
> under obligations, not to discharge my obligations to you, but rather to couple
> my poor name with a name I love and honor, and have it go down on the tide of
> time with the advantage of that name. Nevertheless, I gratefully accept your draft
> for fifty dollars.[139]

Smith likewise provided precious support for many formerly enslaved individuals who found themselves in financial difficulties. Black abolitionists turned
to him when they lacked funds to carry out their projects, including publications: Henry Box Brown requested a loan of $150 to set up his panorama, the

Mirror of Slavery; Jermain W. Loguen asked for his help in publishing *The Rev. J. W. Loguen, as a Slave and as a Freeman* (1859), as did William Wells Brown for *The Black Man* (1863).[140] Since *Bondage and Freedom* came out with a trade publisher, Smith did not need to finance the book directly, but his presence in the dedication did underline Douglass's break with Garrisonianism and his alliance with political abolitionism, which was more interracial and open to the idea of violent resistance to slavery.

Bondage and Freedom should, however, not be read solely as an expression of its author's ideological realignment or his quarrel with the Garrisonians. The "Life as a Freeman" section, after all, only accounts for four chapters, compared to the twenty-one chapters recounting Douglass's life in slavery, which form the bulk of the work. In publishing his second autobiography, Douglass hoped—perhaps above all—to establish himself as a man of letters. It is true that Griffiths's preface (if it is hers) does not frame the work in this light. "The reader is . . . assured . . . that his attention is not invited to a work of ART, but to a work of FACTS," the editor writes, as if the two were mutually exclusive. But she is immediately contradicted by McCune Smith, who praises "that rare polish in [Douglass's] style of writing, which, most critically examined, seems the result of careful early culture among the best classics of our language."[141] The horizon of expectation set by McCune Smith is both aesthetic and political. Even in terms of sheer length, *Bondage and Freedom* presents as a more accomplished work of literature than the *Narrative*. The formulaic title of 1845 has made way for a truly original title. As William L. Andrews argues, the prose in the section on Douglass's life in slavery, particularly his descriptions of his human surroundings, has become richer in scope and depth. "The young jeremiad-writer had painted his past in stark and striking outline," Andrews writes. "The older autobiographer wanted to shade in deeper dimensions to add proportion and perspective to the total portrait."[142] It is perhaps no coincidence that one of the few references to Douglass's experience of writing *Bondage and Freedom* points to its difficulty. "I am busy at work on my book," he wrote to Smith a month prior to publication. "It is more of a Job than at first I supposed it would be—and I am beginning to be weary of it."[143] These efforts should not be read as resulting solely from Douglass's personal ambition. As his letter in the preface suggests, he also aimed to demolish racist stereotypes about the intellectual inferiority of African Americans by writing a book that would dazzle critics.[144] He (or Griffiths) added an appendix with extracts from his best-known speeches, including his masterpiece "What to the Slave Is the Fourth of July?," on the same grounds. The appendix demonstrated that Douglass was a Black intellectual with a significant body of writings to his name and a coherent, radical political vision.

The book's outward appearance also mattered. Working with a trade publisher guaranteed the finished product would match the content. The *Narrative* was a "little volume" sometimes sold in paper wrappers. *Bondage and
Freedom* looked much more impressive, being described as "a very handsome
volume of about 500 pages, got up in the best style of the publishers, and
embellished with a very fine steel engraving of the author" in *Frederick Douglass' Paper*—which doubtless reflected Douglass's own feelings.[145] The spine
was gilt stamped with the title and Douglass's name. This was a major change
from the 1845 *Narrative*, which identified the author only with the words "written by himself." In 1855, Douglass was granted full authorial status on the
spine and title page. The term "author" itself, not used in the *Narrative*, was
repeated in several chapter titles in *Bondage and Freedom*: "The Author's
Childhood," "The Author Removed from His First Home," "The Author's
Parentage," "Personal Treatment of the Author." While such references were
conventional, they nonetheless drew the reader's attention to the work's literary ambitions by staging Douglass's authorship. As Robert S. Levine notes,
Bondage and Freedom showcases "two Douglasses: the Douglass in history who
is part of the story and the older cultural figure."[146] The paratext and the material book both play into the construction of Douglass as an "older cultural
figure." *Bondage and Freedom* is a refined editorial object: the table of contents
is detailed, the title page and dedication elegantly typeset, and each part opens
with an original engraving. In contrast, the *Narrative* is very plain in appearance. The frontispiece portrait in *Bondage and Freedom* also reflects its author's
increasing social confidence. Miller, Orton & Mulligan were contractually
obliged to include "a good *Steel portrait of the Author*."[147] They commissioned
John Chester Buttre, a lithographer and steel-plate engraver renowned for his
numerous portraits of (white) historical and political figures.[148] Buttre engraved
the author's portrait from a daguerreotype that Douglass may have picked
himself. Douglass is no longer shown in profile, but face on. He now has a
beard and his shoulders and chest are fully drawn, not merely sketched in as
in the *Narrative*, highlighting his impressive stature. His tie is neatly knotted
and he wears a decorative tiepin. His gaze is even more "somber and resolute"
than in the *Narrative*.[149] Douglass cuts an imposing figure.

The multiple textual, paratextual, and editorial shifts between the two works
lead John Sekora to categorize them as different genres. "The *Narrative*, for all
its greatness, is not a genuine autobiography," Sekora argues. It is "not so
much a life story as an indictment, an anti-slavery document, the testimony of
an eyewitness." *Bondage and Freedom*, on the other hand, is "a true, full autobiography," marking "a new stage in Douglass's life and prose style."[150] This
suggests that autobiography can be neatly circumscribed as a genre. Yet, as

literary theorist Philippe Lejeune has demonstrated, autobiography is defined by multiple criteria that vary across time and between individuals and are often inconsistent.[151] For antebellum readers, both the *Narrative* and *Bondage and Freedom* could be regarded as autobiographies; Stowe used the term for both.[152] Some contemporary comments do, however, foreshadow Sekora's argument. White abolitionist Samuel J. May's 1869 *Some Recollections of Our Antislavery Conflict* contrasts Douglass's two books. One was a "well-written, intensely interesting autobiography, entitled 'My Bondage and My Freedom,'" the other "a pamphlet which he felt called upon to publish in 1845, in answer to the current assertions that he was an impostor."[153] May only gives the title of *Bondage and Freedom*, and only calls this work an autobiography. For the purposes of my analysis, the distinction is relevant as a reminder that Douglass came to write each work, the *Narrative* and *Bondage and Freedom*, in very different circumstances. The former was written in haste at the outset of his activist career; Douglass shared the details of his life in slavery first and foremost to prove his good faith. In the latter, he strove to make a lasting mark on the American literary record by writing an outstanding text that doubled as a declaration of independence from Garrisonian abolitionism. From this point of view, it is paradoxical that criticism has come to focus on the *Narrative* to the detriment of *Bondage and Freedom*, which Douglass himself undoubtedly considered the finer work. Later in the century, he would come to see his third autobiography, *Life and Times of Frederick Douglass* (1881, 1892), as "his magnum opus."[154]

As had been the case for *Twelve Years a Slave*, the advertising campaign for *Bondage and Freedom* began well before publication. Miller, Orton & Mulligan worked to create a prepublication buzz. The first advertisement appeared in magazines and newspapers from Maine to Michigan in April 1855, announcing the book was "in press."[155] Two months later, another advertisement heralded the imminent publication with the catchy tagline "BE READY FOR THIS! 21 Years a SLAVE—17 Years a FREEMAN."[156] Its eventual publication on 15 August triggered an unprecedented wave of advertising for a Miller, Orton & Mulligan title. The advertising campaign was largely based on an abundance of the (frequently alliterative) "little epigrammatic remarks" scorned by the *Putnam's Monthly*: "The Great Plea for Freedom," "Lions Do Write History!," "Slavery by a Slave!," "A Book by a Bondman!," "Read the Story of His Wrongs!," "The Author Was Bought for 150 Pounds!," "'Hear Me, for My Cause,'" "'I Was in Bonds, But Am Free.'"[157] Several of these slogans foregrounded the apparent incongruity of a enslaved person turned writer, the most ingenious being "From the 'Pen' of a Slave!" Calling on Douglass's atypical authorial background as a sales argument suggests that in 1855, slave narratives were not as clearly identifiable as a genre as is generally claimed. Even in the decade often described as the golden age of the slave narrative, "A Book by a Bondman" could still strike readers as an unusual literary undertaking.

On at least two occasions, Miller, Orton & Mulligan drew on current events to increase sales of Douglass's book. In mid-August 1856, exactly a year after publication, two prominent booksellers, William Strickland and Edwin Upson, were given five days' notice to leave Mobile, Alabama, after "publications of an incendiary and insurrectionary character" were found in their store—one copy of *Autographs for Freedom* and two of *Bondage and Freedom*.[158] A "Vigilance Committee" was appointed to investigate, one of whose members was none other than Josiah Nott, the coeditor of the era's most notorious proslavery polygenist book, *Types of Mankind* (1854).[159] Strickland argued in vain that he was no antislavery campaigner, telling the committee that "[his] early savings for years were invested in slaves."[160] Douglass's publisher immediately seized the opportunity. By late August, the northern press was carrying the following notice:

THE PENALTY in ALABAMA is DEATH
For Selling
MY BONDAGE AND MY FREEDOM
By FREDERICK DOUGLASS.
And for this Foul Crime
TWO BOOKSELLERS OF MOBILE HAVE FLED FOR THEIR LIVES:
Yet, thanks to the Genius of Northern Liberty, the Book is yet freely offered, and largely sold by every Northern Bookseller; and will yet, we trust, be found in every free home throughout our land. . . .
DEATH for SELLING SUCH a BOOK![161]

Censorship was now a unique selling point. Miller, Orton & Mulligan also took advantage of the presidential election that same year to promote *Bondage and Freedom*. The 1856 election, dominated by the issue of slavery, pitted the Democrat James Buchanan (the eventual winner) against John C. Frémont of the Republican Party, then a newly formed political movement opposing the extension of slavery into the western territories. Douglass was realistic about the minuscule Radical Abolition Party's chances of winning the election and made the pragmatic choice to come out in support of the Republican candidate, even though his stance on slavery was more moderate.[162] Douglass's publisher did not wait for his shift in allegiance to sell *Bondage and Freedom* as a pro-Republican work. An advertisement printed in May 1856 invited supporters of the Republican cause to read and share antislavery titles from the Miller,

Orton & Mulligan catalog, including *Bondage and Freedom*.[163] A later advertisement further included books published with the election in mind, such as
the *Republican Manual* and the *Republican Campaign Songster*, under the general title "Popular and Standard Republican Books."[164] Alongside such campaign propaganda, *Bondage and Freedom* had become a "Republican Book."

Bondage and Freedom was distributed far, wide, and fast. It was on sale in
bookstores all over the North, from Harrisburg, Pennsylvania, to Kalamazoo,
Michigan, and Newport, Rhode Island.[165] "'My Bondage and My Freedom' is
read extensively in this city," wrote the Cincinnati correspondent for *Frederick
Douglass' Paper*.[166] On 8 August 1855, the front page of the *New York Daily Tribune* featured no fewer than five advertisements announcing the book was available from various bookstores across the city. Even Miller, Orton & Mulligan's
competitors on the antislavery book market, John P. Jewett and Phillips, Sampson, sold the book in Boston.[167] It could also be ordered from the publishers by
mail at a cost of $1.25. Miller, Orton & Mulligan's highly effective logistics chain
helped them sell five thousand copies of *Bondage and Freedom* within two days
of publication; Douglass could never have hoped to achieve such sales of the
Narrative so quickly back in 1845.[168] Precisely because they were published via
such radically different channels, the claim that *Bondage and Freedom* "was even
more of a success than the 1845 *Narrative*" is somewhat problematic.[169] Sales of
Bondage and Freedom were higher than for the *Narrative* in the weeks and
months following publication, but given *how* it was published, and Douglass's
far higher profile, this is hardly surprising. In fact, the *Narrative* outsold *Bondage and Freedom*. The latter started strongly, as the "FIFTEENTH THOUSAND"
edition of 1855 demonstrates, but then sales began to slow. One 1856 edition is
marked "SEVENTEENTH THOUSAND," and an 1857 edition "EIGHTEENTH THOU-
SAND." The *Narrative*'s itinerant mode of distribution, outside the mainstream
publishing circuit, proved more effective in the long term.

Douglass did not wholly abandon the artisanal model he had used ten years
previously. After the Panic of 1857 bankrupted his publisher, he began promoting *Bondage and Freedom* himself. In 1858, one of his sons sold copies after
certain public meetings—for instance, a lecture in Poughkeepsie, New York,
commemorating West Indian emancipation.[170] The following year, Douglass
announced in his newspaper that anyone sending in the names of five new
subscribers would receive in return a copy of *Bondage and Freedom*, "a book of
nearly FIVE HUNDRED PAGES, neatly bound, and embellished with a LIKENESS
OF THE AUTHOR, together with other engravings."[171] *Bondage and Freedom* was
also for sale at the office of the paper in Rochester.[172] As early as 1855, Douglass
had called on his friends and acquaintances, including some he disagreed with
ideologically. "Please send me any names you may have to whom you think

my Book or paper will be acceptable, and either shall be promptly sent as you
shall direct," he wrote to Benjamin Coates, a Quaker businessman from Philadelphia and one of the best-known supporters of African colonization.[173]
Black abolitionists also acted as relays between Douglass and his audience, as
a letter from Loguen printed in *Frederick Douglass' Paper* reveals:

> Allow me to thank you for your book. I am selling "My Bondage and My Free-
> dom," by Frederick Douglass; and the manner in which it sells, shows that the
> people are awakening to an appreciation of black men's talents for bookmaking.
> And if they are not awakened to a sense of the foul crime and shame of slavery
> by reading *such* a book, "they are joined to their idols; let them alone."[174]

Loguen was inspired by Douglass to publish his own autobiography four years
later.[175] On the whole, the venture proved a profitable one for Douglass. By
the end of the Civil War, he still had "a few thousand dollars . . . saved from
the sale of 'My Bondage and My Freedom,' and the proceeds of my lectures at
home and abroad."[176]

Julia Griffiths brought *Bondage and Freedom* to Britain. Griffiths had returned
to England in the early summer of 1855, planning to head back to the United
States later that year, once she had raised enough from local abolitionists to
keep *Frederick Douglass' Paper* going. She never did make the return journey,
but she kept up a rich correspondence with Douglass that sheds light on her
efforts to promote *Bondage and Freedom*.[177] On a visit to Glasgow, the American abolitionist Parker Pillsbury wrote to Samuel May Jr., "You doubtless
know of Miss Julia Griffiths visit to this country. . . . She has brought the
Proof sheets of Douglass' new book, and is to publish an Edition here, with an
Introduction by Dr. [John] Campbell, or some other equally influential person who will write it." A keen Garrisonian, Pillsbury was openly scornful of
Douglass and his admirers in Glasgow—"our enemies," he called them—who
had "industriously circulated" copies of a speech by Douglass that was apparently unfavorable to the Garrisonian cause.[178] He became obsessed with Griffiths,
constantly tracking her activities.[179] Pillsbury's hostility did not dampen the
enthusiasm of British abolitionists. "The friends here are eager to see a perfect
copy of '*My Bondage and My Freedom*,'" Griffiths wrote in one of her "Letters
from the Old World." "I trust the book will be soon attainable on this side the
Atlantic."[180] In the end, no British publisher picked up Douglass's book, but
several book trade professionals made sure the American edition remained
available, including George Gallie.[181] Gallie, a member of the Glasgow Emancipation Society, played an important role in bringing American antislavery
literature to the British Isles and promoted British books on American slavery.

He helped publish and/or distribute the works of Angelina Grimké, John A. Collins, Henry Clarke Wright, John B. Estlin, and George Thompson. In 1877, Gallie printed an account of a gala held in honor of Josiah Henson. In late 1855, copies of *Bondage and Freedom* were on sale at his bookstore at 99 Buchanan Street, Glasgow.[182]

Unlike the *Narrative, Bondage and Freedom* was not widely distributed via institutional antislavery channels. It made a brief appearance on the list of books on sale at the Pennsylvania Anti-Slavery Society office in late 1855, but its distribution via such channels remained marginal compared to its widespread availability in nonspecialist bookstores.[183] This is due in part to the trade publishing distribution system but can also be attributed to a degree of censorship by the Garrisonians, who were not keen to encourage the circulation of a book that they considered critical of their agenda. Most Garrisonians reacted to the book in the same way, acknowledging Douglass's literary talent in the first part, while critiquing his description of their movement in the second. Echoing Garrison's critical stance, Richard D. Webb, who printed the *Narrative*'s Dublin editions, was reluctant to announce *Bondage and Freedom* in his own *Anti-Slavery Advocate*:

> I saw Douglass's My Bondage & my Freedom lately and read it through. The first portion which is more than three fourths of the book is admirable & I did not see any thing to object to in it. The last part contains imputations against his old friends that I think he must know to be dishonest. Miss Griffiths is putting him before the public here as a disinterested, high minded, Christian spirited, orthodox devoted friend of his race contending with the mean hostility & slanders of the Garrison party. But because this is so, & that I know him to be no saint & full of bitterness & malignity, shall I refuse to notice the best book of the kind ever written by a slave to show the real nature of slavery?[184]

His correspondent, Samuel May Jr., thought it best to simply ignore Douglass as much as possible. He instead advised promoting Samuel Ringgold Ward's *Autobiography of a Fugitive Negro*, published in London that same year:

> I can see no possible reason why you should *not* notice such a book as S. R. Ward's; and abundant reasons why you should notice it. . . . I should make F. Douglass more of our exception, I think, and touch him seldom & slightly. Much notice from us is what he would like, and would be his best capital. Much of his late book is very excellent, but it is villainous and false, beyond credit almost, when he comes to touch upon the American A. S. Society;—altogether too bad to be passed unnoticed, indeed.[185]

It is unlikely that such censorship deprived Douglass of many readers, since his book could be obtained by other means. Yet it sheds light on Garrisonian hostility to Douglass in the mid-1850s. The situation had changed considerably since the publication of the *Narrative*, when white abolitionists used their networks on both sides of the Atlantic to help distribute the work. In this sense, the fact that certain trade publishers were open to slave narratives worked in Douglass's favor, letting him publish *Bondage and Freedom* as he saw fit. It also made it possible for Charles Ball's narrative to be republished, albeit in a fundamentally different manner. Where the rebirth of Douglass's narrative gave the author an opportunity to make himself heard more distinctly and firmly than before, in Ball's case, it made his voice even fainter.

The two versions of Douglass's narrative were published ten years apart, Ball's over two decades apart. As chapter 1 demonstrated, *Slavery in the United States* was initially printed in Lewistown, Pennsylvania, in 1836, then reprinted in New York the following year with the support of the AASS. It reappeared in New York in 1858 with a new title—*Fifty Years in Chains* (fig. 11). In fact, Ball's narrative had never disappeared altogether: it was present in Britain and the United States throughout the 1840s and 1850s in various textual embodiments. British abolitionist Joseph Barker printed extracts from Ball's narrative in *Interesting Memoirs and Documents Relating to American Slavery* in 1846, providing the likely source for a new English edition of *Slavery in the United States* as *The Life of a Negro Slave* that same year. A certain "Mrs. Alfred Barnard" of Norwich reworked and abridged the narrative from 517 to 250 pages. A pamphlet likewise titled *Life of a Negro Slave* came out in Edinburgh in 1847 as part of a successful series of cheap educational texts, the twenty-volume Chambers's Miscellany of Useful and Entertaining Tracts.[186] The thirty-two-page tract was heavily rewritten rather than simply abridged, furthering the process of distorting Ball's voice begun in 1836 by Isaac Fisher. This is the version skewered in a review by the South Carolina journalist D. J. McCord in the *Southern Quarterly Review* early in 1853. McCord claimed *Life of a Negro Slave* was a tissue of "falsehoods and misstatements."[187] In the post–Uncle Tom era, the review did more to raise the profile of Ball's narrative than to discredit it. The same year, *Slavery in the United States* was reprinted in Pittsburgh by John T. Shryock, whose text was very close to the 1836 original. When H. Dayton printed Ball's narrative in turn in 1858 as *Fifty Years in Chains*, he did not revive a long-forgotten text but rather—wittingly or otherwise—seized on a text that had withstood the passage of time and was liable to attract a broad readership.

Attracting readers was what Hiram Dayton was all about. Liedel describes him as a "purveyor of sensation books" and an "[opportunist] of the first

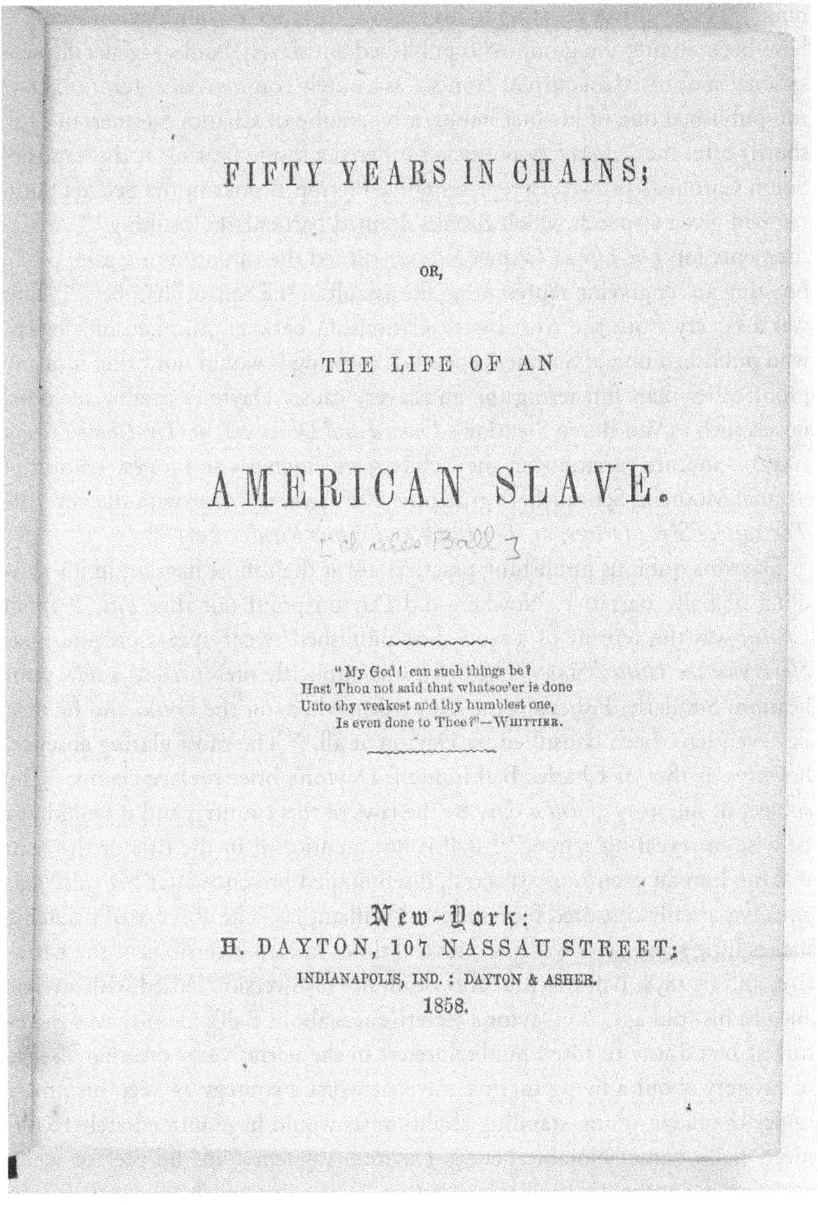

FIFTY YEARS IN CHAINS;

OR,

THE LIFE OF AN

AMERICAN SLAVE.

[Charles Ball]

"My God! can such things be?
Hast Thou not said that whatsoe'er is done
Unto thy weakest and thy humblest one,
Is even done to Thee?"—WHITTIER.

New-York:
H. DAYTON, 107 NASSAU STREET;
INDIANAPOLIS, IND. : DAYTON & ASHER.
1858.

Figure 11. Title page of *Fifty Years in Chains* (Courtesy of
American Antiquarian Society)

rank."[188] No archives attesting to his motivations survive, but Dayton seems to have been among the group who published antislavery books—generally sensationalist or based on current events—as a purely commercial enterprise. Dayton published one of his first books, a biography of Charles Sumner, in 1856, shortly after the antislavery politician suffered a severe beating at the hands of South Carolina's proslavery representative Preston Brooks in the Senate; Sumner had given a speech which Brooks deemed particularly insulting.[189] Advertisements for *The Life of Charles Sumner* turned the caning into a sales pitch, boasting an "engraving representing the assault in the Senate chamber."[190] This was a far cry from the trust-based relationship between Sumner and Jewett, who published one of Sumner's speeches knowing it would not bring him any profit other than furthering the antislavery cause. Dayton's catalog included novels such as Van Buren Denslow's *Owned and Disowned; or, The Chattel Child* (1857)—another variation on the "white slave" theme—and a new edition of Samuel Mosheim Schmucker's gruesome *The Planter's Victim* with the new title *The Yankee Slave Driver; or, The Black and White Rivals* (1857).[191]

Dayton's dubious publishing practices are at their most flagrant in his handling of Ball's narrative. Nowhere did Dayton point out that *Fifty Years in Chains* was the reprint of a work first published twenty years previously as *Slavery in the United States*. The book was implicitly presented as a new publication. Similarly, Fisher's name featured nowhere on the book, and he may not even have been consulted by Dayton at all.[192] The most glaring absence, however, is that of Charles Ball himself. Dayton's brief preface claims, "The subject of the story *is still a slave* by the laws of this country, and it would not be wise to reveal his name."[193] Ball is not mentioned in the title or the text, making him an even more spectral, disembodied presence after his voice was already partially censored by Fisher and William Jay. The absence of his name makes little sense, as it was given several times in earlier versions of the narrative, and by 1858, Ball was probably dead; the 1836 version closed with a reference to his "old age."[194] Dayton's secretiveness about Ball's identity was therefore at best a way to rouse public interest in the narrative by creating a sense of mystery about a living fugitive slave, at worst a strategy to keep his piracy under the radar—long-standing abolitionists would have immediately recognized Ball's name. Notable here is Dayton's vagueness in the preface when asserting the authenticity of the narrative: "The story which follows is *true* in every particular. Responsible citizens of a neighboring State can vouch for the reality of the narrative."[195] Whereas Jay was careful to include certificates and press clippings bearing witness to the truth of Ball's narrative in the 1837 edition, Dayton pointed readers to unnamed "responsible citizens" from an unnamed "neighboring State."

The earliest press reviews, dated January 1858, suggest Dayton's tactics at first went unnoticed. The *National Era* critic was apparently unfamiliar with Ball's narrative and praised the "plain, homely history" whose style he considered akin to Northup's.[196] The following month, however, the *Radical Abolitionist*'s reviewer pointed out that *Fifty Years in Chains* was in fact not a new work. "This work," he wrote, "is highly commended by several respectable journals. We commenced perusing it as a *new* work, but had not proceeded far, before we recognized in this AMERICAN SLAVE under his new dress, our familiar acquaintance CHARLES BALL, whose Narrative, published in 1837, was somewhat extensively circulated among the abolitionists of those times."[197] He went on to write that it was good to see the book printed by a general trade publisher for an audience that would be much wider than the small abolitionist readership of the 1830s. Other antislavery newspapers easily spotted Ball's narrative, including the *National Anti-Slavery Standard* ("it is an old friend with a new name") and—belatedly—the *National Era* ("it is not a new book").[198] As a rule, abolitionist reviewers did not dwell on Dayton's misleading practices. Rather, they were pleased that a powerful antislavery book "long since out of print" was again made available.[199] It mattered little that Ball's identity disappeared incrementally as editions of his narrative continued to appear. Abolitionists no longer saw Ball as a man of flesh and blood but rather as a creature of paper and ink, as suggested by this awkwardly phrased yet eloquent quotation: "Many editions may there be, of the American Slave, Charles Ball."[200]

Several reviews compared the *Slavery in the United States* of 1837 and the *Fifty Years in Chains* of 1858, preferring the latter. The "episodical" style of *Slavery in the United States* was held to be inferior to the more "condensed" prose of *Fifty Years in Chains*.[201] A careful reading reveals that *Fifty Years in Chains* both abridges and rewrites the 1837 narrative, on which Dayton based his own text. While the broad structure of the narrative is more or less the same, there are numerous, complex changes to groups of words or even across several pages, making it difficult to keep track of the textual transformation. A given passage may reorganize, cut, and rewrite paragraphs. Yet the overall process clearly seeks to make the narrative more readable and lively, ridding Fisher's text of what Dayton considered cumbersome passages. For instance, the first three pages of *Slavery in the United States*, where Ball/Fisher write about slavery in general terms, knowledge of slavery in the North, and the nature of the book in hand, are reduced to a single four-line paragraph in *Fifty Years in Chains*, taking the reader straight into the autobiography. "My grandfather was brought from Africa and sold as a slave in Calvert county, in Maryland," the first page of *Fifty Years in Chains* tells us.[202] Other, more discreet changes on the first page follow the same pattern—fewer sweeping statements, less documentary record, and a greater focus on Ball's life and foregrounding of the events that punctuated it. The aforementioned sentence, for example, is shorter than the original: "My grandfather was brought from Africa, and sold as a slave in Calvert county, in Maryland, about the year 1730." Leaving out the year the grandfather arrived in America is typical of Dayton's editorial practice: he omits much factual information he considers unnecessary.[203] Conversely, the first chapter, left untitled in 1837, becomes "SEPARATED FROM MY MOTHER" in 1858. The chapter title adds drama to Ball's narrative, starting it with the key event of the forced separation of an enslaved mother and her child. Similar modifications are found elsewhere. Chapter 15 in *Slavery in the United States* includes a long passage on white southerners that Ball/Fisher clearly identify as a digression: "I shall now return to my narrative," Ball says, before picking up the thread of his autobiography.[204] The corresponding chapter in *Fifty Years in Chains*—chapter 11—drops the digression wholesale, opening instead with Ball's clever tricks to eat his fill on the South Carolina plantation he was then enslaved on.

Dayton clearly set out to give readers what he believed they wanted—adventure and emotion. This also explains the change in title. Whereas *Slavery in the United States* could be a political treatise or history book, Dayton chose *Fifty Years in Chains*, an eye-catching title that echoed other slave narratives, from *Twelve Years a Slave* to Austin Steward's *Twenty-Two Years a Slave, and Forty Years a Freeman* (1857), as well as "outsider" narratives such as Charles Nordhoff's *Nine Years a Sailor* (1857) and Sylvester Crakes's *Five Years a Captive among the Black-Feet Indians* (1858).[205] Dayton intended to make his version of Ball's narrative as reader-friendly as he could. To that end, he abridged Fisher's text but also reshaped the book to draw the attention of potential buyers. Of all the slave narratives published in the antebellum era, *Fifty Years in Chains* is the most visually striking. The original edition is bound in electric blue cloth stamped with gilt ornaments and the title in decorative lettering on the spine; it is thick and the layout generous. Overall the visual effect is a gaudier version of Ticknor & Fields's famous "blue and gold" series, launched in 1856 with a volume of Tennyson's poems.[206] As Michael Winship notes, the success of the "blue and gold" series can be measured by its countless imitations.[207] *Fifty Years in Chains* is a case in point. The upshot for the modern reader is a curious semiotic clash between the violence of the narrative and the gaudy design of the book as artifact.

Dayton's most contradictory signals came at the promotion stage. The advertising campaign generally followed the pattern of *Twelve Years a Slave* and *My Bondage and My Freedom*, with epigrammatic remarks ("'Truth Is Stranger than

Fiction,'" "The Great Sensation Book!"), announcements of high sales figures, and extracts from positive reviews. One unique element was the constant repetition of the claim "Written by Himself."[208] Not only was Ball's narrative not written by himself in 1836, but it was partially modified by Jay in 1837 and thoroughly rewritten by Dayton in 1858. Dayton did not go so far as to include the words on the title page of *Fifty Years in Chains*, but their constant repetition during the advertising campaign reflects his lack of respect for Ball's voice as a formerly enslaved man.

If Dayton's figures are to be believed, *Fifty Years in Chains* (reprinted in 1859 and 1860) enjoyed a degree of success but did not sell the hundred thousand copies the publisher had hoped.[209] In May 1859, a little over a year postpublication, thirteen thousand copies had been sold.[210] In addition to bookstore distribution, Dayton seems to have relied on a network of traveling sales agents, as Derby & Miller had done for *Twelve Years a Slave*. In 1859, he announced he had "150 Agents now in the field."[211] "The agent for this bailiwick is N. R. Forster, who is now canvassing for the work," one Sandusky, Ohio, newspaper wrote.[212] This system made the book available across the North. By 1858, Dayton had joined forces with the Indiana publisher Dayton & Asher, renamed Asher & Company the following year, to distribute the book further west. The publication history of Ball's narrative from 1836 to 1858 is therefore an account of a gradually expanding readership targeted by the publishers behind each edition. In 1836, Fisher and his printer, John W. Shugert, aimed to distribute the work to the people of Lewistown and the surrounding region. Jay and the AASS circulated the 1837 edition among the abolitionist community; in 1858, Dayton hoped to put it in the hands of readers across the North. Yet as Ball's narrative reached an ever-broader audience, it gradually lost its substance as Ball's oral history recorded by Fisher in the mid-1830s was progressively distorted. The edition by a trade publisher in the post–Uncle Tom era hastened the process, more or less stripping the work of its political content to make it an entertainment product, in line with the novelistic turn in antislavery literature that followed the publication of *Uncle Tom's Cabin*. What was left in the end was but a distant echo of Ball's original, singular voice.

Incidents in the Life of *Incidents in the Life of a Slave Girl*

What sets the publishing history of the narrative of Harriet Jacobs apart from other antebellum slave narratives is first of all how long it took to come to fruition. Almost a decade went by between the moment when Jacobs first considered writing an autobiographical narrative and its publication as *Incidents in the Life of a Slave Girl* in 1861, compared to just a few months for *Narrative of the Life of Frederick Douglass*. This lengthy gestation reflects the many hurdles

Jacobs encountered on her journey to authorship. The success of *Twelve Years a Slave*, *My Bondage and My Freedom*, and *Fifty Years in Chains* might suggest that *Uncle Tom's Cabin* had ultimately smoothed the path for antislavery literature and that a formerly enslaved woman would have no difficulty recounting her personal history and having it published in book form. While Jacobs did eventually manage to publish her work, she had to overcome numerous obstacles and setbacks in the process. In the late 1850s, it remained extremely difficult for a formerly enslaved woman to achieve the status of published author. Jacobs struggled with a lack of time and money, attempts by white antislavery advocates to commandeer her work, racial prejudice, and the bankruptcy of the publishers most likely to take on her narrative—making it truly remarkable that it appeared at all, let alone came to the attention of a new readership in the twentieth century after a long period of neglect.

Jacobs escaped to the North in 1842 after famously hiding out for seven years in her grandmother's garret in Edenton, North Carolina. "When I first arrived in Philadelphia," Jacobs writes in her preface to *Incidents*, "Bishop [Daniel] Payne advised me to publish a sketch of my life, but I told him I was altogether incompetent to such an undertaking."[213] It was not just a question of not feeling up to the task. Jacobs had to lie low if she wanted to keep out of the clutches of her former enslavers. As Jean Fagan Yellin has documented in her magisterial biography of Jacobs, James Norcom and his wife made repeated attempts to track her down in the following years. Jacobs worked as a household servant and nanny for the family of author and literary critic Nathaniel Parker Willis in New York City. In 1849, she took up an eighteen-month residence in Rochester, where she ran the Anti-Slavery Reading Room located above Douglass's *North Star* office—a professional experience that likely introduced her to the corpus of antislavery literature. On her return to New York, fresh attempts were made to abduct her. Although she was at the mercy of the recently adopted Fugitive Slave Law, Jacobs steadfastly refused to purchase her freedom from the Norcoms. In 1853, Willis's second wife, Cornelia Grinnell Willis, did so without her knowledge. Jacobs was a free woman.[214]

In Rochester, Jacobs had befriended the Quaker abolitionist and women's rights advocate Amy Post. Like Payne before her, Post suggested Jacobs write out the story of her life now that she was free. "I repeatedly urged her to consent to the publication of her narrative," Post later wrote, "for I felt that it would arouse people to a more earnest work for the disinthralment of millions still remaining in that soul-crushing condition, which was so unendurable to her."[215] Post's suggestion triggered emotional turmoil in Jacobs, due both to her natural sense of discretion and her shame at having suffered sexual harassment at the hands of Norcom. "Your proposal to me has been thought over

and over again but not with out some most painful rememberances," Jacobs
wrote to her Rochester friend in early 1853. Jacobs had until then steered clear
of "Anti-slavery people," as she called them, so as to avoid talking about her
unpleasant experiences; Post was one of the few people she had confided in.
Yet Jacobs gradually came round to the idea of publishing her narrative. She
felt it was her moral duty to do so. "If it could help save another from my fate
it would be selfish and unchristian in me to keep it back," she concluded.[216]
While Frederick Douglass and William Wells Brown took to authorship quite
readily, Jacobs experienced a period of self-doubt about the very possibility of
bearing witness. This was the first of many stumbling blocks she encountered
on the long road to the publication of *Incidents*. In a Victorian cultural context
that did not encourage women to speak out in public and only accepted their
writings insofar as they conformed to a certain ideal of femininity, Jacobs
inevitably found it harder than her male predecessors to put pen to paper.

Jacobs had a clear idea of how the narrative should be structured. "I should
want the History of my childhood and the first five years in one volume and
the next three and my home in the northern states in the secont," she explained
to Post. But her domestic work for the Willis family left her with little time to
write it herself. Nor could she ask her employer for editorial assistance: Nathaniel Parker Willis was "too proslavery" and would certainly disapprove of the
whole project.[217] His wife, Cornelia, suggested contacting Harriet Beecher
Stowe—*Uncle Tom's Cabin* had been published with great fanfare a few months
earlier—and Post soon got in touch with the best-selling author. Jacobs hoped
to spend a month in her company to supply the material she would need to
write the book. Soon after Post sent the letter, however, Jacobs learned in the
press that Stowe would shortly be setting out for England. Jacobs then came
up with another plan to approach her. Maybe Stowe could be persuaded to
take on Jacobs's daughter Louisa, a well-educated and eager young woman,
who would give the English "a very good representative of a Southern Slave."[218]
Cornelia Grinnell Willis agreed to pass on the request. Stowe's reply to the
Post and Willis letters was a disappointment for Jacobs, rousing her to some
anger. Stowe refused to take Louisa with her as "it would subject her to much
petting and patronizing."[219] The infantilizing language of "petting" had long
been used by white abolitionists on both sides of the Atlantic, revealing, as
Hannah-Rose Murray notes, their occasional investment in racial stereotypes.[220] Jacobs criticized Stowe's racism in an ironic reversal of her argument:
"We poor blacks cant have the firmness and stability of character that you
white people have."[221] Stowe did agree to incorporate Jacobs's story into the
work she was soon to publish, *A Key to Uncle Tom's Cabin*, if Willis were willing to vouch for its authenticity. This was hardly what Jacobs had had in

mind. It was important for her to see her account in a standalone volume rather than lost in a sea of biographical vignettes filtered through a white novelist's vision of slavery. Jacobs "wished it to be a history of my life entirely by itsslf . . . and it needed no romance."[222] Willis politely turned the offer down. Jacobs kept writing to Stowe, but her letters went unanswered.

Stowe's rebuff proved a blessing in disguise. It encouraged Jacobs to become an author in her own right. Jacobs was already writing regularly, albeit in a private context, in her correspondence with Post. Words did not always come easily; she often lamented that her "poor pen" did not let her fully express her feelings.[223] In her first public intervention in the national debate on slavery— an open letter printed in the *New York Daily Tribune* in June 1853 in response to a vindication of chattel slavery by Julia Tyler, wife of the former president John Tyler—Jacobs stated that she had never "enjoyed the advantages of an education." Yet she firmly argued her right to denounce slavery and to do so in her own words rather than using someone else as a mouthpiece. The symbolic dimension of this act should not be underestimated: Jacobs was countering the authoritative discourse of the former First Lady with the antagonistic discourse of a "fugitive slave," as she identified herself. In recounting the experience of a young girl who was sexually exploited by her enslaver, she foreshadowed her own later slave narrative. The closing paragraph suggests she was already thinking of writing about her experience herself: "Would that I had one spark from her [Stowe's] store house of genius and talent I would tell you of my own sufferings."[224] Jacobs may still have harbored doubts as to her own "genius and talent," but Yellin is right to claim that "an author was born."[225]

Jacobs had mixed feelings about her new status as an author. In a letter to Black abolitionist William Cooper Nell, she even denied having written the response to Julia Tyler.[226] At the same time, she sent a second letter to the *Tribune* recalling the barbaric murder of a runaway slave in Edenton, followed by a third criticizing the American Colonization Society. She felt a degree of pride in seeing her writings in print and yet downplayed their significance. "Have you seen any more of my scribling?" she shyly asked Post, using a word Nathaniel Hawthorne would notoriously use two years later to discredit female writers.[227] Despite a persistent lack of faith in her writing abilities, Jacobs was learning that her words could weigh in on the slavery debate and arguments against the institution. She soon took the decision to pen her own autographical narrative, sharing the news with her most trusted confidante. "I must write just what I have lived and witnessed myself   dont expect much of me dear Amy   you shall have truth but not talent."[228] Jacobs had finally overcome the self-censorship that had stopped her from fully engaging with her own authorial practice.

Writing the book proved even more of a challenge. The Willis family had just moved to a new residence, Idlewild, in the village of Cornwall, halfway between New York and Albany. Jacobs was kept busier than ever by Nathaniel, Cornelia, and their four—soon five—children. While Douglass and Brown were paid as lecturers for various antislavery societies, Jacobs worked full-time, far from the hubs of reform activity, for a family whom she did not inform of her literary ambitions. Even Cornelia was not told of her plan. "I have not the Courage to meet the criticism and ridicule of Educated people," Jacobs confessed to Post.[229] The aspiring author had little choice but to write in the evenings by candlelight once all the family and their many guests were in bed. Jacobs started working on her manuscript in the last months of 1853. "Just now the poor Book is in its Chrysalis state," she wrote in March 1854, "and though I can never make it a butterfly I am satisfied to have it creep meekly among some of the humbler bugs."[230] William Cooper Nell, on a visit to Idlewild in the summer, encouraged her to keep going and promised to do everything in his power for the book's publication and promotion.[231] Slowed down by sheer drudgery and by her delicate health, Jacobs only managed to produce a draft of her manuscript in 1857, perhaps spurred on by a sense of injustice at the Supreme Court's recent *Dred Scott* decision. As Yellin notes, Jacobs was aware that her narrative might offend the sensibilities of some white middle-class female readers. In an attempt to forestall criticism, she asked Post if she would contribute a preface to the volume, apologizing for requesting such a "sacrifice" from "so good and pure" a person.[232] Post agreed and asked what the preface should include. Jacobs replied,

> I think it would be best for you to begin with our acquaintance and the length of time that I was in your family you advice about giving the history of my life in Slavry mention that I lived at service all the while that I was striving to get the Book out but do not say with whom I lived as I would not use the Willis name neither would I like to have people think that I was living an Idle life— and had got this book out merely to make money—my kind friend I do not restrict you in anything for you know far better than I do what to say.[233]

Post's preface would eventually appear as part of the appendix to *Incidents*. It provides another example of a "gray" paratext, one that bore the name of a white abolitionist but whose content was in fact largely dictated by the Black author herself.

Jacobs also began to think about publication. It was quickly suggested that she should publish simultaneously in the United States and Britain both to get around the problem of the lack of international copyright laws and because

British readers had repeatedly shown a keen interest in slave narratives. Just as she was trying to decide what her best strategy would be, Jacobs received a letter from her brother John S. Jacobs inviting her to join him in England. This was a fine opportunity to catch up with a family member she hadn't seen for years and to work toward a British publication of her narrative. Once again she consulted Post:

> I have been thinking that I would so like to go away and sell my Book—I could then secure a copywright—to sell it both here and in England—and by identify-ing myself with—it I might do something for the Antislavry Cause—to do this I would have to get letters of introduction. from some of the leading Abolitionist of this Country to those of the Old—when you write tell me what you think of it.[234]

Jacobs eventually traveled with Nell to Weymouth, Massachusetts, to meet Maria Weston Chapman, a leading white abolitionist who had spent several years in Europe and was well-known in British antislavery circles. "Harriet had a long talk with Mrs. Chapman and secured her interest in her forthcom-ing Book and any thing she can do toward perfecting it in matter or manner may be relied upon," Nell reported to Post.[235] Chapman also gave Jacobs the letters of introduction she needed to contact British abolitionists. Everything was set for her departure. She set sail for England a few months later.

While the journey put her in touch with many local Garrisonian abolition-ists and African American expatriates and let her spend time in a country where racial prejudice was less flagrant than in the United States, it proved a failure in terms of her plans for publication. The reasons for this failure are unclear, particularly as Jacobs was much appreciated by the people she met in England. She shared her manuscript with Amelia Chesson, daughter of aboli-tionist George Thompson and an active antislavery campaigner herself, and Hannah Waring Webb, the wife of Richard D. Webb. As has been discussed in chapter 2, Richard D. Webb had printed several editions of the narratives of Douglass and Brown, and it is surprising that he did not offer to assist Jacobs in turn; he did, after all, give her manuscript "much attention."[236] Jacobs's account may have presented too much of a challenge to Victorian morals. Not only had Jacobs been sexually harassed by Norcom, but she had initiated a liaison with her white neighbor Samuel Sawyer, later a member of Congress, as a protection against her enslaver. Sawyer was the father of her two children.[237] Thirteen years before, Bristol abolitionist John B. Estlin had fret-ted about a particularly graphic passage in Douglass's *Narrative*, going as far as erasing it in her daughter's copy. Estlin was dead by 1858, but the feeling that

Incidents would be "offensive to English taste" (Estlin's words) and not suitable for British women seems to have lived on.[238] A British edition of *Incidents* would eventually come out a few years later.

Returning from England with no book published and without even having met up with her brother, Jacobs was resolved not to "mention my M S. to my friends again until I had done something with it."[239] Her later correspondence with Post sheds light on the events that eventually led to publication. In 1859, Jacobs submitted her manuscript to the Boston publishers Phillips, Sampson, who over the preceding years had earned a reputation for antislavery literature. Phillips, Sampson agreed to publish it only if it were prefaced by Stowe or Nathaniel Parker Willis; a big name would raise the profile of a narrative written by an obscure African American woman. Asking Willis was still out of the question. Jacobs did have a "second clinch" from Stowe, as she put it, but again her request was refused.[240] By another stroke of misfortune, Moses D. Phillips and Charles Sampson, the two partners at the publishing company, both died later that year, leading to the immediate closure of the business. Discouraged by these turns of events, Jacobs put the manuscript to one side. Not until the fall of 1860 did she try her luck with another Boston-based publishing company, Thayer and Eldridge. William W. Thayer and Charles W. Eldridge were in close contact with several leading lights in abolitionist and Republican circles. Works brought out by the young publishers included the campaign biographies of the two candidates for the Republican ticket at the 1860 presidential election—William H. Seward and Abraham Lincoln—and, in similar vein, James Redpath's successful 1860 biography of antislavery martyr John Brown, *The Public Life of Capt. John Brown*. That same year Thayer and Eldridge also brought out the third edition of Walt Whitman's *Leaves of Grass* and William Douglas O'Connor's novel *Harrington: A Story of True Love*, partly inspired by the life of Solomon Northup. "Our motto was to stimulate home talent, and encourage young authors," Thayer reminisced several decades letter.[241] This time Jacobs was asked to provide a preface penned by the popular white author and Garrisonian abolitionist Lydia Maria Child. Having failed to persuade Stowe, Jacobs was worried about reaching out to "another Sattellite of so great magnitude." She "resolved to make my last effort," however, and was introduced to Child thanks to Nell. In the end procuring Child's agreement proved a vital step in bringing *Incidents* to print.

From the outset of their work together, Child took a considerable interest in Jacobs's narrative. In fact, she did much more than just contribute a preface: she became a full-fledged editor, as the title page of the book clearly indicates (fig. 12). Critics have long debated the nature and scope of Child's involvement. Some have considered her changes to be generally relevant and relatively unobtrusive.

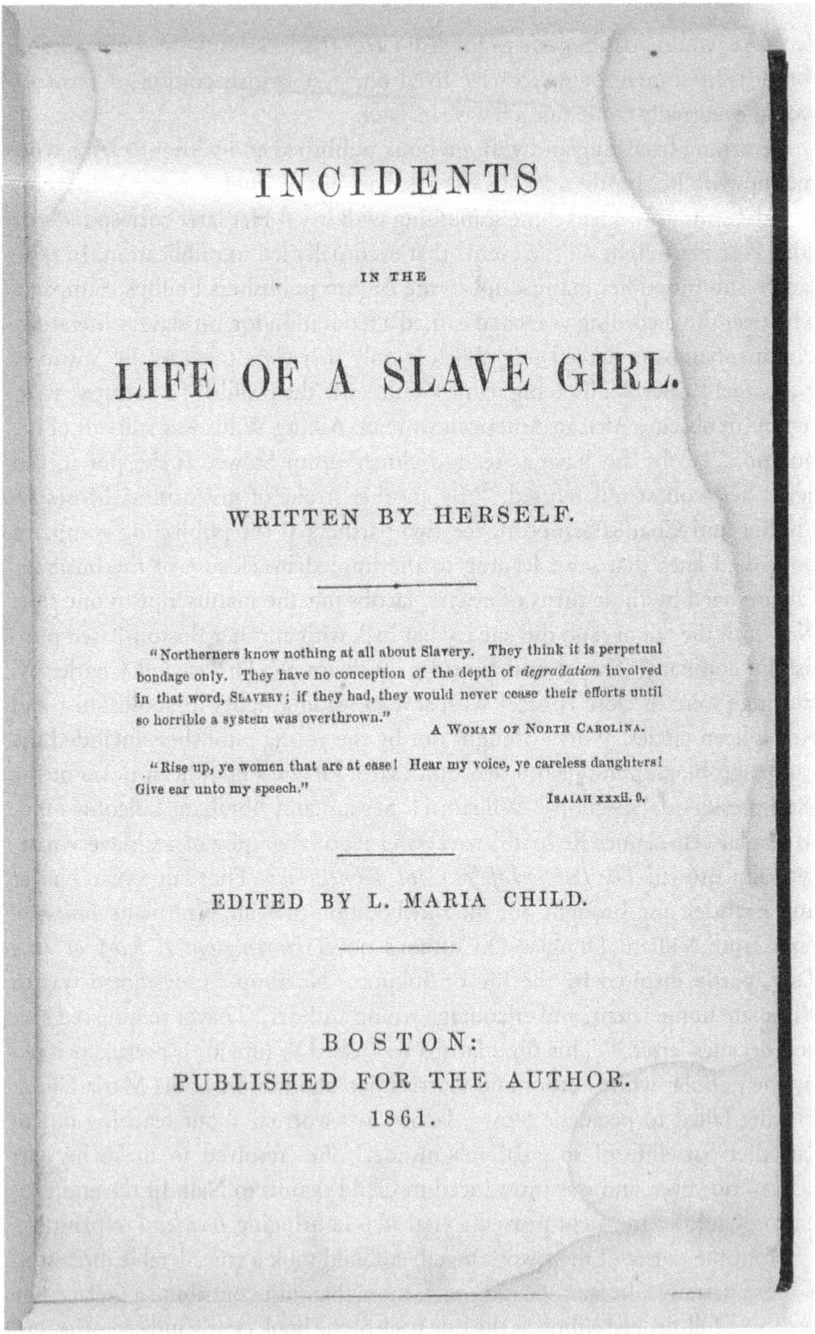

INCIDENTS

IN THE

LIFE OF A SLAVE GIRL.

WRITTEN BY HERSELF.

———

"Northerners know nothing at all about Slavery. They think it is perpetual
bondage only. They have no conception of the depth of *degradation* involved
in that word, SLAVERY; if they had, they would never cease their efforts until
so horrible a system was overthrown."

A WOMAN OF NORTH CAROLINA.

"Rise up, ye women that are at ease! Hear my voice, ye careless daughters!
Give ear unto my speech."

ISAIAH xxxii. 9.

———

EDITED BY L. MARIA CHILD.

———

BOSTON:
PUBLISHED FOR THE AUTHOR.
1861.

Figure 12. Title page of *Incidents in the Life of a Slave Girl*
(Courtesy of American Antiquarian Society)

Incidents, they argue, was "the work of black Harriet Jacobs—and not her editor, white [Lydia] Maria Child."[242] Child was "a practiced and conscientious editor," Yellin writes; she "offered her suggestions in a manner that showed considerable sensitivity toward Jacobs," Carolyn L. Karcher concurs.[243] Other critics have had a less positive view of Child's interventions. Alice A. Deck contends that Jacobs's authorial voice in *Incidents* must compete with Child's intrusive editorial voice. Her editing amounts to nothing less than a "transforming" of the text.[244] What does the evidence say?

Child often praised Jacobs's writing in her private correspondence. She repeatedly claimed that her changes to the manuscript were modest. "I have been busy with your M.S. ever since I saw you; and have only done one third of it," she wrote to Jacobs in August 1860. "I have very little occasion to alter the language, which is wonderfully good, for one whose opportunities for education have been so limited." Jacobs had been provided with books to read by Cornelia Grinnell Willis, Child noted in a letter to her friend Lucy Searle a few months later. "This accounts for the remarkably good style in which the autobiography is written. I abridged, and struck out superfluous words sometimes, but I don't think I *altered* fifty words in the whole volume." Jacobs's own correspondence indicates a considerable degree of literary skill and inventiveness, particularly in her use of metaphor. Her style certainly was "lively" and "dramatic," as Child put it in another letter to Sarah Blake Shaw. Child likely did not change much to the letter of Jacobs's text; some of her minor changes, however, had major consequences, as I discuss below. Moreover, Child did admit to having altered the structure of the work quite significantly. "I am copying a great deal of it," she informed Jacobs, "for the purpose of transposing sentences and pages, so as to bring the story into continuous *order*, and the remarks into *appropriate* places. I think you will see that this renders the story much more clear and entertaining." In the letter to Searle, she explained how she had "put the savage cruelties into one chapter" titled "Sketches of Neighboring Slaveholders" so that sensitive souls could skip it and keep reading without losing the narrative's thread. Child also advised Jacobs to leave out the final chapter on John Brown, a late addition to the manuscript. "It does not naturally come into your story, and the M.S. is already too long."[245] At the same time, she asked Jacobs a series of questions concerning the aftermath of Nat Turner's revolt— "Were any tortured to make them confess? and how? Where any killed?"—in order to flesh out another chapter titled "Fear of Insurrection."[246]

As Albert H. Tricomi convincingly demonstrates, these multiple changes had the effect of blurring the text's generic status, making it more "fiction-like." According to Tricomi, Child reordered the work so as to play down its more militant aspects and, conversely, to foreground its sentimental features. Jacobs's closing

chapter on John Brown, for instance, would have focused the reader's attention on an act of violent resistance against slavery. Shorn of the chapter, *Incidents* concluded instead with the sentimental tableau of the death of Jacobs's
"good old grandmother."[247] The private account of Jacobs's personal life took
precedence over the public expression of her political opinions—something to
which Jacobs never explicitly agreed. Likewise, Child aimed for more sensa-
tionalism and melodrama. By putting all the violent passages into one chapter,
she may have wished to spare sensitive readers but she also made it easy for
sensation seekers to find all the horrific events in one place, their impact mul-
tiplied by their sheer concentration. Her request for further details about the
white backlash in North Carolina following Turner's revolt indicates that she
had no real intention of limiting all references to violence to one chapter.
Child's changes gave the work an entirely new slant, punctuating it with a
series of dramatic "incidents"—a word Jacobs never used in her letters to refer
to her narrative, more often described as a "history" of her life. Further, Child
decided to change the names of various individuals named in the account,
including Jacobs herself, who became Linda Brent. She concealed places and
dates in the southern sections of the narrative, lest anyone be recognized and
persecuted, and "out of delicacy to Mrs. Willis . . . who would not like to have
her name bandied about in the newspapers."[248] Uprooted from an identifiable
geography and chronology and rearranged in accordance with Child's own
literary criteria, Jacobs's work lost some of its autobiographical character and
became more novelistic.[249]

That Child—and, later, reviewers of the book—consistently referred to
Jacobs's narrative as "Linda" rather than its proper title *Incidents in the Life of
a Slave Girl* is no coincidence. Since the eighteenth century, countless women's
novels in Britain had had as their titles the Christian name of their female
protagonists, from Fanny Burney's *Evelina: or, The History of a Young Lady's
Entrance into the World* (1778) and Jane Austen's *Emma* (1815) to Charlotte
Brontë's *Shirley* (1849) and Elizabeth Gaskell's *Ruth* (1853). The tradition had
crossed over to the United States. Ten years before Child revised Jacobs's
manuscript, proslavery author Caroline Lee Hentz had published a novel
titled *Linda; or, The Young Pilot of the Belle Creole* (1850). While the title page
of Jacobs's published narrative mentioned *Incidents in the Life of a Slave Girl*
as the title, the name "Linda" appeared on the spine, creating a (perhaps unin-
tentional) ambiguity over the book's genre. Jacobs did not make any specific
comment as to the title of her book, but she did voice her dissatisfaction
with Child's numerous editorial interventions on at least one occasion. "I
know that Mrs Child will strive to do the best she can more than I can ever
repay," she wrote to Post in late 1860, "but I ought to have been there that we

could have consulted together—and compared our views—although I know that hers are superior to mine yet we could have marked her great Ideas and my small ones together."²⁵⁰ Based on such assertions, Robanna Sumrell Knott insists on how extensive and heavy-handed Child's editing of Jacobs's manuscript actually was. "For someone who describes her editorial adjustments as minimal," Knott writes, Child herself presents evidence that "her changes were more likely of a substantive order." Her letters suggest that she edited "aggressively, possibly modifying the essential argument of the manuscript." Unlike what Karcher argues, Child's tone was often dismissive and she seemed to care little for the author's wishes. Even Knott, however, acknowledges that Jacobs's manuscript would doubtless never have been published without Child's intervention.²⁵¹

Indeed, Child did not just shape Jacobs's manuscript: she was instrumental in seeing it into print. Child was initially reluctant to have the book come out with Thayer and Eldridge. She was concerned that, as a new business, it might not survive in the uncertain economic climate of the late 1850s; the Panic of 1857 had already driven many companies, including publishing firms, into bankruptcy. Yet none of the publishers she contacted would take on the manuscript, and the AASS declined to publish it under its imprint. Child then somewhat peremptorily took over the negotiations with Thayer and Eldridge, who slated *Incidents* for publication in November 1860. She had the copyright and contract put in her own name, negotiated Jacobs's royalty at 10 percent—the average rate for authors working with trade publishers in the mid-nineteenth century—and sorted out various legal details.²⁵² She also contacted Wendell Phillips, who proposed that the committee tasked with handling the Hovey Fund buy and distribute a number of copies—perhaps up to a thousand. As a result, Child asked the publishers to double the print run from one to two thousand copies. Thayer and Eldridge started promoting the book, and publication was imminent when Jacobs and Child learned that the business was on the verge of failure, exactly as Child had feared. Christy Pottroff suggests that the two publishers, having spent too much money on the "ornate and ostentatious" third edition of Whitman's *Leaves of Grass*, found themselves "without the means to fulfill Jacobs's or any other outstanding contract."²⁵³ Not a single copy of *Incidents* had yet been printed. Fortunately for Jacobs, the Boston Stereotype Foundry had already produced the stereotype plates. She was able to buy them outright for half price. Where she found the money is unclear, but Jacobs had the work printed and bound herself.²⁵⁴ After so many efforts to place the book with a publisher, the title page bore not the names of Phillips, Sampson or Thayer and Eldridge but the words so often seen on title pages of antebellum slave narratives: "Published for the Author."

The book was out at long last, despite the countless incidents that had delayed its publication.

Without a trade publisher, Jacobs could not access a large-scale professional distribution network. Jacobs, Child, and Nell thus had to go to great lengths to make sure that copies of *Incidents* ended up in the hands of readers. While Douglass, Brown, and Sojourner Truth had sold copies of their books at anti-slavery meetings and conventions, Jacobs was a more discreet presence in abolitionist circles, and she did not generally give lectures or attend large public events. She just "packed up a trunk of books," Pottroff writes, and traveled for months, "placing her books directly in the hands of her readers."[255] Early in 1862, for instance, she spent some time in Philadelphia, where she was helped by a young antislavery Quaker, Mary Rebecca Darby Smith, who provided her with letters of introduction to local activists, most likely members of the Philadelphia Female Anti-Slavery Society. Jacobs sold them copies of her book: "Your letters has done me good service for which I acknowledge my gratful thanks—I have sold fifty Coppies in all—and the friends that I have meet have encourage me to stay longer," she wrote happily to Smith.[256] At the same time, the African Methodist Episcopal Church's official newspaper, the *Christian Recorder*, brought this "new work put into our hands by the author" to the attention of its African American readers, informing them of Jacobs's presence in Philadelphia: "She is in this city for a few days, and those who wish the book can procure it of her, at No. 107 North Fifth St."[257] Truth had sold copies of her *Narrative* in Black churches; likewise, Jacobs occasionally aimed for specifically Black sites of distribution. As was the case for the narratives discussed in the previous chapter, the embodied nature of these transactions can be seen in various handwritten jottings in original copies of *Incidents*, such as one in the front matter of the copy held at the Schomburg Center for Research in Black Culture: "This book was written by a woman named Harriet Jacobs. . . . This volume was bought from herself."[258]

Child drew on her own networks to facilitate the distribution of *Incidents*. This did not prove an easy task. "The Boston [booksellers] are so shy of touching anything Anti-Slavery, that I find considerable difficulty in extending the sale of the books," she complained to the New Bedford, Massachusetts, abolitionist Daniel Ricketson, before asking him if he could recommend any ways to sell the book in the New Bedford vicinity.[259] She sent a similar request to the poet John Greenleaf Whittier: "Do you think any bookseller, or other *responsible* person in Newburyport [Massachusetts], would be answerable for a few [copies]? They sell here, at retail, $1 a volume. Whoever would take one or two dozen of them might have them at 68 cts per vol. If you think it worth while to send any to Newburyport or Amesbury, please inform me to whom to send."[260] Who knows how many such letters Child sent to antislavery friends across New England? Phillips kept his promise to her, ensuring that a small part of the Hovey Fund was spent purchasing copies of *Incidents*. The Wendell Phillips papers at the Houghton Library contain a receipt for one hundred dollars, suggesting a sale of a far fewer than the thousand copies originally planned when Thayer and Eldridge were set to publish the book.[261] In fact, the entire print run of Jacobs's book was in all likelihood equal to or under a thousand copies, which explains why first editions are rare today. Eric Gardner estimates that there are around one hundred extant copies of the first edition.[262]

Nell remained a staunch supporter of Jacobs's book, which could be bought by contacting him.[263] One of the first articles on *Incidents* to appear in the press was a letter from Nell to Garrison in the *Liberator* announcing the recent publication and underlining how opportune it was: "I feel confident that its circulation at this crisis in our country's history will render a signal and most acceptable service."[264] Unfortunately, the crisis triggered by the secession of the southern states between December 1860 and June 1861 and the launch of hostilities at the Battle of Fort Sumter in April 1861 hindered rather than helped Jacobs's book to reach an audience. The life of a formerly enslaved woman may have seemed trivial compared to the political earthquake of a civil war, and it was hard to promote a single individual's slave narrative when the entire country's attention was caught up by current events. All in all, *Incidents* failed to attract readers outside antislavery circles. It was sold individually by Jacobs, Child, and Nell; it could be obtained at the antislavery offices in Boston, New York, and Philadelphia; African American newspapers such as the *Weekly Anglo-African* carried copies.[265] But this was not enough to bring the book to the attention of a wider audience. *Incidents* was largely ignored by the mainstream press, due both to the polemical nature of its contents and to the context of publication. Even the antislavery press seems to have given it only limited attention. "I am sorry the Liberator and the Standard manifest so little interest in it," Child lamented to a friend.[266] *Incidents* is now as well-known as *Narrative of the Life of Frederick Douglass*, but in its day its distribution across the North was far more restricted.

Jacobs's narrative enjoyed greater success in Britain, where it had failed to find a publisher a few years earlier. The book first circulated informally, with American abolitionists sending copies to British friends and associates, as they had done more than a decade before with the narratives of Douglass and Brown. Mary Anne Estlin's copy, held at Dr. Williams's Library in London, bears the inscription "Mary A. Estlin, of Bristol, Engd. from her friends of the American Antisl: Socy."[267] Jacobs's brother also recommended to Harriet that she send *Incidents* to "different people in England."[268] These people included Frederick W. Chesson, who in 1859 had helped organize the London Emancipation Committee, the principal Garrisonian organization overseas and an important link in the transatlantic abolition movement.[269] Jacobs did more than send him a copy. She shipped the stereotype plates, asking if he could arrange to have an edition of the book published in England. Chesson got in touch with the London publisher William Tweedie, an antislavery and temperance activist who, like Richard D. Webb, Charles Gilpin, and George Gallie, seems to have been particularly interested in the narratives of formerly enslaved men and women. He had brought out William and Ellen Craft's *Running a Thousand Miles for Freedom; or, The Escape of William and Ellen Craft from Slavery* the year before and would publish *The Story of the Life of John Anderson, the Fugitive Slave* in 1863. Tweedie's edition of Jacobs's narrative came out in 1862 under the title *The Deeper Wrong; or, Incidents in the Life of a Slave Girl.* The book was published on the half-profits system, where author (or perhaps in this case, Chesson) and publisher share costs and profits; the arrangement was common in England at the time.[270] Chesson also drew on his press experience to promote the book, sending copies to various individuals and newspapers, while his wife, Amelia, reviewed it in the *Morning Star and Dial. The Deeper Wrong,* she noted, was "the first personal narrative in which one of that sex upon whom chattel servitude falls with the deepest and darkest shadow has ever described her own bitter experience."[271] Some of Chesson's friends, including Henry and Anna Richardson in Newcastle, undertook to distribute the work further. Such individual, informal networks took the work across much of Britain; it was reviewed by papers in London, Newcastle, Plymouth, Edinburgh, and Derry. It must have proved a profitable venture since a second London publisher, Hodson and Son, rushed out a cheap pirate edition of *The Deeper Wrong.* "This is the act of another hungry publisher stooping to take the bread from another's mouth," Chesson complained in his diary. "How much do we need a copyright treaty with America."[272] Chesson and Tweedie considered taking legal steps, but in truth there was nothing they could do, since Hodson had been careful not to keep Tweedie's original title, retaining the American title instead. "If he has a copy of the American edition we shall not be able to get an injunction," Chesson bitterly noted.[273] Tweedie's edition remained a steady seller, however, and in 1863 he was still marketing it in an advertisement at the end of John Anderson's slave narrative.

In the end it took almost a decade for Jacobs's narrative to be written, published, distributed, and read. Jacobs's path to authorship certainly contradicts optimistic claims that in the 1850s "almost any victim of slavery could get published."[274] American trade publishers such as John P. Jewett; Derby &

Miller; H. Dayton; Phillips, Sampson; and Thayer and Eldridge did seek to mine the vein of antislavery literature, including slave narratives, following the success of *Uncle Tom's Cabin*. Yet the narratives they published were often given a melodramatic or sentimental turn to suit the tastes of the broad readership for Stowe's novel. Moreover, it remained difficult for formerly enslaved men and women to achieve publication in the traditional book market. The economically fragile publishing market of the late 1850s could not and would not open up to writings as polemical as those of formerly enslaved people, most of whom had to fall back on alternative publication and distribution networks. Cases like those of Douglass, by then a celebrity in his own right, or Solomon Northup, a free African American with a truly extraordinary life story, remained the exception rather than the rule.

Conclusion

The Slave Narrative Unbound

THE ANTEBELLUM SLAVE narrative is often presented as a unified, coherent whole. This book has demonstrated its profoundly heterogeneous nature. Using the tools of book history and print culture studies, it has striven to "defamiliarize the genre's seeming sameness," as Teresa A. Goddu advises; it has sought to further what Eric Gardner calls its "creative disaggregation."[1] It has identified three major subsets: slave narratives whose publication and distribution were closely controlled by institutional antislavery; self-published narratives with an artisanal distribution model, often sold face-to-face by the formerly enslaved individual within local, national, or international antislavery networks; and narratives published and sold on a grand scale by trade publishers for a general readership. Three slave narratives embody each of these publishing mechanisms: the *Narrative of James Williams* (1838), the *Narrative of the Life of Frederick Douglass* (1845), and *Twelve Years a Slave* (1853)—three texts that "arose in differently organized (if adjacent) literary-social worlds."[2] While *Narrative of the Life of Frederick Douglass* circulated almost exclusively among antislavery campaigners at meetings held by Douglass in the United States and Britain, *Twelve Years a Slave* had to compete with other antislavery writings commercialized by book trade professionals, such as *Uncle Tom's Cabin* (1852), *The White Slave* (1852), and *Ida May* (1854), and more broadly with best sellers such as Fanny Fern's *Fern Leaves from Fanny's Portfolio* (1853) and Maria Cummins's *The Lamplighter* (1854). Douglass and Northup both criticized slavery, but their critiques of the system arose from milieus that are less connected than is often thought. In turn, the *Narrative of James Williams* was a mass-produced work of antislavery propaganda promoting the ideology of the American Anti-Slavery Society (AASS).

Studying slave narratives as material artifacts means studying the specific place of each narrative in antebellum print culture. Such an approach weakens the similarities between the texts. As the introduction points out, this is not to deny any kinship between the various slave narratives, which contemporaries did sometimes consider collectively. Martin R. Delany, for instance, wrote in 1852 that "a number of gentlemen have been authors of narratives, written by themselves, some of which are masterly efforts, manifesting great force of talents. Of such, are those by Frederick Douglass, William Wells Brown, and Henry Bibb."[3] The same year, an article in the Afro-Canadian newspaper *Voice of the Fugitive* came up with an even longer list: "The thrilling narratives of self-emancipated slaves, from the pens of such men as Frederick Douglass, Box Brown, Ellen Craft, Wm. W. Brown, Josiah Henson, Jones, and a host of others, have called the attention of the civilized world to [the] enormity [of the system of slavery]."[4] Nor has it been this book's intention to challenge the slave narrative as a genre in its own right. Douglass, Brown, and Bibb's narratives would not have enjoyed the same critical fortune after the 1960s had they not been presented as part of a single genre whose characteristics could be readily defined and subjected to literary analysis. Yet the archive reveals that the slave narrative is less monolithic than is commonly assumed. A materialist approach not only sheds fresh light on texts that have been abundantly commented, but it also turns the spotlight on a number of less well-known narratives, such as those of Chloe Spear, Peter Wheeler, Leonard Black, Jermain W. Loguen, G. W. Offley, and others. It brings the content and form of the texts into dialog with the circumstances of their production. Discovering the life of Charles Ball in *Slavery in the United States* (1836) and *Fifty Years in Chains* (1858) is not the same reading experience. It is therefore vital to take the context of publication into account for each narrative.

A materialist approach also challenges several preconceptions about slave narratives. First and foremost, it is debatable whether book-length slave narratives were central to institutional antislavery's print culture. The *Narrative of James Williams* was the only slave narrative to be planned, published, promoted, and distributed by an antislavery society. The *Narrative of the Life of Frederick Douglass* and the *Narrative of William W. Brown, a Fugitive Slave* (1847) were undeniably important texts for the abolition movement as a whole, though the AASS was not the driving force behind their publication. These are the antislavery writings that we still read today, rather than the works of Wendell Phillips, Maria Weston Chapman, and Lydia Maria Child. But antebellum white abolitionists who ran antislavery societies did not necessarily give slave narratives the primacy that we give them. In many cases they would have been hard-pressed to do so. A number of narratives that were printed locally on the artisanal model were not intended to be read beyond the author's immediate circle; they never made their way into abolitionist print culture in

Boston, New York, and Philadelphia and could not have served as points of reference for the antislavery argument. These included, among others, the narratives by Leonard Black, William Hayden, Edmond Kelley, William Green, John Thompson—names that have been largely forgotten today yet without whom the slave narrative would not exist as a genre. For this reason, it is an oversimplification to describe slave narratives as "the single most effective publicity tool of the abolitionist movement."[5]

Above and beyond issues of access, white abolitionists did not always seek to root their discourse in writings by formerly enslaved men and women. After a systematic reading of the antislavery press, the correspondence of leading abolitionists, and antislavery society annual reports, what is most striking is not the omnipresence of slave narratives but rather their relative absence. Scholars have often quoted Ephraim Peabody's article hailing the advent of the slave narrative as a new American literary genre, but it should be quoted alongside individuals who did *not* mention slave narratives in contexts where they might be expected to appear. To take just one example, Wendell Phillips gave a speech at the Massachusetts Anti-Slavery Society (MASS) annual convention on 27 January 1853, offering a detailed overview of antislavery literature. On how the slavery system worked, he quoted John Rankin's *Letters on American Slavery* (1826), Theodore D. Weld's *American Slavery as It Is* (1839), and Lydia Maria Child's *An Appeal in Favor of That Class of Americans Called Africans* (1833); on the Bible and slavery, Beriah Green, John G. Fee, and Weld; on constitutional issues, William Jay's *A View of the Action of the Federal Government, in Behalf of Slavery* (1839), William I. Bowditch's *Slavery and the Constitution* (1849), Lysander Spooner's *The Unconstitutionality of Slavery* (1845), and various essays in the *Emancipator* and *Liberator*; on philosophical aspects of abolitionism, Maria Weston Chapman and Edmund Quincy; he also mentions the work of William Goodell, Gerrit Smith, Parker Pillsbury, and Harriet Beecher Stowe and Richard Hildreth's novels.[6] He does not, however, name a single slave narrative. Of course, it is tricky to interpret silence. Yet Phillips here betrays the way certain white abolitionists hierarchized their own political, economic, legal, and philosophical writings over the autobiographical works of formerly enslaved Black men and women. Historian John W. Blassingame came to a similar conclusion more than thirty years ago. "I do not intend to suggest that the abolitionists did not view the narratives as part of their propaganda arsenal," he wrote. "They did. But the narratives were not part of the heavy artillery designed to rout hordes of the enemy. The accounts were rather like rifles valued for their accuracy, enabling the author or editor to pierce the flinty hearts of individual readers."[7]

Notions of popularity and marketability should likewise be reexamined. Scholars of the slave narrative have routinely emphasized how well the narratives sold and how eager northern white audiences were for tales of horror and adventure. Such claims are problematic not only insofar as they overlook a host of "minor" narratives that would never have reached a wide audience but also because they do not reflect the lived experience of most slave narrative authors. This book has pointed out the economic struggles faced by nineteenth-century African American authors and how much time, money, and energy they had to invest in publishing and distributing their books. Describing antebellum slave narratives as a "market phenomenon" and stating that "no Negroes, before or since, have ever experienced less difficulty in getting published" oversimplifies the act of writing and publication at a time when multiple obstacles were still in place.[8] A handful of narratives published in the 1850s did generate vast advertising campaigns and achieved high sales, but they were a mere fraction of the many works on slavery to be published. George Graham's notorious claim that bookshelves in the antebellum era "groan[ed] under the weight of Sambo's woes, done up in covers" is often taken as proof of the popularity of slave narratives, but it in fact referred to the entire output of both pro- and antislavery books.[9] The quotation is usually given without context. It comes from a (highly disparaging) review of *Uncle Tom's Cabin* that does not mention Douglass, Brown, or Bibb; Graham deplored the success of Stowe and her countless imitators. While slave narratives were part of the antislavery corpus, they were not the main target of Graham's attack. *Graham's Magazine* and the *Liberator* both discussed Stowe's novel more often than they did any slave narrative.[10] Truth might have been stranger than fiction, but fiction sold more than truth.

Nina Baym has demonstrated how the novel gained in legitimacy in the United States in the first half of the nineteenth century. The abolition movement itself offers an interesting example. The AASS spoke out against the use of fiction in the antislavery struggle in the 1830s and suspended sales of Hildreth's *The Slave*, as seen in chapter 1; in the 1850s, by contrast, abolitionists were encouraging people to read *Uncle Tom's Cabin*. The "triumph of the novel"—in particular the sentimental novel—had significant consequences for slave narratives, which took a novelistic turn, as shown by the cases of Northup, Ball, and Harriet Jacobs.[11] Yet even these three narratives were less successful than the novels by Stowe, Hildreth, and Mary Hayden Pike. It is understandable that scholars have pointed to the popularity of slave narratives as a rule. It must have seemed all the more pressing to bring them back to prominence if they were thought of as forgotten best sellers. Without understating the success of works like the *Narrative of the Life of Frederick Douglass* and *Twelve Years a Slave*, it is important to measure the challenges faced by Black authors looking to publish their writings in antebellum America, and to read slave narratives in the literary context of the day, which on the eve of the Civil War tended to favor antislavery novels.

Similarly, we need to have a more nuanced understanding of "who read the slave narratives," to use the title of an important essay by Charles H. Nichols.[12] White middle-class northerners composed only part of the readership for slave narratives. Depending on how they were published and distributed, they could also be read by white southerners, African American men and women of the North and South, and even children.[13] The archive of institutional antislavery offers an intriguing instance of two enslaved men reading a slave narrative and an antislavery novel. In 1837 or 1838, William and Jim ran away after reading the narrative of Charles Ball and Hildreth's *The Slave*. A letter from their enslaver appears in the AASS annual report:

> [D]o you Rember the 2 Books you sent out to my sister by me. My 2 Black boys Wm and Jim who lived better & Easier than I did *Read them* & in consequence *Run* off and after 11 Days Rideing and 267$ cost got them & now their places is made wretched by their own conduct as I sold them (Loossing *near* 900$ in price) to a *Trader*. Thus it is, my friend, . . . yr kind present of Books has done a woefull injury to me and my before good boys & to my own purse.[14]

As the case of William and Jim illustrates, slave narratives were not read serially, even by northerners, but depending on a given narrative being available at a given time. This is why comparisons with standardized genres such as westerns and crime novels are not wholly relevant. Readers of crime novels know exactly what they want and what series or publisher will meet their needs; aficionados generally read such books in abundance. One similar genre, historically closer to the slave narrative, is the dime novel, embodied in the latter half of the nine-teenth century by the publisher Beadle and Adams.[15] Slave narratives never constituted a set of texts as readily identifiable as the dime novel, except for the small group of abolitionists at the intersection of the publishing mechanisms discussed in this book. Rethinking the slave narrative outside the generic box it has tended to be put in can only be beneficial for studying the texts themselves, freeing the scholar up to identify their singularities.

In the final analysis, reading slave narratives through the lens of book his-tory leads to the question: What do we talk about when we talk about the slave narrative? The study of the antebellum slave narrative has long been associated with the study of bound books. When we think of the narratives of Douglass, Brown, and Jacobs, we think of the volumes that these authors produced. Their titles are well known, despite their formulaic character. Partly because of their limited number, separately published slave narratives have proved a more easily apprehensible body of texts than the vaster field of slave testimony. "Although I have not made length of text a criterion for selection or rejection," William L. Andrews states in the opening pages of *To Tell a Free Story: The First Century of Afro-American Autobiography, 1760–1865,* "I shall refer only rarely to black first-person narratives that were published in antislavery periodicals, annuals, or anthologies. . . . For my purposes, only separately published items between 1760 and 1865 qualify for extended comment."[16] Anthologies such as Yuval Taylor's *I Was Born a Slave,* Sterling Lecater Bland Jr.'s *African American Slave Narratives,* and William L. Andrews and Henry Louis Gates Jr.'s *Slave Narratives* prioritize full-fledged autobiographies over the shorter pieces referred to by Andrews.[17] The slave narrative has become a discrete entity whose iterations can be precisely counted: "Whereas four slave narratives appeared in the United States and Britain between 1820 and 1829," Lara Langer Cohen writes, "between 1830 and 1839 that number climbed to nine, and between 1840 and 1849 it shot up to twenty-five (twenty-eight, if we include fictionalized slave narratives)."[18]

Slave narrative criticism might have taken a completely different course. One of the earliest scholars of the slave narrative, Marion Wilson Starling, emphasized the sheer variety of venues in which these testimonies appeared between 1703 and 1944: "They are to be discovered in judicial records, broadsides, private printings, abolitionist newspapers and volumes, scholarly journals, church records, unpublished collections, and a few regular publications."[19] Starling herself, however, focused on book-length slave narratives published during the antebellum period—"the most significant period in the literary history of the slave narratives"—setting a trend that found its most stimulating expression in the scholarship of Andrews, Gates, Frances Smith Foster, and others.

That the bound book should be taken as "the measure of literature," as Gardner puts it, comes as no surprise.[20] Books enjoy a degree of visibility that more ephemeral formats cannot have. Books endure through time. Unless they are destroyed—burned by an oppressive regime or pulped by a disappointed publisher—books usually survive censorship, critical failure, or, in the case of slave narratives, "cultural repression." Although they were virtually ignored for a century, collecting dust on the shelves of libraries and secondhand bookstores, copies of *Narrative of the Life of Frederick Douglass, Narrative of William W. Brown,* and *Incidents in the Life of a Slave Girl* remained intact. Not that they were particularly easy to locate. For those pioneering Black scholars working in the 1940s and 1950s, when African American studies were still a long way from being institutionalized, studying slave narratives meant, first and foremost, searching for long-lost books, as Starling reminds us:

It became necessary to go systematically through the card catalogs of the libraries designated as the most likely depositories of slave literature. Entries under the words "Narrative," "Negro," "Slave," "Slavery," "Autobiography," and "Biography" were checked, because special catalog entries labeled "Slave Narratives" proved to be deceptive. Examination of the actual books and card catalog data revealed numerous errors as well as some exciting discoveries.[21]

Book-length slave narratives offer a more comprehensive view of the enslaved individual's psyche than any other primary source possibly can, as well as a more direct one when they are penned by the formerly enslaved person himself or herself. In contrast, most of the pieces that are to be found in antislavery periodicals, almanacs, and gift books are "as-told-to" narratives with sometimes obscure origins. The "Recollections of Slavery by a Runaway Slave," published as five installments in the *Advocate of Freedom* in the summer of 1838, were transcribed by a person known only as "J.," who then had them sent to the *Advocate* through another individual named "A." The fugitive himself was anonymous. Only through painstaking archival research did literary historian Susanna Ashton manage to establish his identity (his name was Jim), allowing his voice to join the chorus of those who had their narrative printed in what the editor of the *Advocate* called a "permanent form."[22] The "permanent form" of the bound book has proved all the more attractive to critics of the slave narrative as narratives published in book form often provide their readers with representations of African American literacy that illustrate the liberating power of the book. One thinks, among other instances, of twelve-year-old Frederick Bailey poring over *The Columbian Orator* ("Every opportunity I got, I used to read this book"); of Josiah Henson and Henry Bibb being taught to read so that they could decipher the Bible by themselves; of G. W. Offley "learning . . . [his] letters" from a "little primer" in little more than a day.[23]

Within the category of bound books, the narratives that have received the most sustained attention are those which were published as full volumes (usually issued in stiff boards covered in cloth) rather than flimsy pamphlets (issued in printed paper wrappers). While *Slavery in the United States*—one of the most voluminous slave narratives published in the antebellum era—has been commented on by literary scholars and historians alike, notwithstanding the fact that it was heavily tampered with by its amanuensis, the self-authored, sixty-three-page *Life and Sufferings of Leonard Black* (1847) has attracted little critical interest. The availability of all texts, regardless of format, on electronic databases such as Documenting the American South, has only begun to help bring attention to lesser-known slave narratives, some of which may usefully disrupt our notion of how a "classic" slave narrative should read. The nineteen-page narrative by Edmond Kelley, *A Family Redeemed from Bondage; Being Rev. Edmond Kelley (The Author), His Wife, and Four Children* (1851), looks nothing like the works of his more eminent counterparts: it is mostly a patchwork of letters, reports, circulars, and legal documents that is no less a "slave narrative" for all that. The writing of the African American self in the antebellum period did not necessarily follow any preconceived notions of originality and narrative linearity. For Kelley, textual production involved a series of reproductions that did not bar him from claiming the status of author, as the title of his narrative parenthetically indicates. Our postmodern sensibility should make us receptive to such unusual textual configurations. For Kelley, the pamphlet format constituted a cheap way to get into print, as he writes in the introduction.[24] While Black pamphleteering as a genre has been the subject of several insightful works, the importance of the pamphlet format to the history of early African American print culture still needs to be fully recognized and documented.

Conversely, the centrality of the bound book as a vehicle for the diffusion of African American letters might have been overestimated. Book publication alone did not guarantee an author critical and commercial success. The narrative of John Thompson provides a case in point. Unlike Douglass and Brown, who had both traveled on the antislavery lecture circuit for several years before they penned their respective narratives, Thompson was virtually unknown in the abolitionist community when he had his own, self-authored narrative published as *The Life of John Thompson, a Fugitive Slave* (1856) in Worcester, Massachusetts. One of the many early African American figures about whom "little is known" outside of the information given in his autobiography, Thompson seems to have spent most of his time in freedom not campaigning for abolition in the North but working as a steward on a whaling vessel as a way to elude recapture.[25] The narrative ends with a detailed account of his seafaring adventures rather than with his introduction to members of the AASS or his subscription to the *Liberator*. As Andrews notes, "Thompson says nothing about participating in the antislavery movement either publicly or privately."[26] His isolation from what Douglass calls "the anti-slavery world" actually shows in the volume, which has none of the authenticating materials that we have come to expect in narratives of fugitive slaves—no letter from a white abolitionist vouching for the authenticity of the story, no recommendation, no runaway advertisements culled from southern newspapers.[27] Prefaced by Thompson himself, the Black narrative does not come sealed within a white envelope. It was more likely the product of gray interactions that took place outside the pages of the printed book. Because he was so little connected to institutional antislavery and had only recently relocated to Worcester with

his family, Thompson apparently never had an opportunity to meet two Worcester men who could have used their influence to promote his *Life*—printer
Henry J. Howland, who later printed one of the numerous editions of the
narrative of Thomas Jones, and his half-brother Joseph A. Howland, a prominent abolitionist and agent of the MASS.[28] Like Leonard Black before him,
who had gone to the editor of the *New Bedford Mercury* for the printing of his
own *Life*, Thompson went to Charles Hamilton, the printer of the *Worcester
Palladium*. Thompson must have come across one of the advertisements that
Hamilton placed in the *Palladium* in early 1856 and paid for the printing himself, possibly with the help of a few benevolent Black and white friends—those
who, after hearing his story, had suggested to him "to put these facts into
permanent form," as he wrote in the preface to the narrative, unwittingly
echoing the editor of the *Advocate of Freedom*.[29]

Printing the book was one thing; having it promoted and circulated was
another matter entirely. Other than a brief, noncommittal review in the *Liberator*, the antislavery press for the year 1856 is devoid of any reference to *The
Life of John Thompson*. The narrative was not advertised in the local press
either—not even in the *Worcester Palladium*. In all likelihood Thompson peddled copies of his book around the region. He may also have sold them at
some of the local abolitionist events—for instance, the antislavery bazaar that
took place in Worcester in September 1856.[30] The Wisconsin Historical Society collections has the only copy with a traceable mark of ownership I have
been able to locate. It belonged to Joseph L. Hall, a Worcester "laborer" who
perhaps was personally acquainted with Thompson or even worked with
him.[31] In any case, the book supports Joanna Brooks's claim that "books conceived and executed as acts of individual entrepreneurial authorship rarely
succeeded in early African America." According to Brooks, Black books fared
better when they were "adapted to mobility, either through their close association with social movements or their production in highly motile shorter
forms."[32] *The Life of John Thompson* was not closely associated with the abolition movement. Nor was it produced in a "highly motile" shorter form: on the
contrary, Thompson's *Life* asserts its bookishness very emphatically. Two of
the copies I have examined, one located at the American Antiquarian Society,
the other at the New-York Historical Society, are bound in brown cloth with
gold lettering and decorations on the spine and front cover (fig. 13). They are
surprisingly beautiful books, whose appearance seems to be in accord with
what Eugene B. McCarthy and Thomas L. Doughton perceive as the distinctly literary quality of the narrative.[33]

Both form and content must therefore have motivated the decision to republish *The Life of John Thompson* as a Penguin Classic in 2011, alongside such

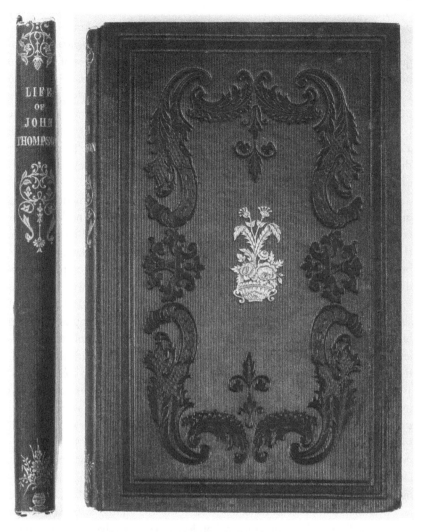

Figure 13. Spine and front cover of *The Life of John Thompson, a Fugitive Slave* (Courtesy of American Antiquarian Society)

canonical titles as *Narrative of the Life of Frederick Douglass*, *Narrative of Sojourner Truth*, and *Incidents in the Life of a Slave Girl*—an unlikely (though much welcome) addition given the book's lack of visibility in the antebellum literary landscape as well as in recent literary criticism. Ironically, the parameters that explain the canonization of the narrative through its inclusion in a "classics" series—notably the fact that it is a book-length slave narrative—are precisely those that account for its "failure" in antebellum America. As the 2013 controversy around the publication of Morrissey's *Autobiography* by Penguin Classics has illustrated, a literary work needs to fit a number of criteria to be recognized by all as a classic.[34] Among other things, a classic is, in Italo Calvino's metaphorical formulation, "a work which constantly generates a pulviscular cloud of critical discourse around it, but which always shakes the particles off."[35] *The Life of John Thompson* is not known to have generated such a cloud. Because it was, to a certain extent, arbitrary, its republication under the Penguin Classics imprint has not resulted in a significant increase in interest for this particular text.

For formerly enslaved men and women in antebellum America, having one's narrative published in book or even pamphlet form was no key to success, if success is to be understood as effective dissemination. Black books in the antebellum era did not circulate well unless they were backed by a white benevolent organization or trade publisher and/or personally and persistently disseminated by the author himself or herself, as Douglass, Brown, Truth, and Jacobs very well knew. In this conclusion, I argue that the political efficacy of slave narratives can best be measured not by the number of copies they sold but by their ability to cross media and genres. Take the example of William and Ellen Craft. Most contemporary readers will be familiar with their narrative as presented in *Running a Thousand Miles for Freedom; or, The Escape of William and Ellen Craft from Slavery* (1860). The book has been reissued twice in the late twentieth century by two leading scholars of African American history (R. J. M. Blackett) and literature (Barbara McCaskill).[36] As a well-known specimen of the genre, it is assumed that *Running a Thousand Miles for Freedom*, like other slave narratives, "went through multiple editions, [was] translated into several European languages, and sold in the tens of thousands"—in other words, that it was popular.[37] In fact, the publication of their book was all but a marginal event in the life and career of the Crafts. *Running a Thousand Miles for Freedom* came out in London in 1860, twelve years after their escape. Despite William Craft's own wishes, it never saw an American edition, apparently because Boston abolitionists did not feel the need to have it reprinted in the United States.[38] Between 1848 and 1860, however, the story of William and Ellen Craft was extensively circulated within the abolitionist mediascape: it was recounted orally at antislavery lectures, conventions, and annual meetings, as well as in private conversations; it appeared in print in newspapers and pamphlets; it was commented on by abolitionists in their correspondence; it was recycled by William Wells Brown in his novel *Clotel* (1853) and by Lydia Maria Child in her play *The Stars and Stripes* (1858); it was illustrated in antislavery almanacs.[39] For American abolitionists, the "slave narrative" of

William and Ellen Craft was the sum of these countless textual, visual, and oral interventions rather than the bound book known as *Running a Thousand Miles for Freedom*. Of course the publication of a self-authored book represented a significant achievement for the Crafts. Blackett suggests that William may have refused to have his story published until he was educated enough to write it himself.[40] Yet the book, which, one reviewer noted, "[did] not contain any facts which had not already been published in another form," was by no means the main channel for the circulation of the Crafts' story.[41] Their narrative can be said to have been truly successful not because it sold in the tens of thousands—it did not—but because it served as a point of reference for abolitionist discourse throughout the 1850s, well before it appeared in book form.

A similar case can be made about Henry Box Brown, whose narrative might well have been the most widely publicized of the antebellum slave narratives. The book itself, written by white abolitionist Charles Stearns and first published in Boston as *Narrative of Henry Box Brown, Who Escaped from Slavery Enclosed in a Box 3 Feet Long and 2 Wide* (1849), was only minimally advertised in the antislavery press. It was neither the main vehicle for the popularization of Brown's story nor the most faithful to the lived experience of the fugitive slave, Stearns's account being "awash with [a] purple prose" that ends up obliterating its subject.[42] What made the transatlantic success of Brown's narrative was its stunning adaptability to all forms and formats. In addition to what has already been mentioned about William and Ellen Craft, the narrative was turned into a children's story in *Cousin Ann's Stories for Children* (1849), a song titled "Escape from Slavery of Henry Box Brown," and a scene in Brown's panorama, the *Mirror of Slavery* (which, incidentally, also included a representation of Ellen Craft disguised as a white man).[43] In Britain, Brown reenacted his escape—he had himself transported in a box from Bradford to Leeds—and in 1857 starred in a play, *The Fugitive Free*, based entirely on his life.[44] As Daphne A. Brooks has argued, "His (auto)biographies, panorama, and public exhibitions, must be considered . . . as concatenate parts that create a sprawling, epic text"—a text so sprawling that it permeated literary genres not strictly associated with antislavery reform such as the city-mysteries novel.[45] Of course William and Ellen Craft and Henry Box Brown are obvious examples of this phenomenon because both their stories revolve around a fundamental trope that is rife with symbolic possibilities—cross-dressing in the case of the Crafts, the box in the case of Brown—and both are therefore eminently suited to all kinds of material transformations. It is no coincidence if their accounts have inspired contemporary novelists (Valerie Martin draws on the story of Ellen Craft in her 2003 novel *Property*) and visual artists (Glenn Ligon reinterprets the escape of Henry Box Brown in his 1993 installation "To Disembark"). But most of the now-canonical slave narratives participated to a certain degree in this economy of reprinting, recirculation, and remediation, as I have shown throughout this book.

This brings us back to one of the fundamental lessons of D. F. McKenzie, the author of *Bibliography and the Sociology of Texts* (1999), who pointed to the importance of loosening the traditional bond in Western literary culture between text and book. "Not all texts are necessarily given in book form," book historian Roger Chartier reminds us in reference to McKenzie, and the "text" of the slave narrative was, in antebellum America, a looser object than suggested by the hefty anthologies now used by students of African American literature.[46] In this sense, slave narratives can be described as "fugitive texts," always liable to be displaced, duplicated, and reincarnated in new forms, following unpredictable trajectories. In October 1842, Lewis Clarke, a fugitive from Kentucky, spoke in Brooklyn to an audience of abolitionists that included Lydia Maria Child; she had learned of the event from her friend Lewis Tappan. A few days later, Child contributed an account of the meeting to the *National Anti-Slavery Standard*, transcribing lengthy passages in the first person, and thereby extending the audience for Clarke's "narrative" beyond a small audience of New York abolitionists to the entire northern readership of the *Standard* and on to other newspapers such as the *Signal of Liberty*, which reprinted extracts from Child's account.[47] One reader of the *Standard* was a young woman living in Concord, Massachusetts. Her name was Helen Thoreau, sister of the famous writer. Helen kept a scrapbook for press clippings from the antislavery publications her family subscribed to. Clarke's account, as retold by Child, caught her eye: she cut it out for her scrapbook.[48] Clarke's "narrative" kept circulating as Helen Thoreau's scrapbook was passed around the members of the Concord Female Anti-Slavery Society; it is easy to imagine the scenes described by Clarke giving rise to a lively discussion among the women of Concord's antislavery community. In the *Standard*, Child wrote, "[Clarke's] discourse . . . *had* no thread, but was as discursive and uncertain as the movements of fallen leaves in the autumn wind." The metaphor is apt: it foreshadows the trajectory of the fugitive's words, swept up in the autumn wind from a Brooklyn meeting hall to the sitting rooms of Concord. This was three years prior to the publication of the *Narrative of the Sufferings of Lewis Clarke*—the "slave narrative" that we read today.

Recent scholarship has emphasized the need to go beyond traditional understandings of the slave narrative. Elizabeth Regosin makes the case for including the African American Civil War Pension Bureau files in the larger body of slave testimony "precisely because they don't fit nicely into the traditional category of African American slave narratives." Writing from the perspective of hemispheric studies, Winfried Siemerling notes that "fully articulated" slave narratives "draw our attention away from other available forms of slave testimony" such as trial documents, committee reports, and so forth; in the Francophone context, Nicholas T. Rinehart likewise argues that, in searching for a French equivalent to the narratives of Douglass or Olaudah Equiano, "we have overlooked forms of testimony produced by slaves and ex-slaves in the New World that do not conform to the generic conventions of the American slave narrative." In his study of freedom suit litigant Polly Wash, Eric Gardner uses court records as a way to "broaden our sense of what might constitute a black story, a black text, a black author, or even a 'slave narrative.'" Like Gardner, Nicole N. Aljoe believes that "definitions of the slave narrative will be most useful if they are sufficiently broad to accommodate the wide variety of styles, forms, and contexts in which the testimonies of slaves have historically appeared." This concerted effort to "think outside the book" has led and will continue to lead to the reemergence of many individual life stories.[49] The slave narrative, however, has always been a more capacious category than what is assumed when we think of it as a series of separately published works. In the absence of a publishing infrastructure that would have facilitated the circulation of Black books in the antebellum period, the stories of formerly enslaved men and women often traveled outside the pages of bound books, in forms that are less easily recoverable today but which might have served them better then. The book often constituted a major incarnation in the material history of a given slave narrative, but book publication per se was not enough for a story to circulate. By reframing the slave narrative as a discursive practice rather than a distinct literary genre with its set of well-defined characteristics—what Gardner terms "the capital-S, capital-N genre of Slave Narratives"—we might not only open up the field of slave testimony to accommodate different kinds of differently told stories, but also better appreciate what "the slave narrative" might have meant to antebellum Americans.[50]

Notes

Introduction

1. John Sekora, "Is the Slave Narrative a Species of Autobiography?," in *Studies in Autobiography*, ed. James Olney (New York: Oxford University Press, 1988), 100.

2. Carla L. Peterson, *"Doers of the Word": African-American Women Speakers and Writers in the North, 1830–1880* (New York: Oxford University Press, 1995), 5.

3. Michael J. Drexler and Ed White, eds., *Beyond Douglass: New Perspectives on African-American Literature* (Lewisburg, PA: Bucknell University Press, 2008); John Ernest, "Beyond Douglass and Jacobs," in *The Cambridge Companion to the African American Slave Narrative*, ed. Audrey Fisch (Cambridge: Cambridge University Press, 2007), 218–31; Deborah Jenson, *Beyond the Slave Narrative: Politics, Sex, and Manuscripts in the Haitian Revolution* (Liverpool: Liverpool University Press, 2011).

4. For a pioneering anthology of writings predating the antebellum slave narrative, see Dorothy Porter, ed., *Early Negro Writing, 1760–1837* (Boston: Beacon Press, 1971).

5. Elizabeth McHenry, *Forgotten Readers: Recovering the Lost History of African American Literary Societies* (Durham, NC: Duke University Press, 2002); Eric Gardner, *Unexpected Places: Relocating Nineteenth-Century African American Literature* (Jackson: University Press of Mississippi, 2009); Lara Langer Cohen and Jordan Alexander Stein, eds., *Early African American Print Culture* (Philadelphia: University of Pennsylvania Press, 2012); George Hutchinson and John K. Young, eds., *Publishing Blackness: Textual Constructions of Race since 1850* (Ann Arbor: University of Michigan Press, 2013); Brigitte Fielder and Jonathan Senchyne, eds., *Against a Sharp White Background: Infrastructures of African American Print* (Madison: University of Wisconsin Press, 2019).

6. Derrick R. Spires, *The Practice of Citizenship: Black Politics and Print Culture in the Early United States* (Philadelphia: University of Pennsylvania Press, 2019), 7.

7. Frances Smith Foster, *Witnessing Slavery: The Development of Ante-bellum Slave Narratives*, 2nd ed. (Madison: University of Wisconsin Press, 1994); Marion Wilson Starling, *The Slave Narrative: Its Place in American History*, 2nd ed. (Washington, DC: Howard University Press, 1988); Charles T. Davis and Henry Louis Gates Jr., eds., *The Slave's Narrative* (Oxford: Oxford University Press, 1985); William L. Andrews, *To Tell a Free Story: The First Century of Afro-American Autobiography, 1760–1865* (Urbana: University of Illinois Press, 1986).

8. Audrey Fisch, introduction to Fisch, *Cambridge Companion*, 1; John Ernest, ed., *The Oxford Handbook of the African American Slave Narrative* (New York: Oxford University Press, 2014).

9. Britt Rusert, "From Black Lit to Black Print: The Return of the Archive in African American Literary Studies," *American Quarterly* 68.4 (2016): 993–1005.

10. Laurence Cossu-Beaumont and Claire Parfait, "Book History and African American Studies," *Transatlantica* 1 (2009), https://journals.openedition.org/transatlantica/4280 ?lang=fr; Teresa A. Goddu, "The Slave Narrative as Material Text," in Ernest, *Oxford Handbook*, 149; Eric Gardner, "Slave Narratives and Archival Research," in Ernest, *Oxford Handbook*, 38. See also Anne Wicke, "Les récits autobiographiques d'esclaves afro-américains: quelques éléments d'histoire éditoriale," in *Figures d'esclaves: Présences, paroles, représentations*, ed. Éric Saunier (Mont-Saint-Aignan: Publications des universités de Rouen et du Havre, 2012), 129–40; Marie-Jeanne Rossignol and Claire Parfait, "William Wells Brown, récits d'esclaves et stratégies d'individuation et de publication," in Saunier, *Figures d'esclaves*, 141–69. I leave out my own essays from this overview.

11. James Green, "The Publishing History of Olaudah Equiano's *Interesting Narrative*," *Slavery and Abolition* 16.3 (1995): 362–75; Vincent Carretta, "'Property of Author': Olaudah Equiano's Place in the History of the Book," in *Genius in Bondage: Literature of the Early Black Atlantic*, ed. Vincent Carretta and Philip Gould (Lexington: University Press of Kentucky, 2001), 130–50; John Bugg, "The Other Interesting Narrative: Olaudah Equiano's Public Book Tour," *PMLA* 121.5 (2006): 1424–42; Akiyo Ito, "Olaudah Equiano and the New York Artisans: The First American Edition of *The Interesting Narrative of the Life of Olaudah Equiano, or Gustavus Vassa, the African*," *Early American Literature* 32.1 (1997): 82–101. Several essays on Abigail Field Mott's 1829 abridgment of Olaudah Equiano's *Interesting Narrative* have also been published recently. See chapter 1, note 167.

12. John Sekora, "Black Message/White Envelope: Genre, Authenticity, and Authority in the Antebellum Slave Narrative," *Callaloo* 32 (1987): 482–515. Although his methodology and conclusions differ from mine, Robert S. Levine does provide essential information about the *Narrative*'s publishing history in *The Lives of Frederick Douglass* (Cambridge, MA: Harvard University Press, 2016), 31–118.

13. Leon Jackson, "The Talking Book and the Talking Book Historian: African American Cultures of Print—The State of the Discipline," *Book History* 13 (2010): 252.

14. Jordan Alexander Stein, "Archive Favor: African American Literature before and after Theory," in *Theory Aside*, ed. Jason Potts and Daniel Stout (Durham, NC: Duke University Press, 2014), 165. On the "reprint revolution" of the late 1960s and Arno Press specifically, see Autumn Womack, "Reprinting the Past/Re-Ordering Black Social Life," *American Literary History* 32.4 (2020): 755–80.

15. Gilbert Osofsky, ed., *Puttin' on Ole Massa: The Slave Narratives of Henry Bibb, William Wells Brown, and Solomon Northup* (New York: Harper & Row, 1969); Arna Bontemps, ed., *Great Slave Narratives* (Boston: Beacon Press, 1969); Robin W. Winks, ed., *Four Fugitive Slave Narratives* (Reading, MA: Addison-Wesley, 1969).

16. William L. Andrews and Henry Louis Gates Jr., eds., *Slave Narratives* (New York: Library of America, 2000).

17. Teresa A. Goddu, *Selling Antislavery: Abolition and Mass Media in Antebellum America* (Philadelphia: University of Pennsylvania Press, 2020), 82.

18. James Olney, "'I Was Born': Slave Narratives, Their Status as Autobiography and as Literature," *Callaloo* 20 (1984): 46.

19. Augusta Rohrbach, "'A Silent Unobtrusive Way': Hannah Crafts and the Literary Marketplace," in *In Search of Hannah Crafts: Critical Essays on The Bondwoman's Narrative*, ed. Henry Louis Gates Jr. and Hollis Robbins (New York: Basic Civitas, 2004), 11; Augusta Rohrbach, *Truth Stranger than Fiction: Race, Realism, and the U.S. Literary Marketplace* (New York: Palgrave, 2002), 35; Robert L. Hall, "Massachusetts Abolitionists Document the Slave Experience," in *Courage and Conscience: Black and White Abolitionists in Boston*, ed. Donald M. Jacobs (Bloomington: Indiana University Press, 1993), 80; Joanne M. Braxton, "Harriet Jacobs' *Incidents in the Life of a Slave Girl*: The Re-Definition of the Slave Narrative Genre," *Massachusetts Review* 27.2 (1986): 382.

20. Meredith L. McGill, "Frances Ellen Watkins Harper and the Circuits of Abolitionist Poetry," in Cohen and Stein, *Early African American Print Culture*, 349n9.

21. James Brewer Stewart, *Holy Warriors: The Abolitionists and American Slavery*, rev. ed. (New York: Hill & Wang, 1997), 142.

22. See Melissa Barton and Brenna Bychowski, "Modeling Black Literature: Behind the Screen with the Black Bibliography Project," in *Ethnic Studies in Academic and Research Libraries*, ed. Raymond Pun, Melissa Cardenas-Dow, and Kenya S. Flash (Chicago: Association of College and Research Libraries, 2021), 217–31.

23. Amy E. Earhart, "An Editorial Turn: Reviving Print and Digital Editing of Black-Authored Literary Texts," in *The Digital Black Atlantic*, ed. Roopika Risam and Kelly Baker Josephs (Minneapolis: University of Minnesota Press, 2021), 44.

24. "Literary Notices," *True Wesleyan*, 7 July 1849.

25. Richard S. Newman, *The Transformation of American Abolitionism: Fighting Slavery in the Early Republic* (Chapel Hill: University of North Carolina Press, 2002); Ira Berlin, *The Long Emancipation: The Demise of Slavery in the United States* (Cambridge, MA: Harvard University Press, 2015); Patrick Rael, *Eighty-Eight Years: The Long Death of Slavery in the United States, 1777–1865* (Athens: University of Georgia Press, 2015); Manisha Sinha, *The Slave's Cause: A History of Abolition* (New Haven, CT: Yale University Press, 2016).

26. Jerry Phillips, "Slave Narratives," in *A Companion to the Literature and Culture of the American South*, ed. Richard Gray and Owen Robinson (Malden, MA: Blackwell, 2004), 44.

27. Henry Louis Gates Jr., ed., *The Classic Slave Narratives* (New York: Penguin, 1987), 3; Stewart, *Holy Warriors*, 142; William L. Andrews, "Slave Narrative," in *The Oxford Companion to African American Literature*, ed. William L. Andrews, Frances Smith Foster, and Trudier Harris (New York: Oxford University Press, 1997), 668.

28. C. Peter Ripley, ed., *The Black Abolitionist Papers*, vol. 3, *The United States, 1830–1846* (Chapel Hill: University of North Carolina Press, 1991), 30–32.

29. Ephraim Peabody, "Narratives of Fugitive Slaves," *Christian Examiner and Religious Miscellany* 47 (1849): 62, 64.

30. Charles H. Nichols, *Many Thousand Gone: The Ex-Slaves' Account of Their Bondage and Freedom* (Leiden: Brill, 1963), xiv; Philip S. Foner, *History of Black Americans*, vol. 2, *From the Emergence of the Cotton Kingdom to the Eve of the Compromise of 1850* (Westport, CT: Greenwood Press, 1983), 457.

31. Sterling Lecater Bland Jr., *Voices of the Fugitives: Runaway Slave Stories and Their Fictions of Self-Creation* (Westport, CT: Greenwood Press, 2000), 43.

32. Foster, *Witnessing Slavery*, 74, 81.

33. Charles T. Davis and Henry Louis Gates Jr., introduction to Davis and Gates, *Slave's Narrative*, xv.

34. Eric Gardner, "Remembered (Black) Readers: Subscribers to the *Christian Recorder*, 1864–1865," *American Literary History* 23.2 (2011): 230.

35. Benjamin Quarles, *Black Abolitionists* (New York: Da Capo Press, 1969).

36. Michaël Roy, "Cheap Editions, Little Books, and Handsome Duodecimos: A Book History Approach to Antebellum Slave Narratives," *MELUS* 40.3 (2015): 85.

37. Erica L. Ball, *To Live an Antislavery Life: Personal Politics and the Antebellum Black Middle Class* (Athens: University of Georgia Press, 2012), 37–61.

38. Mitch Kachun, "Slave Narratives and Historical Memory," in Ernest, *Oxford Handbook*, 22.

Chapter 1. "The General Diffusion of Abolition Light"

1. Manisha Sinha, *The Slave's Cause: A History of Abolition* (New Haven, CT: Yale University Press, 2016), 422.

2. Trish Loughran, *The Republic in Print: Print Culture in the Age of U.S. Nation Building, 1770–1870* (New York: Columbia University Press, 2007), 303–61 (quote at 340); Teresa A. Goddu, *Selling Antislavery: Abolition and Mass Media in Antebellum America* (Philadelphia: University of Pennsylvania Press, 2020), 10–27 (quote at 13).

3. Goddu, *Selling Antislavery*, 1.

4. David Paul Nord, *Faith in Reading: Religious Publishing and the Birth of Mass Media in America* (New York: Oxford University Press, 2004); David Paul Nord, "Benevolent Books: Printing, Religion, and Reform," in *A History of the Book in America*, vol. 2, *An Extensive Republic: Print, Culture, and Society in the New Nation, 1790–1840*, ed. Robert A. Gross and Mary Kelley (Chapel Hill: University of North Carolina Press, 2010), 221–46; Candy Gunther Brown, *The Word in the World: Evangelical Writing, Publishing, and Reading in America, 1789–1880* (Chapel Hill: University of North Carolina Press, 2004).

5. Quoted in Nord, *Faith in Reading*, 38. See also Leon Jackson, "Jedidiah Morse and the Transformation of Print Culture in New England, 1784–1826," *Early American Literature* 34.1 (1999): 2–31.

6. On the U.S. history of stereotyping, see Jeffrey Michael Makala, "Print on Demand: Stereotyping and Electrotyping in the United States Printing Trades and Publishing Industry, 1812–1860" (PhD diss., University of South Carolina, 2018).

7. On the Bible in nineteenth-century America, see Peter J. Wosh, *Spreading the Word: The Bible Business in Nineteenth-Century America* (Ithaca, NY: Cornell University Press, 1994); Paul C. Gutjahr, *An American Bible: A History of the Good Book in the United States, 1777–1880* (Stanford, CA: Stanford University Press, 1999).

8. Scott E. Casper, Jeffrey D. Groves, Stephen W. Nissenbaum, and Michael Winship, eds., *The Industrial Book, 1840–1880*, vol. 3 of *A History of the Book in America* (Chapel Hill: University of North Carolina Press, 2007).

9. Paul J. Polgar, *Standard-Bearers of Equality: America's First Abolition Movement* (Chapel Hill: University of North Carolina Press, 2019), 178, 191.

10. Sinha, *Slave's Cause*, 175, 177, 215.

11. David Turley, *The Culture of English Antislavery, 1780–1860* (London: Routledge, 1991), 48.

12. Richard S. Newman, *The Transformation of American Abolitionism: Fighting Slavery in the Early Republic* (Chapel Hill: University of North Carolina Press, 2002), 180. See pages 89–96 for a discussion of early Black abolitionists' engagement with print culture.

13. For a selection of these pamphlets, see Richard Newman, Patrick Rael, and Phillip Lapsansky, eds., *Pamphlets of Protest: An Anthology of Early African-American Protest Literature, 1790–1860* (New York: Routledge, 2001).

14. Dorothy Porter, introduction to Dorothy Porter, ed., *Early Negro Writing, 1760–1837* (Boston: Beacon Press, 1971), 3.

15. William Hamilton, "An Address to the New York African Society, for Mutual Relief, Delivered in the Universalist Church, January 2, 1809," reprinted in Porter, *Early Negro Writing*, 36–37.

16. Porter, *Early Negro Writing*, 37.

17. Joseph Rezek, "The Orations on the Abolition of the Slave Trade and the Uses of Print in the Early Black Atlantic," *Early American Literature* 45.3 (2010): 670, 673.

18. Peter P. Hinks, *To Awaken My Afflicted Brethren: David Walker and the Problem of Antebellum Slave Resistance* (University Park: Pennsylvania State University Press, 1997), chap. 5. This, at least, is the accepted narrative. See Leon Jackson's forthcoming work on Walker for a revision of this interpretation. On the circulation of the *Appeal*, see also Lori Leavell, "'Not Intended Exclusively for the Slave States': Antebellum Recirculation of David Walker's *Appeal*," *Callaloo* 38.3 (2015): 679–95; on the impact of the *Appeal* on nineteenth-century print-based activism, see Marcy J. Dinius, *The Textual Effects of David Walker's "Appeal": Print-Based Activism against Slavery, Racism, and Discrimination, 1829–1851* (Philadelphia: University of Pennsylvania Press, 2022).

19. "Work for Abolitionists!!," *Liberator*, 15 June 1838.

20. Robert Fanuzzi, *Abolition's Public Sphere* (Minneapolis: University of Minnesota Press, 2003), xii.

21. "Advice," *Liberator*, 26 March 1831.

22. "The Walker Meetings," *North Star*, 4 February 1848; Angelina E. Grimké, *Letters to Catherine E. Beecher, in Reply to an Essay on Slavery and Abolitionism, Addressed to A. E. Grimké* (Boston: Isaac Knapp, 1838), 35.

23. *The Rev. J. W. Loguen, as a Slave and as a Freeman: A Narrative of Real Life* (Syracuse, NY: J. G. K. Truair, 1859), 360.

24. "We shall circulate, unsparingly and extensively, anti-slavery tracts and periodicals." William Lloyd Garrison, "Declaration of Sentiments of the American Anti-Slavery Convention," in *Selections from the Writings and Speeches of William Lloyd Garrison* (Boston: R. F. Wallcut, 1852), 71.

25. On the Great Postal Campaign, see, for instance, Bertram Wyatt-Brown, *Lewis Tappan and the Evangelical War against Slavery* (Baton Rouge: Louisiana State University Press, 1997), chap. 8. For a still useful overview of the AASS's print culture and organizational strategies, see Janet Wilson, "The Early Anti-Slavery Propaganda," *More Books: The Bulletin of the Boston Public Library* 19.9 (1944): 343–60.

26. Richard R. John, *Spreading the News: The American Postal System from Franklin to Morse* (Cambridge, MA: Harvard University Press, 1995), chap. 7.

27. "We shall organize Anti-Slavery Societies, if possible, in every city, town and village of our land. We shall send forth agents to lift up the voice of remonstrance, of warning, of entreaty, and of rebuke." Garrison, "Declaration of Sentiments," 70–71.

28. "'Please Read and Circulate,'" *Friend of Man*, 16 February 1841.

29. "Anti-Slavery Depository," *Emancipator*, 17 May 1838; "Philadelphia Anti-Slavery Depository," *Emancipator*, 28 June 1838.

30. Teresa A. Goddu, "The Antislavery Almanac and the Discourse of Numeracy," *Book History* 12 (2009): 145–48; Goddu, *Selling Antislavery*, 23–25.

31. "Light for the People," *Nantucket Inquirer*, 13 January 1841, quoted in Lloyd Pratt, "Speech, Print, and Reform on Nantucket," in Casper, Groves, Nissenbaum, and Winship, *Industrial Book*, 395–96.

32. Scholarship on antebellum reform movements is abundant. See, for instance, Ronald G. Walters, *American Reformers, 1815–1860*, rev. ed. (New York: Hill & Wang, 1997); Lori D. Ginzberg, *Women in Antebellum Reform* (Wheeling, IL: Harlan Davidson, 2000).

33. Teresa A. Goddu, "Reform," in *The Oxford History of Popular Print Culture*, vol. 5, *US Popular Print Culture to 1860*, ed. Ronald J. Zboray and Mary Saracino Zboray (Oxford: Oxford University Press, 2019), 597.

34. "'Please Read and Circulate.'"

35. "Our Publications," *Emancipator*, 22 March 1838.

36. Several authors have started looking into the publication history of *Narrative of James Williams*. See Lara Langer Cohen, *The Fabrication of American Literature: Fraudulence and Antebellum Print Culture* (Pennsylvania: University of Philadelphia Press, 2012), chap. 3; Goddu, *Selling Antislavery*, chap. 3. For bibliographical approaches to the narrative, see Thomas Franklin Currier, *A Bibliography of John Greenleaf Whittier* (Cambridge, MA: Harvard University Press, 1937), 32–39; Michael Winship, ed., *Bibliography of American Literature*, vol. 9, *Edward Noyes Westcott to Elinor Wylie* (New Haven, CT: Yale University Press, 1991), 115–16, 198, 212, 236.

37. Minutes of the executive committee of the American Anti-Slavery Society, 4 January 1838, 21, Boston Public Library (hereafter cited as Minutes).

38. The following details are drawn from Hank Trent's introduction to *Narrative of James Williams, an American Slave*, ed. Hank Trent (Baton Rouge: Louisiana State University Press, 2013), ix–xlviii, which "confirms Williams was an actual enslaved man in Virginia and Alabama and that most of the slaveholders he mentioned existed" (x).

39. Tappan kept a journal in which he carefully pasted clippings about the *Narrative*. Lewis Tappan Papers, Journals and Notebooks, 159, 164–65, 177, Library of Congress, Washington, DC (hereafter LOC).

40. "'The Slave: or Memoirs of Archy Moore,'" *Emancipator*, 8 March 1838; Minutes, 21 December 1837, 19; 4 January 1838, 24; 18 January 1838, 26. Xiomara Santamarina places the *Narrative of James Williams* within the context of the publication of *The Slave* and makes the case for reading Williams's narrative "as an authentic fiction, rather than as an inauthentic biography." Xiomara Santamarina, "Fugitive Slave, Fugitive Novelist: The *Narrative of James Williams* (1838)," *American Literary History* 31.1 (2019): 24–46 (quote at 27).

41. "Political Hints," *Liberator*, 23 March 1838.

42. See Edward Wagenknecht, *John Greenleaf Whittier: A Portrait in Paradox* (New York: Oxford University Press, 1967).

43. Quoted in Nord, *Faith in Reading*, 119.

44. "Alabama Beacon versus James Williams," *Emancipator,* 30 August 1838, emphasis added.

45. "Interesting Narrative," *Liberator,* 2 February 1838.

46. Letter from Theodore D. Weld to James G. Birney, 12 January 1838, in *Letters of James Gillespie Birney, 1831–1857,* ed. Dwight L. Dumond (New York: Appleton-Century, 1938), 1:446.

47. "James Williams—The Fugitive Slave," *Emancipator,* 25 January 1838.

48. *Emancipator,* 8 February 1838; letter from Theodore D. Weld to James G. Birney, 5 February 1838, in Dumond, *Letters,* 1:451.

49. On Reason's work, see Aston Gonzalez, *Visualizing Equality: African American Rights and Visual Culture in the Nineteenth Century* (Chapel Hill: University of North Carolina Press, 2020), 37–78.

50. "Political Hints."

51. Gonzalez, *Visualizing Equality,* 54.

52. Trent, *Narrative of James Williams,* 12, 13.

53. Robert B. Stepto, *From behind the Veil: A Study of Afro-American Narrative* (Urbana: University of Illinois Press, 1979), 7.

54. Minutes, 15 February 1838, 38; 5 April 1838, 47; 21 June 1838, 76; 20 September 1838, 95.

55. "Narrative of James Williams," *Liberator,* 9 March 1838; "Narrative of James Williams," *Zion's Herald,* 21 March 1838.

56. "In the Press," *Emancipator,* 12 April 1838.

57. "James Williams in Every Family," *Emancipator,* 12 April 1838. According to his own count, Delavan "financed the publication and distribution of more than 36 million antiliquor tracts and periodicals." W. J. Rorabaugh, "Delavan, Edward Cornelius," *American National Biography Online,* https://www.anb.org/view/10.1093/anb/978019 8606697.001.0001/anb-9780198606697-e-1500171.

58. Minutes, 5 April 1838, 47.

59. John, *Spreading the News,* 262.

60. "Conflagration Extra!!," *Emancipator,* 15 November 1838.

61. "From the Far South," *Advocate of Freedom,* 7 June 1838.

62. *New York Commercial Advertiser,* 26 September 1838. Birney wrote elsewhere that "in the slave States" the Williams narrative "had some, though a limited circulation." "Alabama Beacon versus James Williams."

63. "Narrative of James Williams," *Zion's Watchman,* 8 September 1838.

64. "Extract from the Narrative of James Williams," *Liberator,* 16 March 1838; "Extract from the Narrative of James Williams," *Hampshire Gazette,* 28 March 1838.

65. *Emancipator,* 26 July 1838; *Friend of Man,* 11 July 1838. We can infer from the number of copies and how much they cost that it was the cheap edition that was being disseminated in Utica.

66. "Work for Abolitionists!!"; *American Anti-Slavery Almanac, for 1839* (New York: American Anti-Slavery Society, 1838), front and back matter.

67. "Depository of the Ohio A. S. Society," *Philanthropist,* 22 May 1838.

68. "Narrative of James Williams," *Philanthropist,* 22 May 1838.

69. "In the Press," *Emancipator,* 12 April 1838; "Letters from the Editor. No. I," *Friend of Man,* 11 July 1838; "Onondaga Co. Meeting," *Friend of Man,* 25 July 1838.

70. David Paul Nord, "Free Grace, Free Books, Free Riders: The Economics of Religious Publishing in Early Nineteenth-Century America," in *Religion, Media, and the Marketplace*, ed. Lynn Schofield Clark (New Brunswick, NJ: Rutgers University Press, 2007), 38.

71. "A Plan of Distribution," *Emancipator*, 14 June 1838.

72. "Onondaga Co. Meeting."

73. "Alabama Beacon versus James Williams"; "Tricks of Abolitionism," *New York Commercial Advertiser*, 19 September 1838.

74. Leon Jackson, *The Business of Letters: Authorial Economies in Antebellum America* (Stanford, CA: Stanford University Press, 2008), 120–26.

75. *Emancipator*, 5 April 1838.

76. "Alabama Beacon versus James Williams."

77. Quoted in "Alabama Beacon versus James Williams."

78. Letter from Lydia Maria Child to Angelina Grimké, 26 December 1838, in *Letters of Theodore Dwight Weld, Angelina Grimké Weld and Sarah Grimké, 1822–1844*, ed. Gilbert H. Barnes and Dwight L. Dumond (Gloucester: Peter Smith, 1965), 2:732.

79. Letter from Lydia Maria Child to Theodore D. Weld, 29 December 1838, in Barnes and Dumond, *Letters*, 2:735–36.

80. "James Williams," *Emancipator*, 16 August 1838.

81. Minutes, 16 August 1838, 92–93.

82. Lewis Tappan Papers, Journals and Notebooks, 256, LOC.

83. Minutes, 20 September 1838, 95.

84. Minutes, 18 October 1838, 101.

85. "James Williams," *Emancipator*, 25 October 1838.

86. Both *Emancipation in the West Indies* and the Birney/Elmore *Correspondence*, for instance, were for sale at the Wesleyan Book Concern a decade later. "Wesleyan Book Concern," *True Wesleyan*, 10 February 1849.

87. *Philanthropist*, 21 May 1839; *Liberator*, 8 January 1841.

88. "Narrative of James Williams," *African Repository, and Colonial Journal* 15 (1839): 161.

89. "Narrative of Moses Roper," *Liberator*, 30 March 1838.

90. *A Narrative of the Adventures and Escape of Moses Roper, from American Slavery*, 3rd ed. (London: Harvey & Darton, 1839), xii.

91. See, for instance, Theodore Parker, *A Letter to the People of the United States Touching the Matter of Slavery* (Boston: James Munroe & Company, 1848), 34.

92. On *American Slavery as It Is*, see Loughran, *Republic in Print*, 354–59; Ellen Gruber Garvey, "'*facts* and FACTS': Abolitionists' Database Innovations," in *"Raw Data" Is an Oxymoron*, ed. Lisa Gitelman (Cambridge, MA: MIT Press, 2013), 89–102; Julia Bernier, "'Testimony of a Thousand Witnesses': Abolitionist Archives," paper presented at the forty-first annual meeting of the Society for Historians of the Early American Republic, Cambridge, MA, 18–21 July 2019.

93. *American Slavery as It Is: Testimony of a Thousand Witnesses* (New York: American Anti-Slavery Society, 1839), iv.

94. Goddu, *Selling Antislavery*, 73.

95. Letter from Theodore D. Weld to Sarah and Angelina Grimké, 5 January 1838, in Barnes and Dumond, *Letters*, 2:512.

96. Most of these letters are held at the John Jay Homestead State Historic Site (hereafter JJH) in Katonah, New York. My thanks to Allan Weinreb for allowing me access to them, and to David N. Gellman for sending me the text of his paper cited below, which led me to this correspondence.

97. *Slavery in the United States: A Narrative of the Life and Adventures of Charles Ball, a Black Man* (Lewistown, PA: Printed and Published by John W. Shugert, 1836), 400.

98. *History of that Part of the Susquehanna and Juniata Valleys, Embraced in the Counties of Mifflin, Juniata, Perry, Union and Snyder, in the Commonwealth of Pennsylvania* (Philadelphia: Everts, Peck & Richards, 1886), 1:509; *History of Venango County, Pennsylvania* (Chicago: Brown, Runk, 1890), 245–47.

99. *Slavery in the United States* (1836), iii.

100. J. Simpson Africa, *History of Huntingdon and Blair Counties, Pennsylvania* (Philadelphia: Louis H. Everts, 1883), 81.

101. "Prospectus," *Colored American*, 10 February 1838; Minutes, 14 November 1838, 108–9.

102. *Emancipator*, 23 March 1837.

103. Letter from Isaac Fisher to Elizur Wright, 20 October 1837, Elizur Wright Papers, Correspondence, box 4, LOC.

104. Louis P. Masur, *1831: Year of Eclipse* (New York: Hill & Wang, 2001), 57.

105. *Slavery in the United States* (1836), iii–iv, iii, iv.

106. *Emancipator*, 23 March 1837.

107. J. Gerald Kennedy, *Strange Nation: Literary Nationalism and Cultural Conflict in the Age of Poe* (New York: Oxford University Press, 2016), 296.

108. Kennedy, *Strange Nation*, 293.

109. *Slavery in the United States* (1836), 286–87; Trent, *Narrative of James Williams*, 41.

110. Several scholars have pointed out the "encyclopedic" dimension of Ball's narrative. See, for instance, William L. Andrews, *To Tell a Free Story: The First Century of Afro-American Autobiography, 1760–1865* (Urbana: University of Illinois Press, 1986), 84; Christine Levecq, *Slavery and Sentiment: The Politics of Feeling in Black Atlantic Antislavery Writing, 1770–1850* (Durham: University of New Hampshire Press, 2008), 206.

111. Letter from Isaac Fisher to Elizur Wright, 17 July 1836, JJH. See also the introduction to the New York edition: "The author states, in a private communication, that many of the anecdotes in the book illustrative of southern society, were not obtained from Ball, but from other and creditable sources." *Slavery in the United States: A Narrative of the Life and Adventures of Charles Ball, a Black Man* (New York: John S. Taylor, 1837), ii.

112. *Slavery in the United States* (1836), 211, 223.

113. *Slavery in the United States* (1836), 5.

114. "The Life and Adventures of a Fugitive Slave," *Quarterly Anti-Slavery Magazine* 1 (1836): 377.

115. "Prospectus of a New Work, Entitled Slavery in the United States," *Liberator*, 29 August 1835.

116. *Slavery in the United States* (1836), iii.

117. "Prospectus," *Liberator*.

118. *Slavery in the United States* (1836), 116–22, 249–59, 289–96.

119. See, for instance, *A Narrative of the Adventures and Escape of Moses Roper, from American Slavery*, 3rd ed. (London: Harvey & Darton, 1839), 185–93.

120. Scott E. Casper, "Other Variations on the Trade," in Casper, Groves, Nissenbaum, and Winship, *Industrial Book*, 219–22.

121. "Prospectus of a New Work, Entitled Slavery in the United States," *Lewistown Republican and Working Men's Advocate*, 6 October 1835, 3 March 1836.

122. "Prospectus," *Liberator*.

123. Letter from Isaac Fisher to Elizur Wright, 17 July 1836, JJH.

124. *Emancipator*, 23 March 1837.

125. Africa, *History*, 81.

126. Yuval Taylor, ed., *I Was Born a Slave: An Anthology of Classic Slave Narratives* (Chicago: Lawrence Hill, 1999), 1:260; Marion Wilson Starling, *The Slave Narrative: Its Place in American History*, 2nd ed. (Washington, DC: Howard University Press, 1988), 227.

127. "Life and Adventures," 375–93.

128. Nina Baym, *Novels, Readers, and Reviewers: Responses to Fiction in Antebellum America* (Ithaca, NY: Cornell University Press, 1984), 19.

129. "The Life and Adventures of a Fugitive Slave," *Zion's Watchman*, 14 September 1836; "The Life and Adventures of a Fugitive Slave," *Philanthropist*, 14 October 1836; Meredith L. McGill, *American Literature and the Culture of Reprinting, 1834–1853* (Philadelphia: University of Pennsylvania Press, 2003).

130. "A Slave Execution," *Anti-Slavery Record* 2 (1836): 149.

131. "Just Printed," *Lewistown Republican and Working Men's Advocate*, 26 April 1836.

132. Ronald J. Zboray, *A Fictive People: Antebellum Economic Development and the American Reading Public* (New York: Oxford University Press, 1993), 11.

133. "Prospectus," *Liberator*.

134. Letter from Isaac Fisher to William Jay, 30 October 1836, JJH.

135. Charles L. Blockson, *The Underground Railroad in Pennsylvania* (Quantico, VA: Flame International, 1981), 104–5; Forest K. Fisher, *It Happened in Mifflin County: American History with a Central Pennsylvania Connection* (Lewistown, PA: Mifflin County Historical Society, 2009), 189–92. This episode concerns a man named Richard Barnes, Ball's "adopted name" according to Blockson.

136. *History of Venango County*, 246–47.

137. "Life and Adventures," 375.

138. *Third Annual Report of the American Anti-Slavery Society* (New York: Printed by William S. Dorr, 1836), 35.

139. Michael Winship, *American Literary Publishing in the Mid-Nineteenth Century: The Business of Ticknor and Fields* (Cambridge: Cambridge University Press, 1995), 40.

140. "We own no press," James G. Birney wrote in 1838. "Our publications are all printed by contract." *Correspondence, between the Hon. F. H. Elmore, One of the South Carolina Delegation in Congress, and James G. Birney, One of the Secretaries of the American Anti-Slavery Society* (New York: American Anti-Slavery Society, 1838), 18.

141. Minutes, 15 February 1838, 38.

142. Lewis Tappan Papers, Journals and Notebooks, 22, LOC.

143. On the Jay family and slavery, see David N. Gellman, *Liberty's Chain: Slavery, Abolition, and the Jay Family of New York* (Ithaca, NY: Cornell University Press, 2022).

144. In light of what has been emphasized before, it is telling that Jay should have written "as if you were an overseer" rather than "as if you were a slave" and compared the book to a romance. Letter from William Jay to Gerrit Smith, 13 September 1836, JJH.

145. John S. Taylor, "Prospectus of the Cabinet of Freedom," in Thomas Clarkson, *The History of the Rise, Progress, and Accomplishment of the Abolition of the African Slave-Trade by the British Parliament* (New York: John S. Taylor, 1836), 1:2.

146. See Phillip Lapsansky, "Graphic Discord: Abolitionist and Antiabolitionist Images," in *The Abolitionist Sisterhood: Women's Political Culture in Antebellum America*, ed. Jean Fagan Yellin and John C. Van Horne (Ithaca, NY: Cornell University Press, 1994), 203–7; Marcus Wood, *Blind Memory: Visual Representations of Slavery in England and America, 1780–1865* (Manchester: Manchester University Press, 2000), 21–23.

147. "Life and Adventures," 393.

148. Letter from William Jay to Lewis Tappan, 25 March 1837, JJH.

149. *Slavery in the United States* (1837), i.

150. Letter from Isaac Fisher to William Jay, 30 October 1836, JJH.

151. Letter from William Jay to Isaac Fisher, 24 November 1836, JJH.

152. Goddu, *Selling Antislavery*, 180.

153. David N. Gellman, "Abolitionism Makes Strange Bedfellows: George Bush, Gerrit Smith, William Jay, Charles Ball, and Thomas Clarkson in the *Cabinet of Freedom*," paper presented at the thirty-first annual meeting of the Society for Historians of the Early American Republic, Springfield, IL, 16–20 July 2009.

154. "New Books," *Philanthropist*, 12 May 1837; "Books, Pamphlets, Prints," *Liberator*, 8 January 1841; "Anti-Slavery Publications," *Emancipator*, 11 January 1838; "Catalogue," *Pennsylvania Freeman*, 15 January 1846.

155. "Anti-Slavery Library," *New London Gazette and General Advertiser*, 27 June 1838.

156. "Narrative of Charles Ball," *Emancipator*, 15 June 1837.

157. Minutes, 21 June 1838, 76.

158. Letter from Isaac Fisher to William Jay, 30 October 1836, JJH.

159. *Advocate of Freedom*, 26 April, 10 May, 24 May, 21 June, 5 July 1838.

160. "Fiendish Torture," *Liberator*, 2 June 1837; "Narrative of Charles Ball, Who Lived Forty Years as a Slave in Maryland, South Carolina, and Georgia," *Zion's Watchman*, 1 April 1837; "Execution of Two Slaves," *Zion's Herald*, 28 June 1837.

161. *Salem Gazette*, 25 July 1837; *Plaindealer* 1 (1837): 459–62.

162. Teresa A. Goddu, "The Slave Narrative as Material Text," in *The Oxford Handbook of the African American Slave Narrative*, ed. John Ernest (New York: Oxford University Press, 2014), 160.

163. La Roy Sunderland, *Anti-Slavery Manual, Containing a Collection of Facts and Arguments on American Slavery*, 2nd ed. (New York: Printed by S. W. Benedict, 1837), 66–77; *Interesting Memoirs and Documents Relating to American Slavery, and the Glorious Struggle Now Making for Complete Emancipation* (London: Chapman, Brothers, 1846), 264–73.

164. *American Anti-Slavery Almanac, for 1838* (Boston: Isaac Knapp, 1837), 13. For an analysis of this image, see Martha J. Cutter, *The Illustrated Slave: Empathy, Graphic*

Narrative, and the Visual Culture of the Transatlantic Abolition Movement, 1800–1852 (Athens: University of Georgia Press, 2017), 122–23.

165. *Chains and Freedom: or, The Life and Adventures of Peter Wheeler, a Colored Man Yet Living* (New York: E. S. Arnold, 1839), 18.

166. See introduction.

167. James Green, "The Publishing History of Olaudah Equiano's *Interesting Narrative*," *Slavery and Abolition* 16.3 (1995): 372. See also Martha Cutter, "The Child's Illustrated Antislavery Talking Book: Abigail Field Mott's Abridgment of Olaudah Equiano's *Interesting Narrative* for African American Children," in *Who Writes for Black Children? African American Children's Literature before 1900*, ed. Katharine Capshaw and Anna Mae Duane (Minneapolis: University of Minnesota Press, 2017), 117–44; Valentina K. Tikoff, "A Role Model for African American Children: Abigail Field Mott's *Life and Adventures of Olaudah Equiano* and White Northern Abolitionism," in Capshaw and Duane, *Who Writes for Black Children?*, 94–116; Eric D. Lamore, "Olaudah Equiano in the United States: Abigail's Mott 1829 Abridged Edition of the *Interesting Narrative*," in *Reading African American Autobiography: Twenty-First Century Contexts and Criticism*, ed. Eric D. Lamore (Madison: University of Wisconsin Press, 2017), 66–88.

168. "Intellect of Colored Men," *Anti-Slavery Record* 3 (1837): 136.

169. "Gustavus Vassa," *National Enquirer and Constitutional Advocate of Universal Liberty*, 20 July 1837.

170. *Meditations from the Pen of Mrs. Maria W. Stewart* (Washington, DC: Enterprise Publishing Company, 1879), 6. See Marilyn Richardson, ed., *Maria W. Stewart, America's First Black Woman Political Writer: Essays and Speeches* (Bloomington: Indiana University Press, 1987), xix–xx.

171. Max Cavitch, "The Poetry of Phillis Wheatley in Slavery's Recollective Economies, 1773 to the Present," in *Race, Ethnicity and Publishing in America*, ed. Cécile Cottenet (Basingstoke, UK: Palgrave Macmillan, 2014), 216.

172. Joseph Rezek, "The Print Atlantic: Phillis Wheatley, Ignatius Sancho, and the Cultural Significance of the Book," in *Early African American Print Culture*, ed. Lara Langer Cohen and Jordan Alexander Stein (Philadelphia: University of Pennsylvania Press, 2012), 25.

173. Ezra Greenspan, *William Wells Brown: An African American Life* (New York: W. W. Norton, 2014), 273.

174. Lois Brown, "Memorial Narratives of African Women in Antebellum New England," *Legacy* 20.1/2 (2003): 51; Catherine Adams and Elizabeth H. Pleck, *Love of Freedom: Black Women in Colonial and Revolutionary New England* (Oxford: Oxford University Press, 2010), 72–73.

175. Starling, *Slave Narrative*, 210.

176. Susan Paul, *Memoir of James Jackson, the Attentive and Obedient Scholar, Who Died in Boston, October 31, 1833, Aged Six Years and Eleven Months*, ed. Lois Brown (Cambridge, MA: Harvard University Press, 2000), 67. See also Deborah C. De Rosa, *Domestic Abolitionism and Juvenile Literature, 1830–1865* (Albany: State University of New York Press, 2003), 25.

177. *Memoir of Mrs. Chloe Spear* (Boston: James Loring, 1832), 103.

178. See, for example, *Liberator*, 27 July 1833.

179. *Liberator*, 12 May 1832; "Memoir of Chloe Spear," *Liberator*, 26 May 1832; "Literary Notices," *American Baptist Magazine* 12 (1832): 245.

180. On the abolitionists' "juvenile wing," see Sinha, *Slave's Cause*, 254–56.

181. Jackson, *Business of Letters*, 9–52.

182. *Memoir of Mrs. Chloe Spear*, iii.

183. "Catalogue of Publications," *Pennsylvania Freeman*, 21 November 1839; "New Books, for Sale by Isaac Knapp," *Liberator*, 30 June 1837; "The New London Anti-Slavery Library," *New London Gazette and General Advertiser*, 8 January 1840.

184. On Grimes's narrative, see Bryan Sinche, "Self-Publication, Self-Promotion, and the *Life of William Grimes, the Runaway Slave*," *Biography* 42.4 (2019): 825–45.

185. *Chains and Freedom: or, The Life and Adventures of Peter Wheeler, a Colored Man Yet Living. A Slave in Chains, a Sailor on the Deep, and a Sinner at the Cross*, ed. Graham Russell Gao Hodges (Tuscaloosa: University of Alabama Press, 2009), 3.

186. See, for example, Lester's lengthy note on the ACS. *Chains and Freedom* (1839), 85–89.

187. John Nerone, *Violence against the Press: Policing the Public Sphere in U.S. History* (New York: Oxford University Press, 1994), 88.

188. Unwanted copies could be used "for insulation, doll stuffing, wrapping paper, kindling, and a host of other household purposes." Eric Gardner, *Black Print Unbound: The Christian Recorder, African American Literature, and Periodical Culture* (New York: Oxford University Press, 2015), 28. On unsolicited literature, see James Raven, ed., *Free Print and Non-Commercial Publishing since 1700* (Aldershot: Ashgate, 2000).

189. Leah Price, *How to Do Things with Books in Victorian Britain* (Princeton, NJ: Princeton University Press, 2012), 7.

190. *Chains and Freedom* (2009), 2.

191. "Catalogue of Publications," *Pennsylvania Freeman*, 14 November 1839; *Hartford Daily Courant*, 3 February 1840; *Liberator*, 25 December 1840.

192. See, for example, "New Books," *Philanthropist*, 17 July 1838; "Catalogue of Publications," *Pennsylvania Freeman*, 26 December 1839; *Liberator*, 8 January 1841. On Roper in Britain, see Hannah-Rose Murray, *Advocates of Freedom: African American Transatlantic Abolitionism in the British Isles* (Cambridge: Cambridge University Press, 2020), 48–80.

Chapter 2. "My Narrative Is Just Published"

1. Nell Irvin Painter, review of *William Wells Brown: An African American Life*, by Ezra Greenspan, *New York Times*, 14 November 2014.

2. "A Coloured Woman's Interview with a Doctor of Divinity," *National Anti-Slavery Standard*, 29 October 1853.

3. See Manisha Sinha, *The Slave's Cause: A History of Abolition* (New Haven, CT: Yale University Press, 2016), 256–65.

4. Teresa A. Goddu, *Selling Antislavery: Abolition and Mass Media in Antebellum America* (Philadelphia: University of Pennsylvania Press, 2020), 12; Merton L. Dillon, *The Abolitionists: The Growth of a Dissenting Minority* (DeKalb: Northern Illinois University Press, 1974), 126. See also Ronald G. Walters, *The Antislavery Appeal: American Abolitionism after 1830* (Baltimore: Johns Hopkins University Press, 1976), 3–6.

5. Quoted in Henry Mayer, *All on Fire: William Lloyd Garrison and the Abolition of Slavery* (New York: St. Martin's, 1998), 366.

6. Stacey M. Robertson, *Hearts Beating for Liberty: Women Abolitionists in the Old Northwest* (Chapel Hill: University of North Carolina Press, 2010), 127–60.

7. Stanley Harrold, *The Abolitionists and the South, 1831–1861* (Lexington: University Press of Kentucky, 1995), 93.

8. *National Anti-Slavery Standard*, 20 August 1853.

9. *Proceedings of the American Anti-Slavery Society, at Its Second Decade* (New York: American Anti-Slavery Society, 1854), 11–12.

10. See Joseph Barker, "Prospectus," in *Interesting Memoirs and Documents Relating to American Slavery, and the Glorious Struggle Now Making for Complete Emancipation* (London: Chapman, Brothers, 1846), 1–4.

11. *Annual Reports of the American Anti-Slavery Society, by the Executive Committee, for the Year Ending May 1, 1857, and May 1, 1858* (New York: American Anti-Slavery Society, 1859), 189–91. See also Benjamin Quarles, *Black Mosaic: Essays in Afro-American History and Historiography* (Amherst: University of Massachusetts Press, 1988), 70.

12. "The Anti-Slavery Tracts," *Liberator*, 16 March 1855.

13. "Anti-Slavery Tracts," *National Anti-Slavery Standard*, 14 July 1855.

14. Faye E. Dudden, *Fighting Chance: The Struggle over Woman Suffrage and Black Suffrage in Reconstruction America* (Oxford: Oxford University Press, 2011), 23.

15. "Letter from William Goodell," *Liberator*, 21 October 1853.

16. *Sixteenth Annual Report, Presented to the Massachusetts Anti-Slavery Society* (Boston: Printed by Andrews & Prentiss, 1848), 48; letter from Samuel May Jr. to John B. Estlin, 29 April 1850, Rare Books and Manuscripts Department, Boston Public Library (hereafter BPL).

17. Stanley Harrold, *The Abolitionists and the South, 1831–1861* (Lexington: University Press of Kentucky, 1995), 68–69. On the iconography of the branded hand, see Marcus Wood, *Blind Memory: Visual Representations of Slavery in England and America, 1780–1865* (Manchester: Manchester University Press, 2000), 246–50.

18. *Liberator*, 20 February 1846.

19. "Letter from Jonathan Walker," *National Anti-Slavery Standard*, 25 March 1847. Walker also published an undated pamphlet for young readers titled *A Picture of Slavery, for Youth*.

20. "The Fair," *North Star*, 4 February 1848.

21. Harrold, *Abolitionists and the South*, 70; Josephine F. Pacheco, *The Pearl: A Failed Slave Escape on the Potomac* (Chapel Hill: University of North Carolina Press, 2005), 53, 238; "Captain Drayton," *Liberator*, 30 December 1853.

22. Israel Campbell, *An Autobiography. Bond and Free: or, Yearnings for Freedom, from My Green Brier House. Being the Story of My Life in Bondage and My Life in Freedom* (Philadelphia: Published by the Author, 1861), vi; *The Narrative of Lunsford Lane, Formerly of Raleigh, N.C.* (Boston: Printed for the Publisher, 1842), iii.

23. *Liberator*, 12 September 1845.

24. *The Branded Hand: Trial and Imprisonment of Jonathan Walker, at Pensacola, Florida, for Aiding Slaves to Escape from Bondage* (Boston: Published at the Anti-Slavery Office, 1845), v.

25. J. Noel Heermance, *William Wells Brown and Clotelle; A Portrait of the Artist in the First Negro Novel* (Hamden, CT: Archon Books, 1969), 114.

26. Mechal Sobel, "The Revolution in Selves: Black and White Inner Aliens," in *Through a Glass Darkly: Reflections on Personal Identity in Early America*, ed. Ronald Hoffman, Mechal Sobel, and Fredrika J. Teute (Chapel Hill: University of North Carolina Press, 1997), 167.

27. Ann Fabian, *The Unvarnished Truth: Personal Narratives in Nineteenth-Century America* (Berkeley: University of California Press, 2000), 2, 132; Karen A. Weyler, *Empowering Words: Outsiders and Authorship in Early America* (Athens: University of Georgia Press, 2013).

28. Sobel, "Revolution in Selves," 167.

29. John W. Crowley, ed., *Drunkard's Progress: Narratives of Addiction, Despair, and Recovery* (Baltimore: Johns Hopkins University Press, 1999), 3–4.

30. "The Life Insurance," *Massachusetts Spy*, 6 January 1847.

31. *Chains and Freedom: or, The Life and Adventures of Peter Wheeler, a Colored Man Yet Living* (New York: E. S. Arnold, 1839), v; William Wells Brown, *Clotel; or, The President's Daughter* (London: Partridge & Oakey, 1853), chap. 23; Josiah Henson, *Truth Stranger than Fiction: Father Henson's Story of His Own Life* (Boston: John P. Jewett, 1858).

32. *Narrative of Charles T. Woodman, a Reformed Inebriate* (Boston: Theodore Abbot, 1843), v, vi; Gregory P. Lampe, *Frederick Douglass: Freedom's Voice, 1818–1845* (East Lansing: Michigan State University Press, 1998), 313.

33. John W. Crowley, "Slaves to the Bottle: Gough's *Autobiography* and Douglass's *Narrative*," in *The Serpent in the Cup: Temperance in American Literature*, ed. David S. Reynolds and Debra J. Rosenthal (Amherst: University of Massachusetts Press, 1997), 121. See also Erica L. Ball, "Temperance," in *Frederick Douglass in Context*, ed. Michaël Roy (Cambridge: Cambridge University Press, 2021), 162–71.

34. *The Rev. J. W. Loguen, as a Slave and as a Freeman: A Narrative of Real Life* (Syracuse, NY: J. G. K. Truair, 1859), 93–94.

35. Larry Gara, "The Professional Fugitive in the Abolition Movement," *Wisconsin Magazine of History* 48 (1965): 196–204.

36. Donald M. Scott, "Print and the Public Lecture System, 1840–1860," in *Printing and Society in Early America*, ed. William L. Joyce, David D. Hall, Richard D. Brown, and John B. Hench (Worcester, MA: American Antiquarian Society, 1983), 280. See also Donald M. Scott, "Itinerant Lecturers and Lecturing in New England, 1800–1850," in *Itinerancy in New England and New York*, ed. Peter Benes and Jane Montague Benes (Boston: Boston University, 1986), 65–75.

37. Eric Gardner, *Black Print Unbound: The Christian Recorder, African American Literature, and Periodical Culture* (New York: Oxford University Press, 2015), 111.

38. Rhondda Robinson Thomas, "Locating Slave Narratives," in *The Oxford Handbook of the African American Slave Narrative*, ed. John Ernest (New York: Oxford University Press, 2014), 329–35; William L. Andrews, ed., *North Carolina Slave Narratives: The Lives of Moses Roper, Lunsford Lane, Moses Grandy, and Thomas H. Jones* (Chapel Hill: University of North Carolina Press, 2003). For other slave narrative anthologies that focus on specific locales, see Arna Bontemps, ed., *Five Black Lives* (Middletown, CT: Wesleyan University Press, 1971); Eugene B. McCarthy and Thomas L.

Doughton, eds., *From Bondage to Belonging: The Worcester Slave Narratives* (Amherst: University of Massachusetts Press, 2007); Susanna Ashton, ed., *I Belong to South Carolina: South Carolina Slave Narratives* (Columbia: University of South Carolina Press, 2010).

39. C. Peter Ripley, ed., *The Black Abolitionist Papers*, vol. 2, *Canada, 1830–1865* (Chapel Hill: University of North Carolina Press, 1986), 135n4.

40. Harriet E. Wilson, *Our Nig; or, Sketches from the Life of a Free Black* (Boston: Printed by Geo. C. Rand & Avery, 1859), iii, 137.

41. Eric Gardner, "'This Attempt of Their Sister': Harriet Wilson's *Our Nig* from Printer to Readers," *New England Quarterly* 66 (1993): 226–46; Eric Gardner, "Of Bottles and Books: Reconsidering the Readers of Harriet Wilson's *Our Nig*," in *Harriet Wilson's New England: Race, Writing, and Region*, ed. JerriAnne Boggis, Eva Allegra Raimon and Barbara A. White (Durham: University of New Hampshire Press, 2007), 3–26. See also the introduction to Harriet E. Wilson, *Our Nig; or, Sketches from the Life of a Free Black*, ed. P. Gabrielle Foreman and Reginald H. Pitts (New York: Penguin, 2009).

42. *Pennsylvania Freeman*, 15 June 1854. On the 1848 publication of the *Narrative* in Paris, see Michaël Roy, "'Throwing Pearls before Swine': The Strange Publication History of *Vie de Frédéric Douglass, esclave américain* (1848)," *Slavery and Abolition* 40.4 (2019): 727–49.

43. William S. McFeely, *Frederick Douglass* (New York: W. W. Norton, 1991), 115.

44. Gerald Fulkerson, "Textual Introduction," in *The Frederick Douglass Papers*, ser. 2, *Autobiographical Writings*, vol. 1, *Narrative*, ed. John W. Blassingame, John R. Mc-Kivigan, and Peter P. Hinks (New Haven, CT: Yale University Press, 1999), 90–91 (hereafter cited as *FDP* 2, 1:90–91).

45. Frederick Douglass, "The Folly of Our Opponents," *Liberty Bell*, ed. Maria Weston Chapman (Boston: Massachusetts Anti-Slavery Fair, 1845), 166.

46. *Fourteenth Annual Report Presented to the Massachusetts Anti-Slavery Society* (Boston: Printed by Scarlett & Laing, 1846), 50–51.

47. Lampe, *Frederick Douglass*, 261, 305; *Narrative of the Life of Frederick Douglass, an American Slave* (Boston: Published at the Anti-Slavery Office, 1845), 30. See also David W. Blight, *Frederick Douglass: Prophet of Freedom* (New York: Simon & Schuster, 2018), 137.

48. Letter from Wendell Phillips to Elizabeth Pease, 24 February 1845, BPL.

49. Lampe, *Frederick Douglass*, 263, 305–6.

50. *Narrative of the Life of Frederick Douglass, an American Slave* (Boston, 1845), xv.

51. Robert S. Levine, *The Lives of Frederick Douglass* (Cambridge, MA: Harvard University Press, 2016), 41.

52. *Narrative of the Life of Frederick Douglass, an American Slave* (Boston, 1845), viii.

53. Letter from Frederick Douglass to Maria Weston Chapman, 27 October 1844, in *FDP* 3, 1:43.

54. Letter from Lydia Maria Child to Louisa Loring, 22 June 1845, in *Lydia Maria Child: Selected Letters, 1817–1880*, ed. Milton Meltzer and Patricia G. Holland (Amherst: University of Massachusetts Press, 1982), 223.

55. Margaret Fuller, review of *Narrative of the Life of Frederick Douglass*, *New York Daily Tribune*, 10 June 1845. On Fuller's review, see Steven Mailloux, "Misreading as a

Historical Act: Cultural Rhetoric, Bible Politics, and Fuller's 1845 Review of Douglass's *Narrative*," in *Readers in History: Nineteenth-Century American Literature and the Contexts of Response*, ed. James L. Machor (Baltimore: Johns Hopkins University Press, 1993), 3–31; Dwight A. McBride, *Impossible Witnesses: Truth, Abolitionism, and Slave Testimony* (New York: New York University Press, 2001), 75–78.

56. Beth A. McCoy, "Race and the (Para)Textual Condition," *PMLA* 121 (2006): 161.

57. McCoy, "Race and the (Para)Textual Condition," 161.

58. Governing Documents and Records of the New England Anti-Slavery Society, BPL; *Fourteenth Annual Report*, 44.

59. Mayer, *All on Fire*, 350. See also Levine, *Lives of Frederick Douglass*, 46.

60. "Letter from William Goodell."

61. "Narrative of Frederick Douglass," *Liberator*, 20 June 1845, emphasis added.

62. *Narrative of the Life of Frederick Douglass* (Boston, 1845), xv; Frederick Douglass, *My Bondage and My Freedom* (New York: Miller, Orton & Mulligan, 1855), 362–63.

63. The names of Dow and Jackson appear on several copies of what appears to be the "cheap edition" of *Narrative of the Life of Frederick Douglass*, including an 1845 copy held at the Massachusetts Historical Society ("DOW & JACKSON'S Anti-Slavery Press") and an 1847 copy held at the New-York Historical Society ("Dow & Jackson, Printers"). As successors to *Liberator* publisher Isaac Knapp, Dow & Jackson had printed, among other works, several annual reports of the MASS (*Liberator*, 7 August 1840). That Dow & Jackson printed the very first edition of Douglass's narrative remains to be ascertained.

64. Robert S. Levine makes a diametrically opposed argument. Douglass's *Narrative*, he writes, "was in some respects a commodity coming more from Garrison's Anti-Slavery Office than from Douglass himself." Levine compares the Boston edition of the *Narrative* to later editions published in Dublin, showing how Douglass "took back" the *Narrative* from the hands of white abolitionist sponsors. I place the *Narrative* within the context of slave narratives published before (notably *Narrative of James Williams*) and after—hence our differing perspectives. Levine, *Lives of Frederick Douglass*, 31–74 (quote at 74).

65. Lampe, *Frederick Douglass*, 276, 277.

66. Raymond Williams, *The Sociology of Culture* (Chicago: University of Chicago Press, 1995), 44–45.

67. Leon Jackson, *The Business of Letters: Authorial Economies in Antebellum America* (Stanford, CA: Stanford University Press, 2008), 9–52.

68. *National Anti-Slavery Standard*, 19 June 1845; "The National Anti-Slavery Bazaar," *Liberator*, 19 December 1845; "Anti-Slavery Books," *Anti-Slavery Bugle*, 26 March 1847; *Albany Evening Journal*, 12 June 1845; letter from Mary E. Miles to Maria Weston Chapman, 3 December 1845, BPL; "Books on Capital Punishment, &c.," *Liberator*, 11 September 1846; "Books," *Liberator*, 24 May 1850; *New York Evangelist*, 26 June 1845; "Anti-Slavery Books," *Anti-Slavery Bugle*, 8 September 1849.

69. "The Boston Olive Branch," *Liberator*, 2 January 1846.

70. Letter from Samuel May Jr. to Mary Carpenter, 28 August 1845, BPL; letter from John B. Estlin to Samuel May Jr., 1 November 1845, BPL.

71. Jackson, *Business of Letters*, 2.

72. "Fourth Edition," *Liberator*, 2 January 1846.

73. Letter from Henry W. Williams to Stephen S. Foster, 27 February 1846, Abigail Kelley Foster Papers, American Antiquarian Society, Worcester, MA (hereafter AKFP).

74. See Benjamin Fagan, "Journalism," in Roy, *Frederick Douglass in Context*, 108–20.

75. "Book Repository," *National Anti-Slavery Standard*, 5 July 1849.

76. *Oration, Delivered in Corinthian Hall, Rochester, by Frederick Douglass, July 5th, 1852* (Rochester, NY: Printed by Lee, Mann, 1852), 36. On Douglass's "philosophical and tactical about-face," see Waldo E. Martin Jr., *The Mind of Frederick Douglass* (Chapel Hill: University of North Carolina Press, 1984), 31–38 (quote at 31); on the print history of the oration, see Lori Leavell, "The Anticipatory Print Life of Frederick Douglass's July Fourth Speech (1852)," in *Critical Insights: Frederick Douglass*, ed. Jericho Williams (Ipswich, MA: Salem Press, 2020), 105–119.

77. Letters from Henry W. Williams to Stephen S. Foster, 4 August 1845, 27 February 1846, AKFP.

78. Letter from Abby Kelley Foster to Stephen S. Foster, 9 August 1851, AKFP.

79. On the writing of Phillips's two pamphlets and Abby Kelley Foster's growing estrangement from Douglass, see Dorothy Sterling, *Ahead of Her Time: Abby Kelley and the Politics of Antislavery* (New York: W. W. Norton, 1991), 191, 273–75.

80. On Black abolitionists and antislavery factionalism, see Benjamin Quarles, *Black Abolitionists* (New York: Da Capo Press, 1969), 42–47; C. Peter Ripley, ed., *The Black Abolitionist Papers*, vol. 3, *The United States, 1830–1846* (Chapel Hill: University of North Carolina Press, 1991), 22–23.

81. "Slavery in Virginia—Rev. J. C. Bacon," *New York Evangelist*, 19 July 1849. See also "The Destroyer in Our Midst!," *Richmond Enquirer*, 27 April 1849.

82. Harrold, *Abolitionists and the South*, 101.

83. Dickson D. Bruce Jr., *The Origins of African American Literature, 1680–1865* (Charlottesville: University Press of Virginia, 2001), 247.

84. *National Anti-Slavery Standard*, 23 December 1847.

85. "Incendiarism," *National Anti-Slavery Standard*, 28 January 1848.

86. *Extracts from the Narrative of Frederick Douglass* (Philadelphia: n.p., ca. 1845), 32. The Historic Society of Pennsylvania holds a copy.

87. On the eve of the Civil War, 91.7 percent of Delaware's and 49.1 percent of Maryland's Black population was free. Peter Kolchin, *American Slavery, 1619–1877*, rev. ed. (New York: Hill & Wang, 2003), 82.

88. "Falsehood Refuted," *Liberator*, 12 December 1845.

89. Letter from Mary Grew to Maria Weston Chapman, 25 February 1846, BPL.

90. "Gleams of Light," *Liberator*, 26 September 1845.

91. Christopher Phillips, *Freedom's Port: The African American Community of Baltimore, 1790–1860* (Urbana: University of Illinois Press, 1997), 27. On Douglass's time in Baltimore, see Lawrence Jackson, "Baltimore," in Roy, *Frederick Douglass in Context*, 9–20.

92. Dickson J. Preston, *Young Frederick Douglass: The Maryland Years* (Baltimore: Johns Hopkins University Press, 2018), 197.

93. On Douglass's exploitation of print culture in Britain more generally, see Hannah-Rose Murray, *Advocates of Freedom: African American Transatlantic Abolitionism in the British Isles* (Cambridge: Cambridge University Press, 2020), 123–62.

94. "Anti-Slavery Meeting in Belfast," *Northern Whig*, 9 December 1845, in *Frederick Douglass and Ireland: In His Own Words*, ed. Christine Kinealy (Abingdon: Routledge, 2018), 1:254; letter from Frederick Douglass to William Lloyd Garrison, 1 September 1845, in *FDP* 3, 1:48. Douglass refers to South Carolina planter James Henry Hammond's *Two Letters on Slavery in the United States, Addressed to Thomas Clarkson, Esq.* (1845).

95. See Blight, *Frederick Douglass*, 140–42; Levine, *Lives of Frederick Douglass*, 78–84.

96. On the Irish editions of the *Narrative*, see Patricia J. Ferreira, "Frederick Douglass in Ireland: The Dublin Edition of His *Narrative*," *New Hibernia Review* 5.1 (2001): 53–67; Fionnghuala Sweeney, *Frederick Douglass and the Atlantic World* (Liverpool: Liverpool University Press, 2007), 13–36; Tom Chaffin, *Giant's Causeway: Frederick Douglass's Irish Odyssey and the Making of an American Visionary* (Charlottesville: University of Virginia Press, 2014); Levine, *Lives of Frederick Douglass*, 75–118.

97. Letter from George Thompson to Richard D. Webb, 12 August 1845, in *British and American Abolitionists: An Episode in Transatlantic Understanding*, ed. Clare Taylor (Edinburgh: Edinburgh University Press, 1974), 237.

98. Jennifer Regan-Lefebvre, "The Webb Family and Quaker Printing," in *The Oxford History of the Irish Book*, vol. 4, *The Irish Book in English, 1800–1891*, ed. James H. Murphy (Oxford: Oxford University Press, 2011), 122–23. See also Richard S. Harrison, *Richard Davis Webb: Dublin Quaker Printer (1805–72)* (Skibbereen: Brendan Lyons, 1993).

99. "The Anti-Slavery Advocate," *Liberator*, 22 October 1852.

100. "From Richard D. Webb," *Liberator*, 24 October 1845.

101. Letter from Richard D. Webb to Elizabeth Pease, 25 September 1845, BPL.

102. Letter from Frederick Douglass to William Lloyd Garrison, 29 September 1845, in *FDP* 3, 1:58.

103. *American Slavery: Report of a Public Meeting Held at Finsbury Chapel, Moorfields, to Receive Frederick Douglass, the American Slave, on Friday, May 22, 1846* (London: Printed by Christopher B. Christian, 1846), 16.

104. Letter from Frederick Douglass to Richard D. Webb, 6 December 1845, in *FDP* 3, 1:69–70.

105. Letter from William Lloyd Garrison to Richard D. Webb, 12 September 1846, in *The Letters of William Lloyd Garrison*, vol. 3, *No Union with Slaveholders, 1841–1849*, ed. Walter M. Merrill (Cambridge, MA: Belknap Press of Harvard University Press, 1973), 409.

106. Letter from Frederick Douglass to Francis Jackson, 29 January 1846, in *FDP* 3, 1:90.

107. Letter from Richard D. Webb to Elizabeth Pease, 7 October 1845, BPL.

108. John B. Estlin, "Frederick Douglass, the Fugitive Slave," *National Anti-Slavery Standard*, 5 March 1846.

109. On the Estlins, see letter from John B. Estlin to Samuel May Jr., 2 April 1846, BPL; letter from Mary Anne Estlin to Maria Weston Chapman, 1 March 1846, BPL. On the Jenningses, see "Letter from Richard D. Webb," *Liberator*, 26 December 1845.

110. Letter from John B. Estlin to Samuel May Jr., 29 January–1 February 1846, BPL.

111. Letter from Frederick Douglass to Richard D. Webb, 24 December 1845, in *FDP* 3, 1:71.

112. Fulkerson, "Textual Introduction," 88–89.

113. Letter from Richard D. Webb to "My dear friend," 8 July 1849, BPL.

114. Fulkerson mentions the Somers & Isaac edition, but I have been unable to locate a copy. Fulkerson, "Textual Introduction," 89.

115. Audrey A. Fisch, *American Slaves in Victorian England: Abolitionist Politics in Popular Literature and Culture* (Cambridge: Cambridge University Press, 2000), 11–32. On the history of copyright law in the nineteenth century, see Meredith L. McGill, "Copyright," in *The Industrial Book, 1840–1880*, vol. 3 of *A History of the Book in America*, ed. Scott E. Casper, Jeffrey D. Groves, Stephen W. Nissenbaum, and Michael Winship (Chapel Hill: University of North Carolina Press, 2007), 158–78.

116. Letter from Richard D. Webb to Maria Weston Chapman, 16 September 1845, BPL.

117. Letter from Richard D. Webb to Maria Weston Chapman, 30 September 1845, BPL.

118. Letter from Richard D. Webb to Maria Weston Chapman, 16 May 1846, BPL.

119. Letter from Richard D. Webb to Maria Weston Chapman, 26 February 1846, BPL.

120. Letter from John B. Estlin to Samuel May Jr., 29 January–1 February 1846, BPL. See also letter from John B. Estlin to Samuel May Jr., 15 April 1846, BPL.

121. Letter from Frederick Douglass to Richard D. Webb, mid-January 1846, in *FDP* 3, 1:79.

122. Julia Sun-Joo Lee, *The American Slave Narrative and the Victorian Novel* (New York: Oxford University Press, 2010), 3, 4. On author portraits in slave narratives, see also Marcus Wood, "The Slave Narrative and Visual Culture," in Ernest, *Oxford Handbook*, 198–203.

123. Levine, *Lives of Frederick Douglass*, 87. Or, in Colum McCann's novelistic retelling of the episode: "Webb, he thought, had endeavoured to make him look straight-nosed, aquiline, clear-jawed. They wanted to remove the Negro from him." Colum McCann, *TransAtlantic* (London: Bloomsbury, 2013), 46.

124. Letter from Frederick Douglass to Richard D. Webb, 10 February 1846, in *FDP* 3, 1:93.

125. Letter from Richard D. Webb to Henry Clarke Wright, 22 February 1846, Henry Clarke Wright Papers, Houghton Library, Cambridge, MA.

126. Frederick Douglass, review of *A Tribute for the Negro*, by Wilson Armistead, *North Star*, 7 April 1849.

127. John Stauffer, Zoe Trodd, and Celeste-Marie Bernier, *Picturing Frederick Douglass: An Illustrated Biography of the Nineteenth Century's Most Photographed American* (New York: Liveright, 2015), xi–xii.

128. Letter from Richard D. Webb to Maria Weston Chapman, 26 February 1846, BPL.

129. Letter from Frederick Douglass to Richard D. Webb, mid-January 1846, in *FDP* 3, 1:79.

130. Letter from Frederick Douglass to Richard D. Webb, 24 December 1845, in *FDP* 3, 1:71.

131. On Douglass's epistolary practices in Britain and Ireland, see Fionnghuala Sweeney, "Correspondence," in Roy, *Frederick Douglass in Context*, 318–28.

132. Letter from Richard D. Webb to Edmund Quincy, 2 February 1846, in Taylor, *British and American Abolitionists*, 250.

133. Levine, *Lives of Frederick Douglass*, 89.

134. Frances Smith Foster, "Harriet Jacobs's *Incidents* and the 'Careless Daughters' (and Sons) Who Read It," in *The (Other) American Traditions: Nineteenth-Century Women Writers*, ed. Joyce W. Warren (New Brunswick, NJ: Rutgers University Press, 1993), 95.

135. *Narrative of the Life of Frederick Douglass* (Boston, 1845), 62.

136. Letter from John B. Estlin to Richard D. Webb, 5 November 1845, BPL. This letter was clearly written to Webb, not to "James Otis," as indicated in the BPL card catalog.

137. Fisch, *American Slaves in Victorian England*, 1–4.

138. Letter from John B. Estlin to Samuel May Jr., 10 November 1845, BPL.

139. Letter from Samuel May Jr. to John B. Estlin, 29 December 1845, BPL; *Branded Hand*, 27.

140. Letter from John B. Estlin to Richard D. Webb, 13 November 1845, BPL.

141. Letter from John B. Estlin to Samuel May Jr., 29 January–1 February 1846, BPL.

142. *Narrative of the Life of Frederick Douglass, an American Slave* (Dublin: Webb & Chapman, 1845), 62–63.

143. *Narrative of the Life of Frederick Douglass, an American Slave* (Dublin: Webb & Chapman, 1846), 62–63.

144. In *My Bondage and My Freedom*, Douglass calls Caroline a "powerful woman." Douglass, *My Bondage and My Freedom*, 245.

145. Douglass, *My Bondage and My Freedom*, 218.

146. Letter from John B. Estlin to Samuel May Jr., 2 April 1846, BPL.

147. Douglass, *My Bondage and My Freedom*, 218.

148. Douglass, *My Bondage and My Freedom*, 245. For a comparative analysis of the fight against Covey in *Narrative* and *Bondage*, see Robert S. Levine, "Autobiography," in Roy, *Frederick Douglass in Context*, 91.

149. Letter from Richard D. Webb to Edmund Quincy, 2 February 1846, in Taylor, *British and American Abolitionists*, 250; letters from Richard D. Webb to Maria Weston Chapman, 12 October 1845, 26 February 1846, BPL.

150. Letter from Richard D. Webb to Elizabeth Pease, 7 October 1845, BPL.

151. See, for instance, letter from Frederick Douglass to Richard D. Webb, 20 April 1846, BPL.

152. Letter from Frederick Douglass to Richard D. Webb, 26 April 1846, in *FDP* 3, 1:116; letter from Richard D. Webb to Maria Weston Chapman, 16 May 1846, BPL.

153. Letter from Wendell Phillips to Elizabeth Pease, 29 August 1847, BPL. See also letter from Edmund Quincy to Samuel May Jr., 25 February 1846, BPL.

154. *Life and Times of Frederick Douglass* (Boston: De Wolfe & Fiske, 1892), 318.

155. *American Slavery*, 21.

156. Sarah Meer, *Uncle Tom Mania: Slavery, Minstrelsy, and Transatlantic Culture in the 1850s* (Athens: University of Georgia Press, 2005), 4. The phrase "international bestseller" appears in numerous discussions of the *Narrative*. See, for instance, John Stauffer, "Douglass's Self-Making and the Culture of Abolitionism," in *The Cambridge Companion*

to Frederick Douglass, ed. Maurice S. Lee (Cambridge: Cambridge University Press, 2009), 19; Lampe, *Frederick Douglass*, 269; William L. Andrews, "Slave Narrative," in *The Oxford Companion to African American Literature*, ed. William L. Andrews, Frances Smith Foster and Trudier Harris (New York: Oxford University Press, 1997), 668.

157. Henry Louis Gates Jr., ed., *The Classic Slave Narratives* (New York: Penguin, 1987), 7.

158. See Elizabeth McHenry, *Forgotten Readers: Recovering the Lost History of African American Literary Societies* (Durham, NC: Duke University Press, 2002), 118–23; Julia Lee, "Intertextuality," in Roy, *Frederick Douglass in Context*, 329–39. For a specific example of a slave narrator (Aaron) quoting from the work of another slave narrator (Moses Grandy), see *The Light and Truth of Slavery: Aaron's History* (Worcester, MA: Printed for Aaron), 47–48.

159. Letter from Richard D. Webb to "My dear friend," 3 August 1849, BPL.

160. Letter from Edmund Quincy to Caroline Weston, 2 July 1847, BPL.

161. *Narrative of William W. Brown, a Fugitive Slave* (Boston: Published at the Anti-Slavery Office, 1847), v.

162. Letter from Edmund Quincy to Caroline Weston, 2 July 1847, BPL. See also Quincy Family Papers, Journal of Edmund Quincy, 1 July 1847, Massachusetts Historical Society, Boston.

163. *Le Récit de William Wells Brown, esclave fugitif, écrit par lui-même*, trans. and ed. Claire Parfait and Marie-Jeanne Rossignol (Mont-Saint-Aignan: Publications des universités de Rouen et du Havre, 2012), 29.

164. Letters from Samuel May Jr. to John B. Estlin, 15 December 1847, 13 January 1848, BPL.

165. Greenspan, *William Wells Brown*, 150.

166. Letter from Oliver Johnson to Maria Weston Chapman, 15 October 1844, BPL.

167. Greenspan, *William Wells Brown*, 152.

168. Greenspan, *William Wells Brown*, 151.

169. "Narrative of W. W. Brown," *Anti-Slavery Bugle*, 6 August 1847.

170. "W. W. Brown in Upton," *Liberator*, 17 September 1847.

171. "William W. Brown," *Liberator*, 31 March 1848.

172. Michelle Cooper, "The Dissemination of the *Narrative of William W. Brown, a Fugitive Slave*," unpublished essay, 2003, 9. I thank Leon Jackson for sending me a copy of this essay.

173. "New Books," *Liberator*, 29 September 1847; "Book Depository," *National Anti-Slavery Standard*, 5 July 1849; "Anti-Slavery Books," *Anti-Slavery Bugle*, 1 October 1847; "Books!," *Liberator*, 11 February 1848; *Prisoner's Friend*, 11 August 1847.

174. *National Anti-Slavery Standard*, 9 December 1847; "Essex County Anti-Slavery Society," *Liberator*, 15 October 1847; George Adams, *The Massachusetts Business Directory, for the Year 1856* (Boston: George Adams, 1856), 73.

175. "Anti-Slavery Books," *Morning Star*, 20 February 1850.

176. *Narrative of William W. Brown, a Fugitive Slave*, 2nd ed. (Boston: Published at the Anti-Slavery Office, 1848), iv; *Liberator*, 11 February 1848; *Narrative of William W. Brown, a Fugitive Slave*, 3rd ed. (Boston: Published at the Anti-Slavery Office, 1848), iv.

177. Letter from Samuel May Jr. to John B. Estlin, 15 December 1847, BPL.

178. Lara Langer Cohen, "Notes from the State of Saint Domingue: The Practice of Citation in *Clotel*," in *Early African American Print Culture*, ed. Lara Langer Cohen and Jordan Alexander Stein (Philadelphia: University of Pennsylvania Press, 2012), 164. See also John Ernest, *Resistance and Reformation in Nineteenth-Century African-American Literature: Brown, Wilson, Jacobs, Delany, Douglass, and Harper* (Jackson: University Press of Mississippi, 1995), 24.

179. *Liberator*, 20 October 1848; *Narrative of William W. Brown, a Fugitive Slave*, 4th ed. (Boston: Bela Marsh, 1849), iv.

180. *Liberator*, 1 June 1849.

181. *Narrative of William W. Brown* (Boston, 1849), iv.

182. "Social Reform Bookstore," *Liberator*, 30 May 1845; "Books," *Liberator*, 24 May 1850; "Henry Box Brown," *National Anti-Slavery Standard*, 20 September 1849.

183. Massachusetts, vol. 68, 231, R. G. Dun & Co. Credit Report Volumes, Baker Library, Harvard Business School, Cambridge, MA (hereafter HBS).

184. Christopher Mulvey, ed., *"Clotel" by William Wells Brown: An Electronic Scholarly Edition*, 2006, http://rotunda.upress.virginia.edu/clotel/. See also Samantha Marie Sommers, "A Tangled Text: William Wells Brown's *Clotel* (1853, 1860, 1864, 1867)" (BA thesis, Wesleyan University, 2009).

185. Levine, *Lives of Frederick Douglass*, 77.

186. *Récit de William Wells Brown*, 36.

187. Letter from Samuel May Jr. to John B. Estlin, 7 March 1848, BPL; letters from William Lloyd Garrison to Elizabeth Pease, 20 June 1849, 17 July 1849, in Merrill, *Letters of William Lloyd Garrison*, 3:626, 637.

188. Letter from William Lloyd Garrison to Elizabeth Pease, 17 July 1849, in Merrill, *Letters of William Lloyd Garrison*, 3:638.

189. Jeffrey Michael Makala, "Print on Demand: Stereotyping and Electrotyping in the United States Printing Trades and Publishing Industry, 1812–1860" (PhD diss., University of South Carolina, 2018), 217. See also Jonathan Senchyne, "Bottles of Ink, Reams of Paper: *Clotel*, Racialization, and the Material Culture of Print," in Cohen and Stein, *Early African American Print Culture*, 140–42.

190. Letter from Richard D. Webb to "My dear friend," 3 August 1849, BPL.

191. Greenspan, *William Wells Brown*, 192–93, 204, 208–12.

192. Men's Bill Book of a Dublin Printing Office, 1846–1850, 131–32, National Library of Ireland, Dublin.

193. *Narrative of William W. Brown, an American Slave* (London: Charles Gilpin, 1849), 167, 168.

194. *Narrative of the Life of Frederick Douglass* (Dublin, 1845), iii.

195. *Narrative of William W. Brown* (London, 1849), iii.

196. Geoffrey Sanborn, *Plagiarama! Williams Wells Brown and the Aesthetic of Attractions* (New York: Columbia University Press, 2016), 17.

197. "The Late Mr. Charles Gilpin, M.P.," *Times*, 9 September 1874.

198. Greenspan, *William Wells Brown*, 217.

199. The third edition of Pennington's *The Fugitive Blacksmith* lists *Narrative of the Life of Frederick Douglass* as "just published." A copy of Douglass's *Narrative* with Gilpin's name on the title page remains to be located.

200. "New Works," *Publishers' Circular*, 1 September 1849, 294.

201. William Wells Brown, *Three Years in Europe; or, Places I Have Seen and People I Have Met* (London: Charles Gilpin, 1852), 110.

202. Greenspan, *William Wells Brown*, 225–26.

203. Letter from William Lloyd Garrison to Elizabeth Pease, 17 July 1849, in Merrill, *Letters of William Lloyd Garrison*, 3:637–38.

204. Brown, *Three Years in Europe*, 110–16 (quote at 113).

205. Letter from Samuel May Jr. to John B. Estlin, 28 February–9 March 1853, BPL.

206. *Liberator*, 3 September 1847; *Leicester Chronicle*, 16 August 1851.

207. *Liberator*, 25 February 1848; Greenspan, *William Wells Brown*, 279–80.

208. *Eclectic Review* 4, November 1852, 617.

209. Greenspan, *William Wells Brown*, 148.

210. "New Work by William W. Brown," *Liberator*, 3 February 1854.

211. *Sketches of Places and People Abroad* is the subtitle of an expanded version of *Three Years in Europe* published in the United States (*The American Fugitive in Europe: Sketches of Places and People Abroad*, 1855). *Miralda; or, The Beautiful Quadroon* refers to one of the editions of *Clotel*.

212. William Edward Farrison, *William Wells Brown: Author and Reformer* (Chicago: University of Chicago Press, 1969), 314.

213. Greenspan, *William Wells Brown*, 272–73.

214. *Liberator*, 15 February 1850; "Book Repository," *National Anti-Slavery Standard*, 23 May 1850.

215. Letter from Stephen S. Foster to Abby Kelley Foster, 5 August 1850, AKFP.

216. Letter from Stephen S. Foster to Abby Kelley Foster, 27 July 1851, AKFP.

217. *Narrative of William W. Brown* (Boston, 1847), 19–20.

218. Josephine Brown, *Biography of an American Bondman, by His Daughter* (Boston: R. F. Wallcut, 1856), 9.

219. Geoffrey Sanborn, "The Plagiarist's Craft: Fugitivity and Theatricality in *Running a Thousand Miles for Freedom*," *PMLA* 128 (2013): 920n1.

220. Lara Langer Cohen, "Notes from the State of Saint Domingue: The Practice of Citation in *Clotel*," in Cohen and Stein, *Early African American Print Culture*, 163; John Ernest, *Chaotic Justice: Rethinking African American Literary History* (Chapel Hill: University of North Carolina Press, 2009), 76. The slave trader's real name was William Walker.

221. "Recent Deaths," *Boston Evening Transcript*, 8 November 1884.

222. James Finley, "'The Land of Liberty': Henry Bibb's Free Soil Geographies," *ESQ: A Journal of the American Renaissance* 59 (2013): 232.

223. Letter from Wendell Phillips to Elizabeth Pease, 11 February 1848, BPL.

224. Letter from Henry Bibb to Gerrit Smith, 30 December 1848, Gerrit Smith Papers, Syracuse University. All quotes are given with the original spelling and punctuation.

225. AFASS Minute Book, 9 May 1849, 31, Amistad Research Center, Tulane University, New Orleans, LA (hereafter ARC).

226. Letter from George Weir Jr. to Frederick Douglass, in *North Star*, 12 January 1849.

227. Letter from Henry Bibb to Lewis Tappan, 4 March 1850, American Missionary Association Archives, ARC.

228. Letter from Henry Bibb to the executive committee of the American and Foreign Anti-Slavery Society, 6 March 1850, American Missionary Association Archives, ARC.

229. John R. McKivigan, *The War against Proslavery Religion: Abolitionism and the Northern Churches, 1830–1865* (Ithaca, NY: Cornell University Press, 1984), 84–87, 96–99; Chris Padgett, "Hearing the Antislavery Rank-and-File: The Wesleyan Methodist Schism of 1843," *Journal of the Early Republic* 12.1 (1992): 63–84. See also Lucius C. Matlack, *The History of American Slavery and Methodism, from 1780 to 1849: And History of the Wesleyan Methodist Connection of America* (New York: n.p., 1849).

230. "Henry Bibb," *True Wesleyan*, 23 June 1849.

231. "Books for Cash.—On Sale at this Office," *Wesleyan*, 17 November 1853.

232. Harrold, *Abolitionists and the South*, 87, 95–96.

233. Letter from Gerrit Smith to Henry Bibb, 17 July 1849, in *North Star*, 3 August 1849; letter from Lewis Tappan to Louis Alexis Chamerovzow, 17 May 1853, in *A Side-Light on Anglo-American Relations, 1839–1858*, ed. Annie Heloise Abel and Frank J. Klingberg (Lancaster, PA: Association for the Study of Negro Life and History, 1927), 329.

234. Frederick Douglass, review of *Narrative of the Life and Adventures of Henry Bibb, an American Slave, North Star*, 17 August 1849.

235. "Book Repository," *National Anti-Slavery Standard*, 5 July 1849; *Liberator*, 10 August 1849; *Pennsylvania Freeman*, 22 November 1849; "Books," *Liberator*, 24 May 1850.

236. "More Slave Narratives," *Liberator*, 6 July 1849.

237. *Narrative of the Life and Adventures of Henry Bibb, an American Slave* (New York: Published by the Author, 1849), i.

238. *Narrative of the Life and Adventures of Henry Bibb* (1849), xi.

239. Ephraim Peabody, "Narratives of Fugitive Slaves," *Christian Examiner and Religious Miscellany* 47 (1849): 61.

240. Theodore Parker, "The American Scholar," in *Centenary Edition of Theodore Parker's Writings*, ed. George Willis Cooke (Boston: American Unitarian Association, 1907), 8:37.

241. *Anti-Slavery Reporter*, October 1849, 154.

242. John T. Kneebone, "Black, Leonard A.," in *Dictionary of Virginia Biography*, ed. John T. Kneebone et al. (Richmond: Library of Virginia, 1998), 1:514.

243. "Communications," *North Star*, 25 February 1848. See Eric Gardner, *Unexpected Places: Relocating Nineteenth-Century African American Literature* (Jackson: University Press of Mississippi, 2009).

244. See Kathryn Grover, *The Fugitive's Gibraltar: Escaping Slaves and Abolitionism in New Bedford, Massachusetts* (Amherst: University of Massachusetts Press, 2001).

245. *The New Bedford Directory* (New Bedford, MA: Press of Benjamin Lindsey, 1845), 117.

246. Grover, *Fugitive's Gibraltar*, 131; see also 124–26.

247. Kathryn Grover, email to the author, 18 July 2014.

248. Grover, *Fugitive's Gibraltar*, 134.

249. Amreta N. Scott, "A Checklist of New Bedford Imprints from 1840 to 1859 with a Historical Introduction" (MA thesis, Catholic University of America, 1959), 12.

250. *Narrative and Writings of Andrew Jackson, of Kentucky* (Syracuse: Daily and Weekly Star Office, 1847).

251. *The Life and Sufferings of Leonard Black, a Fugitive from Slavery* (New Bedford, MA: Press of Benjamin Lindsey, 1847), 21.

252. Barbara White, "The Integration of Nantucket Public Schools," *Historic Nantucket* 40.3 (1992): 59–62. See also Lloyd Pratt, "Speech, Print, and Reform on Nantucket," in Casper, Groves, Nissenbaum, and Winship, *Industrial Book*, 392–400.

253. *New England Mercantile Union Business Directory* (New York: Pratt, 1849), 117.

254. *Life and Sufferings of Leonard Black*, ii.

255. *Life and Sufferings of Leonard Black*, iii.

256. *Life and Sufferings of Leonard Black*, 50.

257. Bryan Sinche, "The Walking Book," in *Against a Sharp White Background: Infrastructures of African American Print*, ed. Brigitte Fielder and Jonathan Senchyne (Madison: University of Wisconsin Press, 2019), 278.

258. *A Narrative of the Life of Rev. Noah Davis, a Colored Man* (Baltimore: John F. Weishampel Jr., 1859), v.

259. Augusta Rohrbach, *Truth Stranger than Fiction: Race, Realism, and the U.S. Literary Marketplace* (New York: Palgrave, 2002), 39.

260. G. W. Offley Papers, vol. 1, American Antiquarian Society, Worcester, MA.

261. *Life of James Mars, a Slave Born and Sold in Connecticut*, 6th ed. (Hartford: Press of Case, Lockwood, 1868), 36–37.

262. On the already well-documented publishing context of the *Narrative*, see Nell Irvin Painter, *Sojourner Truth: A Life, a Symbol* (New York: W. W. Norton, 1996), 101–12; Margaret Washington, *Sojourner Truth's America* (Urbana: University of Illinois Press, 2009), 156–90. On Truth and Gilbert's collaboration specifically, see Jean M. Humez, "Reading *The Narrative of Sojourner Truth* as a Collaborative Text," *Frontiers* 16.1 (1996): 20–52; Xiomara Santamarina, *Belabored Professions: Narratives of African American Working Womanhood* (Chapel Hill: University of North Carolina Press, 2005), 35–63. For a brief consideration of Truth and print culture, see John Ernest, "Misinformation and Fluidity in Print Culture; or, Searching for Sojourner Truth and Others," *Legacy* 33.1 (2016): 22–24.

263. Mayer, *All on Fire*, 386.

264. William Lloyd Garrison to James Brown Yerrinton, 1 January 1866, BPL. Margaret Washington writes that *Narrative of Sojourner Truth* "was first published in 1850, simultaneously in Boston and New York," but no copy of the 1850 edition seems to have New York listed as place of publication. The second edition, however, was printed in New York by Edward O. Jenkins, later "an ardent Republican in politics." "Note on Editions of Sojourner Truth's *Narrative*," in *Narrative of Sojourner Truth*, ed. Margaret Washington (New York: Vintage, 1993), 125; "Edward O. Jenkins," *American Stationer*, 24 April 1884, 552.

265. Letter from Sojourner Truth to William Lloyd Garrison, 28 August 1851, in Erlene Stetson and Linda David, *Glorying in Tribulation: The Lifework of Sojourner Truth* (East Lansing: Michigan State University Press, 1994), 206.

266. Letter from Sojourner Truth to William Lloyd Garrison, 11 April 1864, in Stetson and David, *Glorying in Tribulation*, 213. See also Washington, *Sojourner Truth's America*, 206.

267. "George Thompson in Union Village," *Liberator*, 28 February 1851; "Notes from the Lecturing Field," *Anti-Slavery Bugle*, 20 September 1851; "From Our Boston Correspondent," *Frederick Douglass' Paper*, 15 June 1855.

268. P. Gabrielle Foreman, "Frederick Douglass's Black Activism," *Black Perspectives*, April 22, 2019, https://www.aaihs.org/frederick-douglasss-black-activism/.

269. "Lecture by Sojourner Truth," *National Anti-Slavery Standard*, 10 December 1853.

270. Daniel Walker Howe, *What Hath God Wrought: The Transformation of America, 1815–1848* (New York: Oxford University Press, 2007), 55. Erica L. Ball also writes that "authors of slave narratives" such as Truth "frequently lectured before the congregations of African American churches and the members of African American voluntary associations." Erica L. Ball, *To Live an Antislavery Life: Personal Politics and the Antebellum Black Middle Class* (Athens: University of Georgia Press, 2012), 38.

271. Letter from Sojourner Truth to Amy Post, ca. 29 May 1851, in Stetson and David, *Glorying in Tribulation*, 205. See also *Narrative of Sojourner Truth: A Bondswoman of Olden Time* (Boston: Published for the Author, 1875), 132.

272. "Patronise Her," *Liberator*, 6 September 1850; "Just Published," *Liberator*, 26 April 1850.

273. See David N. Gellman, *Emancipating New York: The Politics of Slavery and Freedom, 1777–1827* (Baton Rouge: Louisiana State University Press, 2006).

274. Painter, *Sojourner Truth*, 109.

275. Augusta Rohrbach, "Profits of Protest: The Market Strategies of Sojourner Truth and Louisa May Alcott," in *Prophets of Protest: Reconsidering the History of American Abolitionism*, ed. Timothy Patrick McCarthy and John Stauffer (New York: New Press, 2006), 243.

276. Most critics have claimed that the stereotype plates were first used to print the 1850 edition, based on a note to the reader appearing in the 1875 edition: "The first 128 pages of this work are reprinted from stereotype plates, made in 1850." But as Nicole Gray rightly notes, "Stereotyped plates appear to have been made for a new 1853 edition, as the typesetting differs from the 1850 edition." For reasons that remain unclear, Truth's friend James Boyle seems to have owned the plates between the time they were made and 1870, at which point he "made Sojourner a present" of them, as the 1875 edition indicates. It is likely that Truth could not afford the plates herself. *Narrative of Sojourner Truth* (Boston, 1875), iii, 264; Nicole Haworth Gray, "Spirited Media: Revision, Race, and Revelation in Nineteenth-Century America" (PhD diss., University of Texas at Austin, 2014), 189n152; Painter, *Sojourner Truth*, 110.

277. Painter writes that "in 1853, Truth . . . journeyed to Andover, Massachusetts, and asked Stowe directly for a puff," and that "Stowe's puff became the introduction to the late 1853 edition" of the *Narrative*. According to Washington, Truth met the author of *Uncle Tom's Cabin* in 1855. "Needing another reprinting of her *Narrative*," she "extracted an endorsement and introduction from Stowe." Stowe's introduction, it should be noted, is dated October 1855. Painter, *Sojourner Truth*, 130, 318n21; Washington, *Sojourner Truth's America*, 271. Several other African American writers had their works introduced by Stowe in the 1850s, including William C. Nell (*The Colored Patriots of the American Revolution*, 1855), Frank J. Webb (*The Garies and Their Friends*, 1857), and Josiah Henson (*Truth Stranger than Fiction*, 1858).

278. Washington, *Sojourner Truth's America*, 301. See also Carleton Mabee, *Sojourner Truth: Slave, Prophet, Legend* (New York: New York University Press, 1993), 110–15.

279. Quoted in Stetson and David, *Glorying in Tribulation*, 29, 22.

280. "The Abolitionists in New York," *New York Herald*, 5 September 1853.

281. Augusta Rohrbach, *Thinking Outside the Book* (Amherst: University of Massachusetts Press, 2014), 32.

Chapter 3. "Quite a Sensation"

1. John Townsend Trowbridge, *My Own Story: With Recollections of Noted Persons* (Boston: Houghton, Mifflin, 1903), 215.

2. For a recent study of the Fugitive Slave Law, see R. J. M. Blackett, *The Captive's Quest for Freedom: Fugitive Slaves, the 1850 Fugitive Slave Law, and the Politics of Slavery* (Cambridge: Cambridge University Press, 2018).

3. Quoted in Joan D. Hedrick, *Harriet Beecher Stowe: A Life* (New York: Oxford University Press, 1994), 204.

4. Manisha Sinha, *The Slave's Cause: A History of Abolition* (New Haven, CT: Yale University Press, 2016), 436.

5. Michael Winship, "Manufacturing and Book Production," in *The Industrial Book, 1840–1880*, vol. 3 of *A History of the Book in America*, ed. Scott E. Casper, Jeffrey D. Groves, Stephen W. Nissenbaum, and Michael Winship (Chapel Hill: University of North Carolina Press, 2007), 40–69.

6. Michael Winship, *American Literary Publishing in the Mid-Nineteenth Century: The Business of Ticknor and Fields* (Cambridge: Cambridge University Press, 1995), 12.

7. Richard J. Zboray, *A Fictive People: Antebellum Economic Development and the American Reading Public* (New York: Oxford University Press, 1993), 6–7.

8. Jeffrey D. Groves, "Trade Communication," "Courtesy of the Trade," in Casper, Groves, Nissenbaum, and Winship, *Industrial Book*, 130–48.

9. John Tebbel, *A History of Book Publishing in the United States* (New York: R. R. Bowker, 1972), 1:225–27; Zboray, *Fictive People*, 3–4.

10. Ezra Greenspan, *George Palmer Putnam: Representative American Publisher* (University Park: Pennsylvania State University Press, 2000), 362.

11. Ronald J. Zboray and Mary Saracino Zboray, *Literary Dollars and Social Sense: A People's History of the Mass Market Book* (New York: Routledge, 2005), 53.

12. *Narrative of William Hayden, Containing a Faithful Account of His Travels for a Number of Years, Whilst a Slave, in the South* (Cincinnati: Published for the Author, 1846), 8.

13. Claire Parfait, "Early African American Historians: A Book History and Historiography Approach—The Case of William Cooper Nell (1816–1874)," in *Race, Ethnicity and Publishing in America*, ed. Cécile Cottenet (Basingstoke, UK: Palgrave Macmillan, 2014), 34–35.

14. See the introduction to Hannah Crafts, *The Bondwoman's Narrative*, ed. Henry Louis Gates Jr. (New York: Warner, 2002); Julie Bosman, "Professor Says He Has Solved a Mystery Over a Slave's Novel," *New York Times*, 18 September 2013.

15. Eric Gardner, *Black Print Unbound: The Christian Recorder, African American Literature, and Periodical Culture* (New York: Oxford University Press, 2015), 10. See also Todd Vogel, introduction to *The Black Press: New Literary and Historical Essays*, ed. Todd Vogel (New Brunswick, NJ: Rutgers University Press, 2001), 2; Eric Gardner and Joycelyn Moody, introduction to "Black Periodical Studies," ed. Eric Gardner and Joycelyn Moody, special issue, *American Periodicals* 25.2 (2015): 106–7; Benjamin Fagan, *The Black Newspaper and the Chosen Nation* (Athens: University of Georgia Press, 2016).

16. Debra Jackson, "A Black Journalist in Civil War Virginia: Robert Hamilton and the *Anglo-African*," *Virginia Magazine of History and Biography* 116.1 (2008): 47.

17. Martin R. Delany to William Lloyd Garrison, 19 February 1859, in *Martin R. Delany: A Documentary Reader*, ed. Robert S. Levine (Chapel Hill: University of North Carolina Press, 2003), 296, 295.

18. Jerome McGann, introduction to *Blake; or, The Huts from America*, by Martin R. Delany, ed. Jerome McGann (Cambridge, MA: Harvard University Press, 2017), ix.

19. Claire Parfait, *The Publishing History of Uncle Tom's Cabin, 1852–2002* (Aldershot, UK: Ashgate, 2007), 34.

20. Richard Hildreth, *Archy Moore, the White Slave; or, Memoirs of a Fugitive* (New York: Miller, Orton & Mulligan, 1856), ix. On Hildreth and *The Slave*, see Donald E. Emerson, *Richard Hildreth* (Baltimore: Johns Hopkins Press, 1946), 72–80. Like Emerson, I use the introduction to the 1856 edition of the novel as my main source of information regarding its publication history.

21. Leonard L. Richards, *"Gentlemen of Property and Standing": Anti-Abolition Mobs in Jacksonian America* (New York: Oxford University Press, 1970).

22. Quoted in W. Caleb McDaniel, *The Problem of Democracy in the Age of Slavery: Garrisonian Abolitionists and Transatlantic Reform* (Baton Rouge: Louisiana State University Press, 2013), 56.

23. On Eastburn and the *Atlas*, see Frederic Hudson, *Journalism in the United States, from 1690 to 1872* (New York: Harper & Brothers, 1873), 390–94; *American Dictionary of Printing and Bookmaking* (New York: Howard Lockwood, 1894), 158. Thomas Gossett wrongly claims that Eastburn (whom he calls Eastham) "lost his contract as official printer for the city of Boston" as a result of printing *The Slave*. Thomas F. Gossett, *"Uncle Tom's Cabin" and American Culture* (Dallas: Southern Methodist University Press, 1985), 148.

24. "Uncle Tom, The White Slave, Ida May and the N. Y. Evening Post," *Boston Evening Telegraph*, 13 November 1854.

25. *Liberator*, 30 June 1838.

26. *Liberator*, 12 June 1846.

27. *Fourth Annual Report of the American Anti-Slavery Society* (New York: Printed by William S. Dorr, 1837), 58.

28. Andrew Reed and James Matheson, *A Narrative of the Visit to the American Churches, by the Deputation from the Congregational Union of England and Wales* (New York: Harper & Brothers, 1835), 2:186.

29. "An Apology for Drs. Reed and Matheson's Narrative, by Their American Publishers," *Slavery in America* 6 (December 1836): 142–43.

30. *Fifteenth Annual Report Presented to the Massachusetts Anti-Slavery Society* (Boston: Printed by Andrews & Prentiss, 1847), 38.

31. Anne Marsh-Caldwell, *Tales of the Woods and Fields* (New York: Harper & Brothers, 1836), 274n.

32. *Fourth Annual Report*, 58–59.

33. Circular of the American Anti-Slavery Society for help in obtaining subscribers for the *National Anti-Slavery Standard*, 25 July 1845, Rare Books and Manuscripts Department, Boston Public Library (hereafter BPL). See "Marie, ou Esclavage aux Etats-Unis," *National Anti-Slavery Standard*, 17 July 1845.

34. "Book Notices," *National Anti-Slavery Standard*, 24 December 1846.

35. Hosea Easton, *A Treatise on the Intellectual Character, and Civil and Political Condition of the Colored People of the U. States* (Boston: Isaac Knapp, 1837), 42, 41.

36. "Anti-Slavery Book Store," *Liberator*, 26 May 1834.

37. Kristen Doyle Highland, "Mapping the Bookstore in Nineteenth-Century New York City," Columbia Book History Colloquium, 25 March 2014.

38. Graham Russell Gao Hodges, *David Ruggles: A Radical Black Abolitionist and the Underground Railroad in New York City* (Chapel Hill: University of North Carolina Press, 2010), 60, 67–68.

39. *Anti-Slavery Almanac for 1846* (New York: Finch & Weed, 1845), back matter.

40. "New Publications," *New York Daily Tribune*, 23 August 1845; "New Work on Slavery," *Emancipator* (Boston), 10 December 1845; *New York Evangelist*, 26 June 1845.

41. *New York Evangelist*, 29 May 1845.

42. Zboray, *Fictive People*, 3–4.

43. Michael Winship, "'The Greatest Book of Its Kind': A Publishing History of *Uncle Tom's Cabin*," *Proceedings of the American Antiquarian Society* 109 (2002): 309–32; Parfait, *Publishing History of Uncle Tom's Cabin*. See also Sarah Meer, *Uncle Tom Mania: Slavery, Minstrelsy, and Transatlantic Culture in the 1850s* (Athens: University of Georgia Press, 2005.

44. Donald Edward Liedel, "The Antislavery Novel, 1836–1861" (PhD diss., University of Michigan, 1961), 137.

45. Liedel, "The Antislavery Novel," 116–21.

46. On John P. Jewett, see Michael Winship, "John Punchard Jewett, Publisher of *Uncle Tom's Cabin*: A Biographical Note with a Preliminary List of His Imprints," in *Roger Eliot Stoddard at Sixty-Five: A Celebration* (New York: Thornwillow Press, 2000), 85–114; Parfait, *Publishing History of Uncle Tom's Cabin*, 35–37; Tebbel, *History of Book Publishing*, 1:426–29.

47. Charles Sumner, *White Slavery in the Barbary States* (Boston: John P. Jewett, 1853); *The Landmark of Freedom* (Boston: John P. Jewett, 1854); *The Crime against Kansas* (Boston: John P. Jewett, 1856); Giles B. Stebbins, *Facts and Opinions Touching the Real Origin, Character, and Influence of the American Colonization Society* (Boston: John P. Jewett, 1853), 94; Josiah Henson, *Truth Stranger than Fiction: Father Henson's Story of His Own Life* (Boston: John P. Jewett, 1858). On the *Autographs for Freedom*, see Meaghan M. Fritz and Frank E. Fee Jr., "To Give the Gift of Freedom: Gift Books and the War on Slavery," *American Periodicals* 23.1 (2013): 60–82. On the "Juvenile Anti-Slavery Toy Books," see Deborah C. De Rosa, *Domestic Abolitionism and Juvenile Literature, 1830–1865* (Albany: State University of New York Press, 2003), 28–30.

48. Letter from John P. Jewett to Charles Sumner, 3 March 1854, in Michael Winship, "'Yours for Freedom': John P. Jewett Writes to Charles Sumner," *Harvard Library Bulletin* 24.2 (2013): 9, 12.

49. Letter from Jewett to Sumner, 3 March 1854, 12. On Sumner in Congress, see Manisha Sinha, "The Caning of Charles Sumner: Slavery, Race, and Ideology in the Age of the Civil War," *Journal of the Early Republic* 23.2 (2003): 242.

50. Donald E. Liedel, "The Puffing of *Ida May*: Publishers Exploit the Antislavery Novel," *Journal of Popular Culture* 3 (1969): 287–306. See also Jessie Morgan-Owens, *Girl in Black and White: The Story of Mary Mildred Williams and the Abolition Movement* (New York: W. W. Norton, 2019). On Phillips, Sampson, see Tebbel, *History of Book Publishing*, 1:424–26.

51. Letter from John P. Jewett to Charles Sumner, 25 February 1854, in Winship, "Jewett," 9.

52. On Derby & Miller and their successors, see Peter Dzwonkoski, ed., *American Literary Publishing Houses, 1638–1899* (Detroit, MI: Gale, 1986), 1:116.

53. Liedel, "Antislavery Novel," 201.

54. Harriet Beecher Stowe, "Anti-Slavery Literature," *Independent*, 21 February 1856.

55. "Speech of J. M. McKim, at Glasgow," *National Anti-Slavery Standard*, 8 October 1853.

56. George R. Graham, "Editor's Table. Personal," *Graham's Magazine*, March 1853, 365.

57. Liedel, "Antislavery Novel," 96–97.

58. Nina Baym, *Novels, Readers, and Reviewers: Responses to Fiction in Antebellum America* (Ithaca, NY: Cornell University Press, 1984), 223. On the "waning of the anti-fiction prejudice" in the 1840s and 1850s, see also Barbara Hochman, *Uncle Tom's Cabin and the Reading Revolution: Race, Literacy, Childhood, and Fiction, 1851–1911* (Amherst: University of Massachusetts Press, 2011), chap. 3 (quote at 81).

59. Liedel, "Antislavery Novel," 85; "Uncle Tomitudes," *Putnam's Monthly*, January 1853, 97–102; George R. Graham, "Black Letters; or Uncle Tom-Foolery in Literature," *Graham's Magazine*, February 1853, 209–15.

60. John Dixon Long, *Pictures of Slavery in Church and State* (Philadelphia: Published by the Author, 1857), 7–10.

61. James D. Hart, *The Popular Book: A History of America's Literary Taste* (New York: Oxford University Press, 1950), 113; David Brown, *Southern Outcast: Hinton Rowan Helper and "The Impending Crisis of the South"* (Baton Rouge: Louisiana State University Press, 2006), 89–90.

62. Joel Myerson and Daniel Shealy, eds., *The Journals of Louisa May Alcott* (Athens: University of Georgia Press, 1997), 98.

63. Alfred Brophy and Autumn Barrett, "Why Haven't Publishers Apologized for Their Books That Glorify Slavery?," *Fortune*, 2 February 2018, http://fortune.com/2018/02/02/charlottesville-va-book-publishers-slavery/.

64. Madeleine B. Stern, *Books and Book People in Nineteenth-Century America* (New York: R. R. Bowker, 1978), 11–14; Hart, *Popular Book*, 93.

65. New York, vol. 31, 43, R. G. Dun & Co. Credit Report Volumes, Baker Library, HBS.

66. William Hosmer, *The Higher Law, in Its Relations to Civil Government* (Auburn, NY: Derby & Miller, 1852), 203.

67. *Radical Abolitionist* 1.3, October 1855, 21.

68. Scott E. Casper, *Constructing American Lives: Biography and Culture in Nineteenth-Century America* (Chapel Hill: University of North Carolina Press, 1999), 2.

69. Melissa J. Homestead, *American Women Authors and Literary Property, 1822–1869* (Cambridge: Cambridge University Press, 2005), 223–24 (quotes at 224, 223).

70. See Carol Wilson, *Freedom at Risk: The Kidnapping of Free Blacks in America, 1780–1865* (Lexington: University Press of Kentucky, 1994); David Fiske, *Solomon Northup's Kindred: The Kidnapping of Free Citizens before the Civil War* (Santa Barbara, CA: Praeger, 2016); Richard Bell, *Stolen: Five Free Boys Kidnapped into Slavery and Their Astonishing Odyssey Home* (New York: 37 INK, 2019).

71. "The Kidnapping Case," *New York Daily Times*, 20 January 1853. See also "From Washington," *New York Daily Times*, 19 January 1853.

72. *Twelve Years a Slave: Narrative of Solomon Northup, a Citizen of New-York, Kidnapped in Washington City in 1841, and Rescued in 1853, from a Cotton Plantation Near the Red River, in Louisiana* (Auburn: Derby & Miller, 1853), xv–xvi.

73. "Solomon Northrop; or, 12 Years a Slave," *Essex County Republican*, 13 August 1853. Northup's name was (and still is) frequently misspelled as "Northrup" or "Northrop."

74. Sue Eakin and Joseph Logsdon, introduction to *Twelve Years a Slave*, by Solomon Northup, ed. Sue Eakin and Joseph Logsdon (Baton Rouge: Louisiana State University Press, 1968), xii–xiv; David Fiske, Clifford W. Brown, and Rachel Seligman, *Solomon Northup: The Complete Story of the Author of Twelve Years a Slave* (Santa Barbara, CA: Praeger, 2013), 110–12. Both Wilson and Fisher, John W. Blassingame writes, "had little or no connection with professional abolitionists." John W. Blassingame, introduction to *Slave Testimony: Two Centuries of Letters, Speeches, Interviews, and Autobiographies* (Baton Rouge: Louisiana State University Press, 1977), xviii.

75. Sam Worley, "Solomon Northup and the Sly Philosophy of the Slave Pen," *Callaloo* 20.1 (1997): 244.

76. Northup, *Twelve Years a Slave* (1853), 155.

77. Northup, *Twelve Years a Slave*, 209.

78. Lisa Brawley, "Frederick Douglass's *My Bondage and My Freedom* and the Fugitive Tourist Industry," *NOVEL: A Forum on Fiction* 30.1 (1996): 98.

79. Sue Eakin, introduction to *Solomon Northup's Twelve Years a Slave and Plantation Life in the Antebellum South*, ed. Sue Eakin (Lafayette, LA: Center for Louisiana Studies, University of Louisiana at Lafayette, 2007), ix.

80. Liedel, "Antislavery Novel," 50–51.

81. Still's true story was in fact more complicated. See Edlie L. Wong, *Neither Fugitive nor Free: Atlantic Slavery, Freedom Suits, and the Legal Culture of Travel* (New York: New York University Press, 2009), 114–15.

82. Harriet Beecher Stowe, *A Key to Uncle Tom's Cabin* (Boston: John P. Jewett, 1853), 173–74.

83. Northup, *Twelve Years a Slave* (1853), 226.

84. Robert B. Stepto, "Sharing the Thunder: The Literary Exchanges of Harriet Beecher Stowe, Henry Bibb, and Frederick Douglass," in *New Essays on Uncle Tom's Cabin*, ed. Eric J. Sundquist (Cambridge: Cambridge University Press, 1986), 135, 136.

85. Zora Neale Hurston, "What White Publishers Won't Print," in *Within the Circle: An Anthology of African American Literary Criticism from the Harlem Renaissance to the Present*, ed. Angelyn Mitchell (Durham, NC: Duke University Press, 1994), 118.

86. "More Uncle Tom," *Daily Picayune*, 26 January 1855, in *Twelve Years a Slave*, by Solomon Northup, ed. Henry Louis Gates Jr. and Kevin M. Burke (New York: W. W. Norton, 2017), 224.

87. "'Uncle Tom's Cabin.'—No. 2," *Albany Evening Journal*, 18 July 1853.

88. "An Oneida Journal," *Circular*, 29 March 1855.

89. Roy E. Finkenbine, "'Who Will . . . Pay for their Sufferings?': New York Abolitionists and the Failed Campaign to Compensate Solomon Northup," *New York History* 95.4 (2014): 639.

90. *Syracuse Daily Standard*, 4 April 1853.

91. Parfait, *Publishing History of Uncle Tom's Cabin*, 39.

92. *New York Daily Times*, 15 April 1853; "Solomon Northup's Kidnappers," *Wesleyan*, 20 July 1854; "Solomon Northrop; or, 12 Years a Slave."

93. Fiske, Brown, and Seligman, *Solomon Northup*, 116; Eakin and Logsdon, introduction to Northup, *Twelve Years a Slave*, xxii–xxiii.

94. Letter from Kate E. R. Pickard to Peter Still, 9 May 1856, Peter Still Papers, Rutgers University.

95. Walter Sutton, *The Western Book Trade: Cincinnati as a Nineteenth-Century Publishing and Book-Trade Center* (Columbus: Ohio State University Press, 1961), 134–49; Walter Sutton, "The Derby Brothers: 19th-Century Bookmen," *University of Rochester Library Bulletin* 3.2 (1948), https://rbscp.lib.rochester.edu/2444.

96. Quoted in Gavin Jones and Judith Richardson, "Proslavery Fiction," in *The Cambridge Companion to Slavery in American Literature*, ed. Ezra Tawil (Cambridge: Cambridge University Press, 2016), 108.

97. Quoted in Fiske, Brown, and Seligman, *Solomon Northup*, 112.

98. *Cayuga Chief*, 19 April 1853; *New York Daily Times*, 15 April 1853; *National Era*, 21 April 1853; *Frederick Douglass' Paper*, 29 April 1853; *Norton's Literary Gazette and Publishers' Circular*, 15 April 1853, 71; *Literary World*, 23 April 1853.

99. "Editorial Notes.—Cursive and Discursive," *Putnam's Monthly*, April 1855, 440–41. See Liedel, "Antislavery Novel," 110–12. See also Lara Langer Cohen, *The Fabrication of American Literature: Fraudulence and Antebellum Print Culture* (Philadelphia: University of Pennsylvania Press, 2012), 23–64.

100. Winship, "Manufacturing and Book Production," 63.

101. *Publishers' Circular*, 16 June 1853, 222, 230.

102. *Norton's Literary Gazette and Publishers' Circular*, 15 August 1853, 137.

103. *Littell's Living Age*, 10 September 1853.

104. *Connecticut Courant*, 1 October 1853; *Norfolk Democrat*, 11 November 1853; *Alexandria Gazette*, 20 October 1853.

105. *Albany Evening Journal*, 16 July, 30 July, 2 August 1853.

106. *Frederick Douglass' Paper*, 18 November 1853.

107. Leon Jackson, *The Business of Letters: Authorial Economies in Antebellum America* (Stanford, CA: Stanford University Press, 2008), 3.

108. Fiske, Brown, and Seligman, *Solomon Northup*, 117–18.

109. "Book and Tract Depository of the American and Foreign Anti-Slavery Society," *American Jubilee*, March 1854, 8; *Pennsylvania Freeman*, 28 August 1853; *Liberator*, 23 December 1853, 23 March 1855; "Literary Notices," *Frederick Douglass' Paper*, 29 July 1853, 5 August 1853; "Twenty-First Anniversary of the American Anti-Slavery Society," *National Anti-Slavery Standard*, 20 May 1854; "Narrative of Solomon Northup," *National Anti-Slavery Standard*, 18 March 1854.

110. Letter from Samuel May Jr. to John B. Estlin, 20 December 1853, BPL.

111. *Liberator*, 26 August 1853; *Norton's Literary Gazette and Publishers' Circular*, 15 August 1853, 137.

112. H. C. Carey, *Letters on International Copyright* (Philadelphia: A. Hart, 1853), 50.

113. Liedel, "Antislavery Novel," 148n56. A new edition came out under the imprint of C. M. Saxton in 1859.

114. *Narrative of the Life of Frederick Douglass, an American Slave*, ed. Benjamin Quarles (Cambridge, MA: Belknap Press of Harvard University Press, 1960), xiii.

115. J. C. Derby, *Fifty Years among Authors, Books and Publishers* (New York: G. W. Carleton, 1884), 63.

116. Finkenbine, "Failed Campaign," 644.

117. Fiske, Brown, and Seligman, *Solomon Northup*, 118–22.

118. On Henson, see Robin W. Winks, "The Making of a Fugitive Slave Narrative: Josiah Henson and Uncle Tom—A Case Study," in *The Slave's Narrative*, ed. Charles T. Davis and Henry Louis Gates Jr. (Oxford: Oxford University Press, 1985), 112–46.

119. "The Life of Frederick Douglass," *Christian Ambassador*, 18 August 1855.

120. On Douglass in Rochester, see Nancy A. Hewitt, "Rochester," in *Frederick Douglass in Context*, ed. Michaël Roy (Cambridge: Cambridge University Press, 2021), 34–45.

121. Frederick Douglass, *My Bondage and My Freedom* (New York: Miller, Orton & Mulligan, 1855), vi–vii.

122. Frederick Douglass, "The Heroic Slave," in *Autographs for Freedom*, ed. Julia Griffiths (Boston: John P. Jewett, 1853), 174–239. On Douglass and Griffiths, see Frank E. Fee Jr., "To No One More Indebted: Frederick Douglass and Julia Griffiths, 1849–63," *Journalism History* 37.1 (2011): 12–26; Janet Douglas, "A Cherished Friendship: Julia Griffiths Crofts and Frederick Douglass," *Slavery and Abolition* 33.2 (2012), 265–74; Leigh Fought, *Women in the World of Frederick Douglass* (New York: Oxford University Press, 2017), 124–51.

123. Jane Marsh Parker, "Reminiscences of Frederick Douglass," in *Douglass in His Own Time: A Biographical Chronicle of His Life, Drawn from Recollections, Interviews, and Memoirs by Family, Friends, and Associates*, ed. John Ernest (Iowa City: University of Iowa Press, 2014), 46, 47.

124. Gerald Fulkerson, "Textual Introduction," in *The Frederick Douglass Papers*, ser. 2, *Autobiographical Writings*, vol. 2, *My Bondage and My Freedom*, ed. John W. Blassingame, John R. McKivigan, and Peter P. Hinks (New Haven, CT: Yale University Press, 2003), 288 (hereafter cited as *FDP* 2, 2:288); Alex W. Black, "Frederick Douglass, Julia Griffiths, and Collaborative Autobiography," paper presented at the Frederick Douglass Across and Against Times, Places, and Disciplines conference, Paris, 11–13 October 2018.

125. Susan M. Ryan, "Douglass, Melville, and the Moral Economies of American Authorship," in *Frederick Douglass and Herman Melville: Essays in Relation*, ed. Robert S. Levine and Samuel (Chapel Hill: University of North Carolina Press, 2008), 90.

126. Douglass, *My Bondage and My Freedom*, 361, 362, 398.

127. "A Faithful Correction and Willing Acknowledgement," *National Anti-Slavery Standard*, 12 January 1856.

128. Letter from Frederick Douglass to William Lloyd Garrison, 13 January 1856, in *The Life and Writings of Frederick Douglass*, vol. 5, *Supplementary Volume, 1844–1860*, ed. Philip S. Foner (New York: International Publishers, 1975), 372.

129. Anna Mae Duane, *Educated for Freedom: The Incredible Story of Two Fugitive Schoolboys Who Grew Up to Change a Nation* (New York: New York University Press, 2020), 121.

130. "National Council of the Colored People," *Frederick Douglass' Paper*, 18 May 1855.

131. Robert S. Levine, *The Lives of Frederick Douglass* (Cambridge, MA: Harvard University Press, 2016), 157.

132. See Jim Casey, "Colored Conventions," in Roy, *Frederick Douglass in Context*, 293–304.

133. See Kellie Carter Jackson, *Force and Freedom: Black Abolitionists and the Politics of Violence* (Philadelphia: University of Pennsylvania Press, 2019).

134. Douglass, *My Bondage and My Freedom*, xxxi.

135. "Faithful Correction."

136. Letter from Lewis Tappan to Louis Alexis Chamerovzow, 10 November 1855, in *A Side-Light on Anglo-American Relations*, ed. Annie Heloise Abel and Frank J. Klingberg (Lancaster, PA: Association for the Study of Negro Life and History, 1927), 363.

137. See John R. McKivigan, "The Frederick Douglass–Gerrit Smith Friendship and Political Abolitionism in the 1850s," in *Frederick Douglass: New Literary and Historical Essays*, ed. Eric J. Sundquist (Cambridge: Cambridge University Press, 1990), 205–32.

138. John Stauffer, *The Black Hearts of Men: Radical Abolitionists and the Transformation of Race* (Cambridge, MA: Harvard University Press, 2001), 19.

139. Letter from Frederick Douglass to Gerrit Smith, 14 August 1855, in *The Life and Writings of Frederick Douglass*, vol. 2, *Pre-Civil War Decade*, ed. Philip S. Foner (New York: International Publishers, 1950), 266.

140. Jeffrey Ruggles, *The Unboxing of Henry Brown* (Richmond: Library of Virginia, 2003), 83; letter from Jermain W. Loguen to Gerrit Smith, 23 March 1859, Gerrit Smith Papers, Syracuse University; letter from William Wells Brown to Gerrit Smith, 4 September 1862, Gerrit Smith Papers, Syracuse University.

141. Douglass, *My Bondage and My Freedom*, v, xxix.

142. William L. Andrews, *To Tell a Free Story: The First Century of Afro-American Autobiography, 1760–1865* (Urbana: University of Illinois Press, 1986), 218.

143. Letter from Frederick Douglass to Gerrit Smith, 18 July 1855, Gerrit Smith Papers, Syracuse University.

144. Douglass, *My Bondage and My Freedom*, vii.

145. "Douglass' Narrative," *Anti-Slavery Bugle*, 10 October 1845; *Frederick Douglass' Paper*, 21 September 1855.

146. Robert S. Levine, "Autobiography," in Roy, *Frederick Douglass in Context*, 90.

147. Frederick Douglass Papers, Legal File, Copyrights, 1845–1881, Library of Congress, Washington, DC.

148. Celeste-Marie Bernier and Andrew Taylor, *If I Survive: Frederick Douglass and Family in the Walter O. Evans Collection* (Edinburgh: Edinburgh University Press, 2018), 682.

149. See Julia Lee's discussion of the *Narrative* portrait in chapter 2.

150. John Sekora, "'Mr. Editor, If You Please': Frederick Douglass, *My Bondage and My Freedom*, and the End of the Abolitionist Imprint," *Callaloo* 17.2 (1994): 620, 610.

151. Philippe Lejeune, *Le Pacte autobiographique* (Paris: Seuil, 1996), 45.

152. Stowe, "Anti-Slavery Literature."

153. Samuel J. May, *Some Recollections of Our Antislavery Conflict* (Boston: Fields, Osgood, 1869), 293, 295. On postbellum autobiographical writings by abolitionists, see

Julie Roy Jeffrey, *Abolitionists Remember: Antislavery Autobiographies and the Unfinished Work of Emancipation* (Chapel Hill: University of North Carolina Press, 2008).

154. Levine, *Lives of Frederick Douglass*, 9. *Bondage and Freedom* has been receiving more attention recently. See Frederick Douglass, *My Bondage and My Freedom*, ed. Celeste-Marie Bernier (Oxford: Oxford University Press, 2019); Frederick Douglass, *My Bondage and My Freedom*, ed. Nick Bromell and R. Blakeslee Gilpin (New York: W. W. Norton, 2020).

155. *Portland Transcript*, 7 April 1855; *Michigan Farmer*, 1 May 1855.

156. *New York Daily Times*, 21 July 1855; *Independent*, 26 July 1855; *Cayuga Chief*, 17 July 1855; *Christian Ambassador*, 28 July 1855; etc.

157. *Frederick Douglass' Paper*, 31 August 1855; *New York Daily Times*, 1 August, 6 August 1855; *National Anti-Slavery Standard*, 11 August 1855; *Independent*, 9 August 1855; *Frederick Douglass' Paper*, 17 August 1855; *Albany Evening Journal*, 4 August 1855; *Puritan Recorder*, 2 August 1855; *Milwaukee Daily Sentinel*, 6 August 1855; *Ballou's Pictorial Drawing Room Companion*, 29 August 1855.

158. "The 'Incendiary Publications' in Mobile," *New York Daily Times*, 23 August 1856.

159. "The Mobile Development," *Daily Dispatch*, 27 August 1856. On Nott, see Eric Herschthal, "Science and Technology," in Roy, *Frederick Douglass in Context*, 257.

160. "The Incendiary Publications in Mobile. Statement of Mr. Strickland in Regard to His Expulsion," *New York Daily Times*, 30 September 1856.

161. *New York Daily Tribune*, 30 August 1856.

162. Stauffer, *Black Hearts of Men*, 293n24.

163. *Independent*, 1 May 1856.

164. *New York Daily Tribune*, 8 August 1856.

165. "My Bondage and My Freedom," *Church Advocate*, 4 October 1855; "Pedlers Ware," *Kalamazoo Gazette*, 22 February 1856; "New Books," *Newport Mercury*, 10 November 1855.

166. "From Our Cincinnati Correspondent," *Frederick Douglass' Paper*, 26 October 1855.

167. *Puritan Recorder*, 30 August 1855; *Ballou's Pictorial Drawing Room Companion*, 22 September 1855.

168. *Liberator*, 24 August 1855.

169. John Stauffer, "Frederick Douglass's Self-Fashioning and the Making of a Representative American Man," in *The Cambridge Companion to the African American Slave Narrative*, ed. Audrey Fisch (Cambridge: Cambridge University Press, 2007), 208.

170. *FDP* 1, 2:214.

171. *Frederick Douglass' Paper*, 22 April 1859.

172. *Frederick Douglass' Paper*, 17 August 1855.

173. Letter from Frederick Douglass to Benjamin Coates, 17 April 1856, in Foner, *Life and Writings*, 2:288. On Coates, see Emma J. Lapsansky-Werner and Margaret Hope Bacon, eds., *Back to Africa: Benjamin Coates and the Colonization Movement in America, 1848–1880* (University Park: Pennsylvania State University Press, 2005).

174. "Letter from Rev. J. W. Loguen," *Frederick Douglass' Paper*, 9 November 1855.

175. On the publication history of Loguen's narrative, see Carol M. Hunter, *To Set the Captives Free: Reverend Jermain Wesley Loguen and the Struggle for Freedom in*

Central New York, 1835–1872 (New York: Garland, 1993), 17–30; Jennifer A. Williamson, introduction to *The Rev. J. W. Loguen, as a Slave and as a Freeman: A Narrative of Real Life*, ed. Jennifer A. Williamson (Syracuse, NY: Syracuse University Press, 2016).

176. *Life and Times of Frederick Douglass* (Boston: De Wolfe & Fiske, 1892), 455.

177. Erwin Palmer, "A Partnership in the Abolition Movement," *University of Rochester Library Bulletin* 26.1/2 (1970–71), https://rbscp.lib.rochester.edu/3476.

178. Letter from Parker Pillsbury to Samuel May Jr., 6 September 1855, BPL.

179. Stacey M. Robertson, *Parker Pillsbury: Radical Abolitionist, Male Feminist* (Ithaca, NY: Cornell University Press, 2000), 109.

180. "Letters from the Old World.—No. V," *Frederick Douglass' Paper*, 12 October 1855. On Griffiths's transatlantic letters to Douglass, see Sarah Meer, "Old Master Letters and *Letters from the Old World*: Julia Griffiths and the Uses of Correspondence in Frederick Douglass's Newspapers," in *The Edinburgh Companion to Nineteenth-Century American Letters and Letter-Writing*, ed. Celeste-Marie Bernier, Judie Newman and Matthew Pethers (Edinburgh: Edinburgh University Press, 2016), 377–90.

181. Promotional material for *My Bondage and My Freedom*, undated, University of Manchester Library, *JSTOR Primary Sources*, https://www.jstor.org/stable/60237900 ?seq=1#metadata_info_tab_contents.

182. "American Slavery," *British Banner*, 20 November 1855.

183. *National Anti-Slavery Standard*, 15 December 1855.

184. Letter from Richard D. Webb to Samuel May Jr., 21 December 1855, BPL.

185. Letter from Samuel May Jr. to Richard D. Webb, 16 January 1856, BPL. See Samuel Ringgold Ward, *Autobiography of a Fugitive Negro: His Anti-Slavery Labours in the United States, Canada, and England* (London: John Snow, 1855).

186. Jonathan Rose, *The Intellectual Life of the British Working Classes* (New Haven, CT: Yale University Press, 2001), 187.

187. *Southern Quarterly Review*, January 1853, 206. See Blassingame, introduction to *Slave Testimony*, xxiii–xxvi.

188. Liedel, "Antislavery Novel," 198, 203. Dayton's first name appears in *Wilson's Business Directory of New York City* (New York: John F. Trow, 1858), 36.

189. See Sinha, "Caning of Charles Sumner."

190. D. A. Harsha, *The Life of Charles Sumner* (New York: H. Dayton, 1858), back matter.

191. Harsha, *The Life of Charles Sumner*, back matter.

192. That Fisher died in 1858 may not be entirely coincidental. J. Simpson Africa, *History of Huntingdon and Blair Counties, Pennsylvania* (Philadelphia: Louis H. Everts, 1883), 81.

193. *Fifty Years in Chains; or, The Life of an American Slave* (New York: H. Dayton, 1858), 7.

194. *Slavery in the United States: A Narrative of the Life and Adventures of Charles Ball, a Black Man* (Lewistown, PA: Printed and Published by John W. Shugert, 1836), 400.

195. *Fifty Years in Chains* (1858), vii.

196. *National Era*, 7 January 1858.

197. *Radical Abolitionist*, February 1858, 56.

198. *National Anti-Slavery Standard*, 13 March 1858; *National Era*, 26 August 1858.

199. *National Anti-Slavery Standard*, 13 March 1858.

200. *Radical Abolitionist*, February 1858, 56.

201. *National Era*, 26 August 1858; *Radical Abolitionist*, February 1858, 56.

202. Ball, *Fifty Years in Chains* (1858), 9.

203. *Slavery in the United States: A Narrative of the Life and Adventures of Charles Ball, a Black Man* (New York: John S. Taylor, 1837), 15–16.

204. *Slavery in the United States* (1837), 292.

205. The only edition of Ball's narrative currently in print uses the 1837 text with the catchier 1858 title. Charles Ball, *Fifty Years in Chains*, ed. Philip S. Foner (Mineola, NY: Dover, 2003).

206. Jeffrey D. Groves, "Judging Literary Books by Their Covers: House Styles, Ticknor and Fields, and Literary Promotion," in *Reading Books: Essays on the Material Text and Literature in America*, ed. Michele Moylan and Lana Stiles (Amherst: University of Massachusetts Press, 1996), 84.

207. Winship, *American Literary Publishing*, 124.

208. *New York Daily Tribune*, 9 February 1858; *Independent*, 6 May 1858; *National Era*, 26 August 1858; etc.

209. *National Era*, 9 September 1858.

210. *New York Daily Tribune*, 20 May 1859.

211. *New York Daily Tribune*, 20 May 1859.

212. *Daily Commercial Register*, 29 May 1858.

213. *Incidents in the Life of a Slave Girl*, ed. Lydia Maria Child (Boston: Published for the Author, 1861), 6.

214. See Jean Fagan Yellin, *Harriet Jacobs: A Life* (New York: Basic Civitas, 2004). My discussion of the publishing history of *Incidents* is largely indebted to Yellin's biography. See chapters 8 and 9 in particular on the genesis and publication of the book.

215. *Incidents in the Life of a Slave Girl*, 304. On Post, see Nancy A. Hewitt, *Radical Friend: Amy Kirby Post and Her Activist Worlds* (Chapel Hill: University of North Carolina Press, 2018).

216. Letter from Harriet Jacobs to Amy Post, after 27 December 1852 and before 14 February 1853, in *Harriet Jacobs Family Papers*, ed. Jean Fagan Yellin (Chapel Hill: University of North Carolina Press, 2008), 1:190, 191 (hereafter cited as *HJFP*, 1:190, 191).

217. Letter from Harriet Jacobs to Amy Post, *HJFP*, 1:191.

218. Letter from Harriet Jacobs to Amy Post, 14 February 1853, in *HJFP*, 1:193.

219. Letter from Harriet Jacobs to Amy Post, 4 April 1853, in *HJFP*, 1:194–95.

220. Hannah-Rose Murray, *Advocates of Freedom: African American Transatlantic Abolitionism in the British Isles* (Cambridge: Cambridge University Press, 2020), 150–52.

221. Letter from Harriet Jacobs to Amy Post, ca. May 1853, in *HJFP*, 1:196.

222. Letter from Harriet Jacobs to Amy Post, 4 April 1853, in *HJFP*, 1:195.

223. Letter from Harriet Jacobs to Amy Post, 4 April 1853, in *HJFP*, 1:194.

224. "Letter from a Fugitive Slave," *New York Daily Tribune*, 21 June 1853, in *HJFP*, 1:198, 200.

225. Yellin, *Harriet Jacobs*, 123.

226. Letter from William Cooper Nell to Amy Post, 31 August 1853, in *William Cooper Nell: Selected Writings, 1832–1874*, ed. Dorothy Porter Wesley and Constance Porter Uzelac (Baltimore: Black Classic Press, 2002), 352.

227. "America is now wholly given over to a d—d mob of scribbling women," Hawthorne wrote to his publisher in 1855. Quoted in Leland S. Person, *The Cambridge Introduction to Nathaniel Hawthorne* (Cambridge: Cambridge University Press, 2007), 24.

228. Letter from Harriet Jacobs to Amy Post, 9 October 1853, in *HJFP*, 1:206.

229. Letter from Harriet Jacobs to Amy Post, 11 January 1854, in *HJFP*, 1:209.

230. Letter from Harriet Jacobs to Amy Post, March 1854, in *HJFP*, 1:213.

231. Letters from William Cooper Nell to Amy Post, 13 June and 21 July 1854, in *HJFP*, 1:217.

232. Letters from Harriet Jacobs to Amy Post, 18 May and 8 June 1857, in *HJFP*, 1:235.

233. Letter from Harriet Jacobs to Amy Post, 21 June 1857, in *HJFP*, 1:237.

234. Letter from Harriet Jacobs to Amy Post, 21 June 1857, in *HJFP*, 1:237.

235. Letter from William Cooper Nell to Amy Post, 22 September 1857, in *HJFP*, 1:238.

236. Letter from Harriet Jacobs to Anne Warren Warren Weston, 28 June 1858, in *HJFP*, 1:250.

237. Yellin, *Harriet Jacobs*, 138.

238. See chapter 2.

239. Letter from Harriet Jacobs to Amy Post, 8 October 1860, in *HJFP*, 1:282.

240. Letter from Harriet Jacobs to Amy Post, 8 October 1860, in *HJFP*, 1:282.

241. William W. Thayer, "Autobiography of William Wilde Thayer," unpublished manuscript (Indianapolis, 1892), 17. On Thayer and Eldridge, see Albert J. Von Frank, "The Secret World of Radical Publishers: The Case of Thayer and Eldridge of Boston," in *Boston's Histories: Essays in Honor of Thomas H. O'Connor*, ed. James M. O'Toole and D. Quigley (Boston: Northeastern University Press, 2004), 52–70.

242. Jean Fagan Yellin, "Texts and Contexts of Harriet Jacobs' *Incidents in the Life of a Slave Girl: Written by Herself*," in Davis and Gates, *Slave's Narrative*, 262.

243. Yellin, *Harriet Jacobs*, 141; Carolyn L. Karcher, *The First Woman in the Republic: A Cultural Biography of Lydia Maria Child* (Durham, NC: Duke University Press, 1994), 436.

244. Alice A. Deck, "Whose Book Is This? Authorial versus Editorial Control of Harriet Brent Jacobs' *Incidents in the Life of a Slave Girl: Written by Herself*," *Women's Studies International Forum* 10.1 (1987): 39.

245. See Bruce Mills, "Lydia Maria Child and the Endings to Harriet Jacobs's *Incidents in the Life of a Slave Girl*," *American Literature* 64.2 (1992): 255–72.

246. Letter from Lydia Maria Child to Harriet Jacobs, 13 August 1860, in *The Collected Correspondence of Lydia Maria Child, 1817–1880*, ed. Patricia G. Holland and Milton Meltzer (Millwood, NY: Kraus Microform, 1980), 46/1243 (hereafter cited as *CC*, 46/1243); letter from Lydia Maria Child to Lucy Searle, 4 February 1861, in *CC*, 47/1282; letter from Lydia Maria Child to Sarah Blake Sturgis Shaw, ca. February–March 1861, in *CC*, 48/1298.

247. Jacobs, *Incidents in the Life of a Slave Girl*, 303.

248. Letter from Lydia Maria Child to John Greenleaf Whittier, 4 April 1861, in *CC*, 48/1300.

249. Albert H. Tricomi, "Harriet Jacobs's Autobiography and the Voice of Lydia Maria Child," *ESQ: A Journal of the American Renaissance* 53.3 (2007): 216–52 (quote at 225).

250. Letter from Harriet Jacobs to Amy Post, 8 November 1860, in *HJFP*, 1:284.

251. Robanna Sumrell Knott, "Harriet Jacobs: The Edenton Biography" (PhD diss., University of North Carolina at Chapel Hill, 1994), 321–51 (quotes at 340 and 335).

252. Susan S. Williams, "Authors and Literary Authorship," in Casper, Groves, Nissenbaum, and Winship, *Industrial Book*, 91.

253. Christy Pottroff, "Harriet Jacobs, Publisher and Activist," *Avidly*, 18 November 2019, http://avidly.lareviewofbooks.org/2019/11/18/harriet-jacobs-publisher-and-activist/.

254. Letter from Lydia Maria Child to Harriet Jacobs, 27 September 1860, in *HJFP*, 1:280–81; letter from Harriet Jacobs to Amy Post, 8 October 1860, in *HJFP*, 1:282–83; letter from Lydia Maria Child to Wendell Phillips, 2 December 1860, in *HJFP*, 1:285–86.

255. Pottroff, "Harriet Jacobs, Publisher and Activist."

256. Letter from Harriet Jacobs to Mary Rebecca Darby Smith, 14 January 1862, in *HJFP*, 1:361–62.

257. "Linda," *Christian Recorder*, 11 January 1862, in *HJFP*, 1:361.

258. Anonymous inscription, 11 May 1861, in *HJFP*, 1:352.

259. Letter from Lydia Maria Child to Daniel Ricketson, 14 March 1861, in *CC*, 47/1295.

260. Letter from Lydia Maria Child to John Greenleaf Whittier, 4 April 1861, in *CC*, 48/1300.

261. Harriet Jacobs to Francis Jackson, 1 February 1861, in *HJFP*, 1:295.

262. One was sold in an eBay auction in 2005 for over two thousand dollars. Eric Gardner, "Fortune-Telling on eBay: Early African American Textual Artifacts and the Marketplace," in *Everyday eBay: Culture, Collecting, and Desire*, ed. Ken Hillis, Michael Petit and Nathan Scott Epley (New York: Routledge, 2006), 66, 73n13.

263. "Linda," *Liberator*, 8 February 1861, in *HJFP*, 1:327.

264. "Linda, the Slave Girl," *Liberator*, 25 January 1861, in *HJFP*, 1:294.

265. "Linda," *Weekly Anglo-African*, 13 April 1861, in *HJFP*, 1:349.

266. Letter from Lydia Maria Child to Henrietta Sargent, 9 February 1861, in *CC*, 47/1285.

267. Inscription of Mary A. Estlin, *Incidents in the Life of a Slave Girl*, March 1861, in *HJFP*, 1:334–35.

268. Letter from Harriet Jacobs to Amy and Isaac Post, 18 June 1851, in *HJFP*, 1:355.

269. *HJFP*, 1:lxvi.

270. Diary of Frederick W. Chesson, 18 January 1862, in *HJFP*, 1:364; Williams, "Authors and Literary Authorship," 92.

271. *Morning Star and Dial*, 10 March 1862, in *HJFP*, 1:366.

272. Diary of Frederick W. Chesson, 31 March 1862, in *HJFP*, 1:382.

273. Diary of Frederick W. Chesson, 1 April 1862, in *HJFP*, 1:389.

274. See the introduction.

Conclusion

1. Teresa A. Goddu, "The Slave Narrative as Material Text," in *The Oxford Handbook of the African American Slave Narrative*, ed. John Ernest (New York: Oxford University Press, 2014), 150; Eric Gardner, "Slave Narratives and Archival Research," in Ernest, *Oxford Handbook*, 41.

2. Richard H. Brodhead, *Cultures of Letters: Scenes of Reading and Writing in Nineteenth-Century America* (Chicago: University of Chicago Press, 1993), 5.

3. Martin R. Delany, *The Condition, Elevation, Emigration, and Destiny of the Colored People of the United States* (Philadelphia: Published by the Author, 1852), 128n.

4. "American History Coming to Light," *Voice of the Fugitive*, 20 May 1852.

5. Richard S. Newman, *Abolitionism: A Very Short Introduction* (New York: Oxford University Press, 2018), 83.

6. *Twenty-first Annual Report Presented to the Massachusetts Anti-Slavery Society by Its Board of Managers, January 26, 1853* (Boston: Printed by Prentiss & Sawyer, 1853), 101–32.

7. John W. Blassingame, ed., introduction to *Slave Testimony: Two Centuries of Letters, Speeches, Interviews, and Autobiographies* (Baton Rouge: Louisiana State University Press, 1977), xxx.

8. Augusta Rohrbach, *Truth Stranger than Fiction: Race, Realism, and the U.S. Literary Marketplace* (New York: Palgrave, 2002), 29; Benjamin Quarles, *Black Abolitionists* (New York: Da Capo Press, 1969), 66.

9. See, for instance, Henry Louis Gates Jr., *Figures in Black: Words, Signs, and the "Racial" Self* (New York: Oxford University Press, 1987), 82; Frances Smith Foster, *Witnessing Slavery: The Development of Ante-bellum Slave Narratives*, 2nd ed. (Madison: University of Wisconsin Press, 1994), 144–45; Rohrbach, *Truth Stranger than Fiction*, 46.

10. Sarah Meer notes that *Uncle Tom's Cabin* appeared in almost every issue of the *Liberator* in 1852. Sarah Meer, *Uncle Tom Mania: Slavery, Minstrelsy, and Transatlantic Culture in the 1850s* (Athens: University of Georgia Press, 2005), 1.

11. Nina Baym, *Novels, Readers, and Reviewers: Responses to Fiction in Antebellum America* (Ithaca, NY: Cornell University Press, 1984), chap. 2.

12. Charles H. Nichols, "Who Read the Slave Narratives?," *Phylon Quarterly* 20.2 (1959): 149–62.

13. For a more detailed investigation of readers of slave narratives, see Michaël Roy, "'Neither *be*, nor *own*, a slave!': Lire les récits d'esclaves africains-américains dans l'Amérique antebellum," *Revue française d'études américaines* 150 (2017): 98–118.

14. *Fifth Annual Report of the Executive Committee of the American Anti-Slavery Society* (New York: Printed by William S. Dorr, 1838), 112n.

15. See Albert Johannsen, *The House of Beadle and Adams and Its Dime and Nickel Novels: The Story of a Vanished Literature*, 3 vols. (Norman: University of Oklahoma Press, 1950–62).

16. William L. Andrews, *To Tell a Free Story: The First Century of Afro-American Autobiography, 1760–1865* (Urbana: University of Illinois Press, 1986), 19.

17. Yuval Taylor, ed., *I Was Born a Slave: An Anthology of Classic Slave Narratives*, 2 vols. (Chicago: Lawrence Hill Books, 1999); Sterling Lecater Bland Jr., ed., *African American Slave Narratives: An Anthology*, 3 vols. (Westport, CT: Greenwood Press, 2001); William L. Andrews and Henry Louis Gates Jr., eds., *Slave Narratives* (New York: Library of America, 2000).

18. Lara Langer Cohen, *The Fabrication of American Literature: Fraudulence and Antebellum Print Culture* (Pennsylvania: University of Philadelphia Press, 2012), 105.

19. Marion Wilson Starling, *The Slave Narrative: Its Place in American History*, 2nd ed. (Washington, DC: Howard University Press, 1988), xxvi. Starling's monograph is

adapted from her 1946 doctoral dissertation, "The Slave Narrative: Its Place in American Literary History."

20. Eric Gardner, *Unexpected Places: Relocating Nineteenth-Century African American Literature* (Jackson: University Press of Mississippi, 2009), 7.

21. Starling, *Slave Narrative*, 338.

22. "Recollections of a Runaway Slave," *Advocate of Freedom*, 2 August 1838; Susanna Ashton, "Re-collecting Jim: Discovering a Name and a Slave Narrative's Continuing Truth," *Commonplace* 15.1 (2014), http://commonplace.online/article/re-collecting-jim/.

23. *Narrative of the Life of Frederick Douglass, an American Slave* (Boston: Published at the Anti-Slavery Office, 1845), 39; *The Life of Josiah Henson, Formerly a Slave, Now an Inhabitant of Canada* (Boston: Arthur D. Phelps, 1849), 62–66; *Narrative of the Life and Adventures of Henry Bibb, an American Slave* (New York: Published by the Author, 1849), 21; *A Narrative of the Life and Labors of the Rev. G. W. Offley, a Colored Man, and Local Preacher* (Hartford, CT: n.p., 1860), 9–10. Later African American autobiographical narratives have also frequently emphasized their subjects' interactions with books. See Booker T. Washington, *Up from Slavery* (New York: W. W. Norton, 1995), 18; Richard Wright, *Black Boy* (New York: Harper Perennial, 2020) 244–53; *The Autobiography of Malcolm X* (London: Penguin, 2011), 263–87; Ta-Nehisi Coates, *Between the World and Me* (New York: Spiegel & Grau, 2015), 46–48.

24. *A Family Redeemed from Bondage; Being Rev. Edmond Kelley (The Author), His Wife, and Four Children* (New Bedford, MA: Published by the Author, 1851), 3.

25. On the "little is known" refrain, see Eric Gardner, "Accessing Early Black Print," *Legacy* 33.1 (2016): 27; John Ernest, "Life beyond Biography: Black Lives and Biographical Research," *Commonplace* 17.1 (2016), http://commonplace.online/article/life-beyond-biography/.

26. William L. Andrews, ed., *The Life of John Thompson, a Fugitive Slave* (New York: Penguin, 2011), xxvii.

27. *Narrative of the Life of Frederick Douglass*, 116.

28. *Proceedings of the Worcester Society of Antiquity, for the Year 1889* (Worcester, MA: Published by the Society, 1890), 147; *The Experience of Thomas H. Jones, Who Was a Slave for Forty-Three Years* (Worcester, MA: Printed by Henry J. Howland, 1857).

29. *The Life of John Thompson, a Fugitive Slave; Containing His History of 25 Years in Bondage, and His Providential Escape* (Worcester, MA: Published by John Thompson, 1856), v.

30. "The Eighth Worcester Anti-Slavery Bazaar," *Worcester Palladium*, 20 August 1856.

31. *The Worcester Almanac, Directory, and Business Advertiser, for 1856* (Worcester, MA: Henry J. Howland, 1855), 118.

32. Joanna Brooks, "The Unfortunates: What the Life Spans of Early Black Books Tell Us about Book History," in *Early African American Print Culture*, ed. Lara Langer Cohen and Jordan Alexander Stein (Philadelphia: University of Pennsylvania Press, 2012), 50, 51.

33. Eugene B. McCarthy and Thomas L. Doughton, eds., *From Bondage to Belonging: The Worcester Slave Narratives* (Amherst: University of Massachusetts Press, 2007), 40.

34. British pop singer Morrissey demanded that Penguin publish his autobiography under their "classics" imprint, a request that the publishing house eventually

satisfied, claiming that the book was "a classic in the making." See "Morrissey Inks Memoir Deal with Penguin Classics," *Guardian*, 4 October 2013.

35. Italo Calvino, "Why Read the Classics?," in *Why Read the Classics?*, trans. Martin McLaughlin (Boston: Mariner Books, 2014), 6.

36. *Running a Thousand Miles for Freedom: The Escape of William and Ellen Craft from Slavery*, ed. R. J. M. Blackett (Baton Rouge: Louisiana State University Press, 1999); *Running a Thousand Miles for Freedom: The Escape of William and Ellen Craft from Slavery*, ed. Barbara McCaskill (Athens: University of Georgia Press, 1999).

37. William L. Andrews, "Slave Narrative," in *The Oxford Companion to African American Literature*, ed. William L. Andrews, Frances Smith Foster, and Trudier Harris (New York: Oxford University Press, 1997), 668.

38. Letter from William Craft to Samuel May Jr., 29 May 1860, Boston Public Library; letter from Samuel May Jr. to Wendell Phillips, 14 June 1860, Wendell Phillips Papers, Houghton Library, Cambridge, MA.

39. I borrow the notion of an abolitionist mediascape from Teresa A. Goddu, "Antislavery Media," unpublished paper.

40. Blackett, *Running a Thousand Miles for Freedom*, ix.

41. Quoted in Barbara McCaskill, *Love, Liberation, and Escaping Slavery: William and Ellen Craft in Cultural Memory* (Athens: University of Georgia Press, 2015), 59.

42. Jeffrey Ruggles, *The Unboxing of Henry Brown* (Richmond: Library of Virginia, 2003), 63.

43. Ruggles, *The Unboxing of Henry Brown*, 58–59, 65, 89. On Black panoramists drawing images from slave narratives, see Teresa A. Goddu, *Selling Antislavery: Abolition and Mass Media in Antebellum America* (Philadelphia: University of Pennsylvania Press, 2020), 203–7; Aston Gonzalez, *Visualizing Equality: African American Rights and Visual Culture in the Nineteenth Century* (Chapel Hill: University of North Carolina Press, 2020), 114, 124, 127.

44. Hannah-Rose Murray, *Advocates of Freedom: African American Transatlantic Abolitionism in the British Isles* (Cambridge: Cambridge University Press, 2020), 175–83.

45. Daphne A. Brooks, *Bodies in Dissent: Spectacular Performances of Race and Freedom, 1850–1910* (Durham, NC: Duke University Press, 2006), 69; Carl Ostrowski, "Slavery, Labor Reform, and Intertextuality in Antebellum Print Culture: The Slave Narrative and the City-Mysteries Novel," *African American Review* 40.3 (2006): 494–96.

46. Roger Chartier, *Au bord de la falaise: L'histoire entre certitudes et inquiétude* (Paris: Albin Michel, 2009), 305–6.

47. Lydia Maria Child, "Lewis Clark. Leaves from a Slave's Journal of Life," *National Anti-Slavery Standard*, 20 October, 27 October 1842; "A White Slave's Experience," *Signal of Liberty*, 9 January 1843. The *Signal of Liberty* was the official organ of the Michigan State Anti-Slavery Society.

48. The scrapbook pages are available on the Black Abolitionist Papers electronic database. On Helen Thoreau's scrapbook, see Robert A. Gross, "Helen Thoreau's Antislavery Scrapbook," *Yale Review* 100.1 (2012): 103–20; on scrapbooking in nineteenth-century America, see Ellen Gruber Garvey, *Writing with Scissors: American Scrapbooks from the Civil War to the Harlem Renaissance* (Oxford: Oxford University Press, 2013); on antislavery in Concord, see Sandra Harbert Petrulionis, *To Set This World Right: The*

Antislavery Movement in Thoreau's Concord (Ithaca, NY: Cornell University Press, 2006).

49. Elizabeth Regosin, "Lost in the Archives: The Pension Bureau Files," in Ernest, *Oxford Handbook*, 120; Winfried Siemerling, "Slave Narratives and Hemispheric Studies," in Ernest, *Oxford Handbook*, 345; Nicholas T. Rinehart, "Finding Francophone Equiano (in All the Wrong Places)" (BA thesis, Harvard University, 2014), 3; Gardner, *Unexpected Places*, 41; Nicole N. Aljoe, introduction to *Journeys of the Slave Narrative in the Early Americas*, ed. Nicole N. Aljoe and Ian Finseth (Charlottesville: University of Virginia Press, 2014), 4; Augusta Rohrbach, *Thinking Outside the Book* (Amherst: University of Massachusetts Press, 2014). Gardner also draws attention to Civil War and postbellum "Information Wanted" notices—placed in newspapers by African American women and men separated from family by slavery and war—as "brief slave narratives." More controversially, David Waldstreicher describes runaway advertisements as "the first slave narratives" in the United States. Eric Gardner, *Black Print Unbound: The Christian Recorder, African American Literature, and Periodical Culture* (New York: Oxford University Press, 2015), 83; David Waldstreicher, "Reading the Runaways: Self-Fashioning, Print Culture, and Confidence in Slavery in the Eighteenth-Century Mid-Atlantic," *William and Mary Quarterly* 56.2 (1999): 247. On enslaved testimony in both the French and British colonial contexts, see also Sophie White, *Voices of the Enslaved: Love, Labor, and Longing in French Louisiana* (Chapel Hill: University of North Carolina Press, 2019); Sophie White and Trevor Burnard, eds., *Hearing Enslaved Voices: African and Indian Slave Testimony in British and French America, 1700–1848* (New York: Routledge, 2020).

50. Gardner, *Unexpected Places*, 194n36.

Index